Richard Taylor

Prodigals

A Vietnam Story

Richard Taylor

Prodigals

A Vietnam Story

CASEMATE
Havertown, PA

Published by
CASEMATE
2114 Darby Road, Havertown, PA
Telephone: 610-853-9131

Typeset and design by
Savas Publishing & Consulting Group

ISBN 1-932033-19-X

First edition, first printing

Cataloging-in-Publication data is available
from the Library of Congress

Printed in the United States of America

To Vietnam Veterans, their loved ones and families.

To Sandy, Paige, Scott, Amy,
and my mother and father—my loved ones.

To those who helped me along the way.

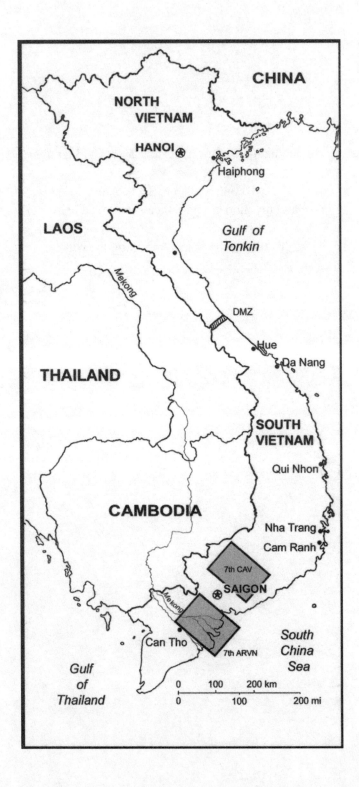

Contents

Preface
xiii

List of Abbreviations
xvii

Chapter 1. History Repeats Itself
1

Chapter 2. The Long Journey
5

Chapter 3. Good Morning, Vietnam
13

Chapter 4. Sliders
17

Chapter 5. Assignment: Mekong Delta
23

Chapter 6. Rude Awakening
31

Chapter 7. Storm Clouds over the Double Y
41

Chapter 8. Trouble at the Double Y
49

Chapter 9. Friendly Fire
57

Contents (continued)

Chapter 10. River Assault
61

Chapter 11. Into Snoopy's Nose
67

Chapter 12. Changes
77

Chapter 13. Sudden Death
83

Chapter 14. East of the Sun
89

Chapter 15. Unfriendly Fire
93

Chapter 16. Big Storm
99

Chapter 17. Gates of Hell
111

Chapter 18. Storm Unremitting
117

Chapter 19. Mopping Up
125

Chapter 20. Rats of a Different Sort
133

Chapter 21. Blessed Respite
139

Chapter 22. Clock Winding Down
145

Contents (continued)

Chapter 23. Revival
155

Chapter 24. Returning
163

Chapter 25. Garry Owen
169

Chapter 26. Combat Assault
181

Chapter 27. War Zone D
193

Chapter 28. Green
197

Chapter 29. High-Angle Hell
205

Chapter 30: Operation Mercer
215

Chapter 31. Reorienting
225

Chapter 32. Bruised Heart
231

Chapter 33. Recovery
239

Chapter 34. Artillery Zone
249

Chapter 35. Back to Bravo
253

Contents (continued)

Chapter 36. Backs to the Wall
259

Chapter 37: Staff Wars
267

Chapter 38. Delta Demons
275

Chapter 39. News From Home
283

Chapter 40. All or Nothingt
287

Chapter 41. Which Way Home?
293

Chapter 42. Fragments
297

Chapter 43. Saint Christopher
307

Postmortem / Acknowledgments
313

End Notes
319

Index
327

Maps and Illustrations

Theater Map
Frontis

7th ARVN Area of Operations
22

My Tho
27

Dinh Tuong Province
45

Tet Offensive
98

1st Cavalry Area of Operations
179

Ambush: South of Camp Gorvad
183

Operation Mercer
208

Photographs follow page 142

Life is either a daring adventure, or nothing.

— Helen Keller

"Suicide is Painless"

Preface

Written in Manila in 1993, on the 25th anniversary
of the Tet General Offensive of 1968

Music from the theme of the old M*A*S*H 4077 television series flows like blood from an open wound. This time, the pain is in my head—a hangover from last night's excess of San Miguel beer—accompanying an uncertain emptiness I attempt unsuccessfully to fill this time every year.

This year the taste is especially sweet, spiked by memories of my first stop in the Philippine Islands. The old song from the M*A*S*H classic returns in January each year like a warm monsoon in winter, and I foolishly try to discover whether suicide is indeed painless.

Each year I make it a point to have an extra drink on January 30, as I did in 1968. The resulting hangover is self-inflicted punishment I willingly bear for having survived. I nurture my own private hell on these special occasions. My annual observance is a ritual of honor.

In 1968, I was a twenty-three-year-old first lieutenant who had been in the army all of eighteen months, four of them spent in Vietnam's Mekong River delta. Cloaked in the ideals of John Kennedy, I was responsible for advising South Vietnamese Army officers in the defense of their own country against the rebellious Ho Chi Minh. I was a bit short on experience but I hoped, at least, that I could be a positive influence. Let's not kid ourselves—I was the conduit for an arsenal of American firepower directed toward an enemy, intent to kill him before he killed us.

My anguish began on a patrol in the Plain of Reeds, where we discovered large caches of weapons and ammunition—staggering in their volume. Even at that time it seemed strange to me that the Viet Cong would leave so much material buried in large bunkers that far south after humping it all the way down the Ho Chi Minh Trail—but what did I know of grand strategy? I was only a green lieutenant. Later, the answer to that riddle would be made abundantly clear to the world.

The Chinese New Year was upon us. The opposing forces agreed to a ceasefire so the Vietnamese on both sides could spend this traditional period celebrating their ancestors with their families. Many would travel about the country to do that—just like in the United States, which we thought of as the "real world." Our battalion was reduced to about twenty-five percent of its normal strength. Even the battalion's senior American advisor decided to visit friends in the northern provinces of Vietnam during that holiday season. After all, it was the season to be jolly. Only Master Sergeant Mendenhall and I were left to advise our Vietnamese in the event the unthinkable happened. I was confined to the Catholic seminary in My Tho, keeping a bullet wound clean to avoid infection. Mendenhall's instructions were to call me if anything unusual happened.

It was January 29. With the war zone quiet and no fighting anywhere, I went to the team bar to celebrate the Tet holidays and to lick my wounds over having been shot by "friendly fire." I knew how to celebrate well in those days.

About midnight I drifted off to sleep, if you can call it that, in a barracks-type room with eight other rear-echelon warriors. I was abruptly awakened by the noise of a B-40 rocket erupting through the wall over my head, the impact sending plaster over us like hailstones in a storm. Following a moment of stunned silence, the sounds of yelling men running to battle positions erupted like another explosion. Other real bursts joined the cacophony as outgoing fire rose to equal the noise of incoming.

The next morning, January 30,1968, I staggered out into the bright light of the hallway looking for breakfast, only to discover everyone lined up in battle positions wearing helmets and flack jackets, pointing rifles in self-defense. The sounds of rifle fire, which replaced holiday firecrackers, came from the direction of the city of My Tho. I wished it would stop. It did not.

Someone grabbed my arm and informed me I was wanted in the radio room. My Vietnamese battalion was on the march, and Master Sergeant Mendenhall was trying to reach me. The battalion was marching down the road toward the sound of gunfire and an American officer was needed to accompany it. I didn't see any other volunteers, but I didn't expect to. Everyone I saw was wide-eyed and pale-faced.

I stood beside the seminary gate and watched and waited while the battalion marched past; the troops had the most fearful expressions on their faces I had ever seen. I held my position until a single, taller American with a radio approached. I walked into the road, fell alongside Master Sergeant Mendenhall, and asked for an update. He was happy to have company but could not tell me much. I sensed his alarm at the situation. His unspoken concern caused my own to escalate with each step.

Approaching My Tho, the sounds of gunfire grew closer and more distinct. We left the paved road and had advanced two blocks when intense machine gun fire ripped through our ranks at close range. After a few moments to regroup we resumed our advance into the hellish fires of war.

At that moment both life and death began for me. I would never again be the person I was before, and the trials I faced would remain permanently etched into my self-definition. I'll never forget them. I don't want to forget them, because thus began my most private and defining experience—and not an experience that I enjoyed. I was afraid of dying at any moment. Sometimes we were close to death, or perhaps we did die in some measurable way. On the other hand, one never lives as fully as when facing death—and we witnessed both in their most graphic terms.

The roller coaster of the Tet Offensive proceeded on a grand scale, larger than any arena in the world—gladiators fighting to the death while the world witnessed the events in daily edited, abbreviated, and exaggerated news clips.

But survival can be bittersweet. Every year, right after the rejoicing of Christmas, as serious attempts at New Year resolves fade into dreams, the prodigals of a January past return to cloud my view. I hope others understand that a little too much to drink on this occasion is a private celebration of life, as well as another escape from death.

Suicide is not painless.

—— Richard Taylor

List of Abbreviations

AID	Agency for International Development
APC	Armored Personnel Carrier (M-113)
ARVN	Army of the Republic of Vietnam
CIB	Combat Infantry Badge
CIDG	Civilian Irregular Defense Group
CP	Command Post
FB	Fire Base
FSB	Fire Support Base
G-1/S-1	Personnel Staff
G-2/S-2	Intelligence Staff
G-3/S-3	Operations Staff
G-4/S-4	Logistics Staff
G-5/S-5	Civil Affairs Staff
LAW	Light Antitank Weapon, M-72
LZ	Landing Zone
MARS	Military Affiliate Radio System

Medevac	Medical Evacuation, usually by helicopter
MP	Military Police
MRF	Mobile Riverine Force
NLF	National Liberation Front
NVA	North Vietnamese Army
PA&E	Pacific Architects and Engineers
PF	Popular Forces
PRU	Provincial Reconnaissance Unit
Psyops	Psychological Operations
PX	Post Exchange
RAG	River Assault Group
RF	Regional Forces
ROTC	Reserve Officers Training Course
R&R	Rest and Recuperation
Ruff-puff	South Vietnamese territorial forces, including regional and popular forces (RF/PF)
TOC	Tactical Operations Center
USO	United Services Organization
VC	Viet Cong
VNAF	Vietnamese Air Force
XO	Executive Officer

"In the Mekong Delta, South Vietnamese rangers killed 33 Viet Cong in a battle southwest of Saigon. In fighting which raged for several hours, seven Vietcong were captured along with four crew weapons and two mortars."

—*Atlanta Constitution,* August 17, 1967

1

History Repeats Itself

August 19, 1967

I was ready to pull the trigger.

If I had to kill, I could do it. I was trained, and I knew if it came to that, I would commit myself to the chilling prospect. After all, I had grown up hunting small game in south Georgia, my grandfather had presented me with a shotgun at fourteen, and I bought my first pistol at sixteen. I followed the buildup of hostilities in Southeast Asia for two years in high school, four years in military school, and another year in the U.S. Army. The military had steeled my spine and conditioned my mind and body for the trials I was to face. I was proficient in an array of destructive tools, a soldier anxious to take my place on the battlefield.

I tasted the salty sweat on my upper lip. My khaki shirt clung to my back from the tortuous non-air-conditioned car ride. I welcomed a flight to the other side of the world, to a place I had studied from afar. The worst part of it was this, the very beginning. I waited with the two most significant people in my life, my mother and father. We stood in awkward silence, not knowing what to say to one another.

I was a trained professional, prepared for every hardship man or nature could throw at me—petrified by what I had to endure. Passengers moved about us in the busy airport in Jacksonville, Florida. Despite the cooled air in the terminal, I was very hot and uncomfortable. My father was dressed in a jacket, tie, and hat; my mother was in a Sunday-best dress. I felt we were at a funeral—mine.

My mother broke the awkward silence. "What will you be doing in Vietnam, son?"

Oh, I wished she had not asked that question. I knew I was going to be an advisor to the South Vietnamese army. But I had been in the army for only a little over a year myself. I knew that I would respond to my personal challenges, but I didn't really think I had much advice to offer people who were already fighting their war.

"I'll work with the South Vietnamese, Mom. I won't know my job until I get there." I tried to sound confident and in control. "I'll write as soon as I can." A trickle of sweat crept down my leg. For a moment, I thought I had wet my pants. I excused myself to go to the bathroom, just in case. Using paper towels, I dried my chest, waist, and legs beneath my uniform. The image of a pale soldier in the mirror startled me, since I believed I was alone. Then I recognized my own reflection. No wonder my mother looked at me as if I were a dead man—I looked like one!

Returning to the passenger area near the gate, I noticed that my parents had taken a seat on a bench. I wished they hadn't done that because I felt better standing. My mother had tears in her eyes, and my father's chin quivered as he asked, "You'll be going to San Francisco?"

It was a question I knew had already been answered. "Actually, I'll fly to Atlanta and take a connecting flight to San Francisco. There, I'll take a helicopter to Oakland, and then a taxi the army depot." I reviewed the itinerary again for the third or fourth time.

My father had served in the U.S. Navy in the Pacific Theater in World War II. I remembered sitting on the floor with my mother when I was two years old, listening to a seventy-eight rpm record of his voice talking to us from Hawaii. We listened to it over and over. Despite that, I didn't think he knew how I felt. He had gone in a general mobilization to save the nation from attacking forces of Japan. No one was sure why I was going to this little guerilla war. But even without clear definition this was my grand adventure. The purpose would evolve later, along with the outcome. I was going to war in Vietnam; my country wanted me to go, and I was a volunteer. That was good enough for me.

My flight was announced. I shook my father's hand and hugged my mother. "I'll write," I promised. I was not afraid of the war, but I was terrified of losing control of my own emotions at that moment.

"Goodbye." It sounded so final as my father said it.

"Write when you can, and take care of yourself," my mother added.

"Bye," I managed as I turned to walk up the gangway to board the plane. No further discussion was possible just then, although our feeling's were about to burst out all over. No utterance could be allowed that might trigger that eruption.

Some things never change: young, idealistic men going off to war, breaking the hearts of their mothers and fathers, fiancées, and children; fearful of the undertaking ahead, but more afraid of showing anxiety or breaking down at a defining moment of manhood.

I had already spent a year in the stateside army after being commissioned a Regular Army second lieutenant through the ROTC program at North Georgia College. In the 101st Airborne Division, I had taken my responsibilities as a platoon leader and company executive officer seriously; I had also taken every possible opportunity to attend training, and I mastered basic airborne, jumpmaster, pathfinder, and the infantry officer's basic training before receiving my orders to the dreaded Military Assistance Command, Vietnam, known as MACV. I aspired to go overseas with my own beloved 101st Airborne Division, not as an advisor to the Vietnamese but as a fighting man in a U.S. combat unit, so I had been disappointed at the advisor's role assigned to me.

Nevertheless, I had trained at the Military Assistance Training and Advisors Course at Fort Bragg, North Carolina, learned about Vietnamese culture, geography, organizations, and a little of the language, and after all this preparation accepted my assignment as a start, not an end, to my campaign as an American soldier. I had very little understanding then of what could really be changed by one person, much less an army or even a great nation. I'm not sure I really cared—I just wanted to break away and ride the waves of time and history.

As I found my seat on the plane, I could envision my parents swallowing their emotional strain all the way home. Their stoic natures had not allowed for a public expression of their emotions any more than mine had. For myself, I was shaking inside so badly that it must have been written on my face. I didn't know what to do with my hands. I hoped drinks would be served soon, but I would have to change planes in Atlanta before taking the long flight to San Francisco.

I found myself sitting next to a beautiful girl about my age, who was anxious to make small talk. Just my luck that this was the only time in my life that I was sitting next to an attractive stranger who wanted to get acquainted, and my heart pounded so fast that I couldn't catch my breath. My windpipe was so constricted from holding back a groan that I might never talk again. I spent the rest of the flight trying to master my swirling emotions. After a couple of beers in Atlanta and on the flight to San Francisco, I finally felt that I was in control again, at least of the present situation if not the future. I was almost grateful to have lost the beautiful stranger in the airport; I couldn't have carried on that charade any longer.

Oakland and San Francisco were a blur of in-processing and out-processing. The army had, of course, long before mastered the art of processing people. You started by standing in line, and after that, just followed the leader. Oakland Army Depot seemed sleazy, but it was nicer than the surrounding neighborhood. I met another officer at the processing center and we decided to make the most of our last night in civilization. I don't remember his name or much of the evening except for singing "I Left My Heart in San Francisco" at a little bar in Jack London Square.

The journey had finally begun. I was on my way to make my own personal history, and discover whether I would blink in the face of it. My father had gone to war and returned, and our ancestors had done the same. History repeats itself. This wasn't anything new. But it was incredibly new to me, and that's what counted.

"U.S. B52 bombers raided a big Communist military buildup in the fifth consecutive day of strikes by the eight-engine Stratofortresses on both sides of the demilitarized zone."

—*Atlanta Constitution,* August 19, 1967

2

The Long Journey

August 21–22, 1967

The bus ride from Oakland Army Depot to the Norton Air Force Base departure field was long and lonely, until we arrived at the gate. There the bus was greeted by a group of protesting hippies and flower children opposing the war. Decked out in sack dresses, ponytails, and beads, and carrying posters and flowers, they were the peaceful personification of news clips I had often scoffed at. Now faced with their presence, I wondered what they were thinking about the men in khaki uniforms. I already knew what they thought about our country's involvement in the war. We passed without incident: we outnumbered the hippies, and the air police were nearby.

The convoy of buses parked, and we unloaded through the diesel fumes of their idling engines to then hang around the terminal. "Terminal" seemed to me a very appropriate word. For an hour and a half rosters were checked and people counted. I took my time boarding, since officers were instructed to board last, and found myself in a first-row seat on the aisle, across from the galley. We were on a Braniff Airways Military Airlift Command flight, a no-frills commercial flight chartered by the military to ferry troops overseas.

The flight from California to Hawaii was long but uneventful; everyone was settling in for the longer trip from Hawaii to Clark Air Force Base in the Philippines. When we deplaned in Hawaii, we were instructed to leave on the plane anything we had carried aboard, since we would be reboarding by row number and returning to the same seats. I headed with others to the bar to have a refreshing 10 a.m. beer.

Once the new aircrew was ready we were called to reboard. By this time I was over the jitters, but I must have resembled a lost puppy. I reclaimed my prized first-row aisle seat. The flight attendants, who had been busy with preflight checks during takeoff, sat in the folding jumpseats directly in front of the first row. I made eye contact with an attractive young woman with short brown hair who was seated directly across from me. Fortunately, this encounter progressed much better than the one on the flight from Jacksonville to Atlanta, when my voice had frozen in my throat.

I could not take my eyes off her during takeoff—except when she said, "You'll have a nice view of Diamond Head from the window right after takeoff." I wondered if she could be trying to make me stop staring at her.

I glanced out the porthole. "You make this trip often?"

"Too often, I think. All of us are volunteers. No one is assigned to a Vietnam flight that doesn't want to go."

"This is my first trip," I said, aware that the army captain sitting next to me in the middle seat was wearing two rows of medals from a previous combat tour, and the lieutenant colonel by the window wore a virtual salad of color on his chest from this and other wars. The lieutenant colonel was designated flight commander, which meant that he was responsible for the discipline of the troops on board. It dawned on me that the officers were seated in the first few rows in the front of the airplane, while the enlisted men were occupying most of the other seats. I didn't have any medals except for the badges from army training. I felt naked and as green as I actually was; I hoped the cute flight attendant wouldn't notice.

When the seatbelt sign was turned off, the stewardesses excused themselves to serve drinks, nonalcoholic only, and prepare an in-flight meal.

The nice woman I had been talking to quickly offered the officers a drink first, directly from the galley. I wasn't sure if it was because we were officers or sitting in front, but I sensed something more than just that. When she handed me a glass of Coke our hands brushed, and my heart leaped to my throat. I had felt a stirring the moment we sat facing one another; her touch ignited a spark inside me.

My stewardess served from the galley. I watched her every move as unobtrusively as possible, trying to be nonchalant but not succeeding. She was either interested or aware of my interest, because our eyes met often, but it was difficult to talk while she worked. I stood beside the galley door, ostensibly to stretch my legs, and we were able to talk at eye level while she worked.

Finally the food and drinks were finished and cleared away. Someone announced that the movie would be *Don't Drink the Water*, and the lights were turned down.

My stewardess came over to the front row of officers.

"There are a few empty seats if anyone wants to move back and watch the movie. You won't be able to see the screen from up here." Two of the girls pulled the jumpseat down to sit across from us again.

"Or we could talk and play cards," my girl suggested.

The lieutenant colonel stood. "I think I'll walk around and visit the troops, then find an empty seat and get some sleep."

I stayed firmly planted where I was. "Cards are fine by me."

"My name's Jill," announced the other stewardess.

"And I'm Peggy," followed my girl, strumming my heartstrings with the sound of her name.

The captain and I respectively introduced ourselves as Tom and Richard—Dick to my friends.

Peggy and Jill broke out two new decks of cards and shuffled them on the serving trays in front of the seats. I had played hearts before, but never with two decks. I was assured that this made it more interesting, but I was already completely interested. It had everything to do with playing hearts, but not cards.

By the time the second movie started playing cards had grown old. Peggy put the serving trays away and brought back pillows and blankets. Tom moved over into the empty seat next to the window and settled back for some rest.

Peggy sat down, again facing me, and we talked for a few minutes. Jill excused herself without explanation for parts unknown.

After a few minutes, Peggy asked, "Do you mind if I sit in that empty middle seat? These pull-down seats aren't very comfortable."

With the jump seat down, we could stretch our legs out, ensuring that no one sat there. The seats went back, and with pillows and short blankets we were quite cozy.

"What do you think about the war?" Peggy asked.

"I don't know about the politics, but if our country is involved, then I think it's my duty to go. Besides, this is the biggest thing in the world, and I wouldn't miss it." I looked into her warm, brown eyes for my answer. "What do you think?"

Peggy held my gaze. "I support our troops—that's why I volunteer for these flights—but I always wonder about all the protests and demonstrations. Doesn't that bother you?"

"Yeah," I said, "but I don't focus on that. They have the right to protest. You make these flights often. What do other soldiers think about it?"

"I think they feel like you do—a little confused about why we're there, but determined to go because we are. Of course, some are against it, and others are just nervous." Peggy placed her hand lightly on my arm. "How about you? Are you okay?"

My God, could she read my mind? "Yeah, I'm okay. I'm a little jittery," I confessed. "This is all new to me, but I'm confident in myself and my training. I'll be all right. . . . I think."

Her fingers interlaced with mine under the blanket. "We aren't supposed to do this. Do you mind?"

"I won't tell anyone if you don't." We both drifted for a while. I felt warm and secure for the first time in days.

The second movie ended too soon. People stirred in the cabin again. The lieutenant colonel returned to his seat, Tom moved back to the center, and Peggy folded blankets and fluffed pillows like a normal stewardess. Only I could see she was an angel looking after me.

"I'll talk to you later." She returned to the galley to prepare breakfast.

I felt empty. Releasing her hand had broken something inside me; I was vulnerable again. I pretended to sleep, but I peeked through heavy lids to catch glimpses of this beautiful person who had somehow touched me deeply in only a few minutes. I saw her glancing back while she went about her business. I knew she was grateful to have something to do with her hands. Mine felt like they were strapped to an electric chair for the final countdown.

We exchanged a few words here and there during breakfast, and it was hard not to yell, "Stop this plane! Peggy and I want to get off and go to Canada."

When our landing was announced at Clark Air Force Base in the Philippines, Peggy and Jill returned to their jumpseats. The sky was black outside the porthole window.

"Will you continue on with us to Vietnam?" I asked Peggy, hopefully.

She shook her head slowly. "No, they require a fresh crew for the final part of the flight to pick up soldiers leaving Vietnam and bring them back to Clark. They are only on the ground in Vietnam a short time, but it's too many hours for one crew. You'll be on the ground at Clark for a couple of hours while the new crew prepares the aircraft and refuels for the trip to Saigon and back."

"What will you do?"

"We'll ride a bus to a hotel for crew rest. I'll take the flight to Vietnam tomorrow. That one is always hardest because . . . I'll need to get some rest."

"Could we talk once we get on the ground at Clark?"

Again she shook her head. "I wish we could, but that's strictly forbidden. I don't think I could do it anyway."

"Why not? I want to talk to you. That's all."

"It's very hard to say goodbye . . . over and over. It's just too hard." Tears welled in her eyes, and she pulled out a tissue, ignored the seatbelt sign, and rushed directly to the rest room.

I felt Jill staring at me, and the silence from Tom and the lieutenant colonel was chilling. I knew they were listening, but I didn't care.

At the last possible moment Peggy returned to her seat. I knew it was only because it was required for landing. She was not one to break regulations, not usually. Now she was implacable and we didn't speak or look directly at one another. I diverted my attention to the airfield as we taxied across Clark. The rows of B-52 Stratofortress bombers, their long wingtips almost touching the ground, were breathtaking and brought me abruptly back to reality. We were two people going about our duty because it was the right thing to do, but wanting very much to do otherwise. Once committed, there was no turning back. Military Airlift Command, Braniff

Airlines, and the entire U.S. Army represented by the lieutenant colonel two seats away absolutely ensured that there would be no backsliding.

The airplane stopped rolling, and I thought my heart had stopped at the same time. Peggy opened the passenger exit door and directed the ground crew rolling the ramp ladder into place. From my seat I was positioned to be the first person off the plane. I wanted to be last.

I found myself standing on top of the ramp with her. She simply said, "Take care of yourself."

I couldn't speak at all. My voice was frozen again. I knew I would be unable to say what I wanted to, anyway. So I took her in my arms and kissed her on her lips. It lasted only a few seconds, but I felt her arms encircle me. I broke our embrace and turned away while I still could.

My knees wobbled as I climbed down the ramp and crossed the tarmac to the terminal. The oppressive humidity of the Philippine night air enveloped me like a wet blanket, even worse after the altitude and dry air of the airplane. My khaki uniform shirt clung to my back again, and I was grateful, as I wiped the sweat from my face, that I could collect tears from my cheeks without anyone noticing. I repeated the move several times while slowly crossing the steaming tarmac. As we entered the terminal, I remember someone asking as he stared into my bloodshot eyes. "Hard flight?"

I couldn't sit down in the waiting area. I paced about and wandered into the latrine to regain my composure. I washed my face and hands with cold water before going back to the bright lights of the passenger area to pace some more.

I was jarred back to the real world when Tom touched my arm. "They're calling your name, Lieutenant!"

I stared at him, not understanding, until I heard over the intercom: "Lieutenant Taylor, you have a call on the house phone. Lieutenant Taylor, please pick up the house phone at the information desk."

My hand shook. Something must have happened at home, and I would have to return to Jacksonville for a family emergency. I didn't want to imagine anything happening to one of my parents, especially after the difficult departure from Jacksonville. I lifted the phone.

"Are you okay?" said the voice on the other end.

I was confused for a few seconds. Then I muttered, "Where are you?"

"I'm in the crew lounge," Peggy said, "but I wanted to talk to you again."

"Come down here. This is crazy. I want to see you. I *need* to see you." I scanned the upper windows frantically, trying to catch a glimpse of her.

"I can't do it. I want to—but I'd lose my job." Her voice broke a little, stabbing in my chest. "I don't think I could handle it again."

"Let's get out of here. Let's meet outside, *please*." I could see no one in the windows above, so I concentrated on the voice on the phone.

"Dick, I really do want to but I can't. And you don't need this either. Not now—maybe someday."

"That's impossible! I don't even know your last name, or your address or phone number."

"Drake. My name is Peggy Drake."

"How will I find you, Peggy?"

"You'll have to contact me through Braniff. I don't know where I'll be, or if I'll be married, or what. You may not want to, or. . . ."

"I want to write you," I pleaded.

"No. I can't do it. I can't get attached. I'm not strong enough. Something might happen, and I can't go on this way. You can't expect me to. It's not fair!"

"Peggy, do you feel the way I do? If you do, we have to meet again."

"Dick, call me after the war. Call Braniff. I'll tell them it's okay to give my number to you...if it still is. But not now! It has to be later."

"Peggy, don't leave it like this. Please, give me something more." I knew I was losing her.

"They're calling me to go. I have to catch the bus," she said between sobs.

"Peggy, I love you. I want to see you again."

"Bye, Dick. Please take care of yourself, and come back in one piece." The phone went dead.

"Peggy, Peggy . . . shit." She was gone.

My heart was broken. No, it was removed. I was a dead man walking. I no longer cared about the war, the army, the goddamned politicians, or the Vietnamese. Maybe she was right. She was telling me that she could not develop a close attachment with a young man on his way to war. Many of us went home on cargo planes instead of passenger flights.

If this was only the journey to war, how would I ever survive the war? Peggy was right. How would either of us be able to take it? It was too much to ask. Thank God, it was time to reboard the plane to finish the long trip.

Let's get it over with.

"While a note of optimism is creeping into intelligence reports on progress of war in Vietnam, pessimism suddenly has taken hold in the U.S. The public is becoming more and more insistent that the war in Vietnam either be won, or be de-escalated by an American pullback."

—*U.S. News & World Report, August 28. 1967*

3

Good Morning, Vietnam

August 23-24, 1967

An explosion welcomed me to the Vietnam War, but it was not the dramatic attack I had been trained to handle. I was fully prepared to defend myself, but I soon discovered that the enemy was everywhere, in our minds as well as our physical presence.

The final leg of the trip from the Philippines to Saigon was melodramatic. When I left Jacksonville, I'd anticipated arriving in Saigon with adrenaline pumping, all senses honed to a sharp edge, and keenly aware of all my training. I expected to rush from the airplane directly into a raging battle.

My imagined baptism of fire was built on a myth. In reality, I was dog tired from nearly forty-eight hours with virtually no sleep, emotionally wrecked by farewells with my parents and with Peggy. Frantic last-hurrah partying in Oakland had not helped, either. When I saw bursts of light through the airplane's porthole, I didn't know whether we were flying into a lightning storm or over explosions of bombs and artillery. I no longer cared. In my exhausted condition, I just wanted to end the long journey and face whatever was thrown at me. Most of all I wanted to sleep, and I desperately wanted to stretch my legs.

A gruff Air Force sergeant met us in the middle of the night. He lined us up, drill sergeant fashion, into proper lines for transportation to our next destination. I was dismayed to discover heat and humidity were actually worse in Saigon than in the Philippines. The passenger terminal at Tan San Nhut was austere in contrast to Jacksonville, Atlanta, and San Francisco; this facility made even the barren terminal at Clark Field appear elegant. We were standing in a tin barn with a concrete floor and not much else; this busiest airport in the world had all the ambience of a chicken coop.

Most of our group reported to a desk with a sign overhead reading "U.S. Army-Vietnam." From there, transportation to Camp Alpha was arranged. At Camp Alpha the lucky ones were processed and transported to U.S. units. Twenty-five unfortunate souls reported to the MACV desk for routing to Koepler Compound in downtown Saigon. At the MACV compound we would go through roughly the same procedures as the blessed ones, except we were to be shipped on to advisory teams with the ARVN—the Army of the Republic of Vietnam.

Following instructions from our hard-bitten non-commissioned officer (NCO), we struggled to pile all our duffel bags into the back seats of the bus and then sat near the front. I didn't want to be separated from my bag, but the driver announced: "Put your bags in the back and you sit in the front. That way you greenhorns won't trip over your bags when you scramble out the doors if we're ambushed!"

Maybe this was the real war after all. I felt naked without a weapon. Heightening my uneasiness, I noticed the windows of the bus had heavy wire screens over them and opened only a couple of inches to allow the hot, stifling air inside. Everyone in the bus tried to appear nonchalant, but I knew they were as nervous as I was—or at least I hoped they were. The bus moved forward, which forced hot air to circulate around us like a draft created when a door opens to a steaming sauna.

Our driver and sole defender picked up the only M16 rifle in the bus, dramatically chambered a round, and placed it back in the rifle rack mounted near his seat. He turned around in his seat and eyed us doubtfully. "Hang on. We'll be driving through Saigon at high speed." He shoved the gear of the idling troop transport into place and the vehicle jerked ahead, transmission grinding.

"High speed" was an understatement. We took the first turn so fast that our baggage in back tumbled across the seats to the other side. The steady drone and gentle bumps of the airplane were replaced by a bone-jarring ramble; everyone hung on for dear life. The rattling vehicle leaned precipitously with all its weight on one side. Saigon's haunted streets were vacant, except for occasional policemen, like white mice with their small stature and white shirts.

Our bus clattered through a guarded gate at Koepler Compound somewhere in the middle of town. We had safely made it this far. A MACV supply sergeant, who issued each of us one sheet, one pillow, and one pillowcase as we stepped off the bus, accentuated the inauspicious arrival. "Find any empty bunk and get some sleep." He pointed in the direction of a series of stucco buildings.

The new replacements scattered to search for unoccupied beds in dark rooms. I checked my Timex; it was already 5:30 a.m. I was exhausted from jet lag but believed I could muster enough strength left to crash into a bed. I had no other choice. I struggled with my duffel bag and the clean sheet, searching for any empty bunk to collapse on.

I realized the sleeping quarters were in an old hotel or office building constructed around a large courtyard. A high stone fence with barbed wire and glass shards buried in the concrete on top protected the perimeter. The barracks consisted of small rooms, each offering two sets of steel double bunks, and nothing else. I easily found an empty top bunk, dropped my bag on the floor, and attempted to spread my single sheet over the dingy mattress so that there would be something between my naked skin and the crawling things I imagined inside the mattress.

Finally, at long last, I stretched out on the musty mattress, which had welcomed at least a hundred sweaty soldiers to the war zone. I tried to close my bloodshot eyes as the first rays of daylight seeped through a screen door. A slow-turning ceiling fan revolved just over my head, offering a slight breeze. If I was careful sitting up I would not stick my head into the swishing blades. But my eyes would not stay closed. I was in Vietnam; I could not spend my first hours here sleeping. Lying on my back, pretending to sleep, I watched a gecko climb the walls and ceiling to catch flies, listened to the faint whir of the fan, and finally drifted into a gray zone between sleep and consciousness.

Then, movement in the dark shadows of the room yanked my untangled nerves into a knot.

Fatigue vanished and my senses surged into power drive. Using honed observation skills I saw a crouching figure skulk into the room, being careful not to let the screen door slam behind. The stranger was dressed in black pants, a white shirt, and the type of conical hat I knew was worn by the enemy. Hunched over, the invader stealthily slid a bundle into the far corner of the room and retreated very quietly out the screen door, once again careful not to let the door slam. I was still naked and without a weapon, my heart and mind racing.

My training kicked in. I responded without thinking. Rolling to the edge of the top bunk, I dropped off the bed, careful not to raise my head into the whirring fan. I hit the floor hard. Quickly on my feet, I grabbed the mystery bundle and rushed to the door.

I hurled the package through the screen door into the open courtyard yelling "bomb!" at the top of my lungs. I flung myself to the floor and covered my head with my arms, waiting for the inevitable explosion.

The explosion was not the Viet Cong bomb I expected; it was the shrill cries and curses of a Vietnamese cleaning lady as she gathered her lunch scattered about the courtyard.

Good morning, Vietnam!

"Lt. General Thieu and his running mate, Lt. General Ky, shared the platform with rival civilian presidential tickets in My Tho for the first time. Thieu said they "do not promise to do everything in the next four years." My Tho is a war-shabby Mekong Delta city of 67,000. Meanwhile, a bus hit a mine on Provincial Road 26, 12 miles to the southeast."

—*New York Times,* August 27, 1967

4

Sliders

August 25-26, 1967

Humiliated by my episode with the cleaning lady's lunch, I did not want to be seen leaving the room, so I climbed back onto my top bunk and pretended to sleep. I discovered that the exertion had caused me to start sweating again in the heat and humidity, so I just lay quietly on my damp sheet and tried to attract all the air I could from the whirring fan above. Discordant sounds of Vietnamese music circulated with the stale air. The shrill music was disagreeable to my senses, but I would eventually grow accustomed to the sound, and even learn to appreciate it.

The noise of other Americans moving about in the morning light increased, and mounting hunger trumped my embarrassment. I convinced myself that I could blend in with the others and that the bomb incident would soon be forgotten. I made a mental note to move to another bed lest the cleaning lady have a Viet Cong friend. I eased into my smelly khaki uniform, rummaged around for a shaving kit, and walked in the general direction of the common bathroom. As I shaved the aroma of cooking food drifted into the latrine.

I followed my nose to the nearest excuse for a four-star restaurant on the premises. It turned out to be a snack bar run by Philippine laborers. As I entered the door, grease from the grill attacked my nose while steam watered my eyes. The grill was covered with eggs, bacon, and hamburgers, cooking together with hamburger grease running into the eggs, and bacon grease oozing onto the hamburgers.

In the food line, I ran into 1st Lt. Mike Jefferson, with whom I'd served in the 101st Airborne Division until he preceded me to Vietnam. We caught up on old times, quickly getting to the present, as we waited for chow.

"How long have you been in country, Mike?"

"Four months." I noticed he had lost weight. "I was with an ARVN infantry battalion, but a position opened in the Vietnamese airborne, and I got it."

"So you'll get jump pay again? Lucky!" An extra $110 a month came with the hazardous duty. I thought it odd that he would get $110 a month for jumping out of an airplane, but only $55 a month for being shot at.

He nodded. "Yeah, but I'm looking forward to it for other reasons. The ARVN weren't too bad, but the airborne is a cut above, as you know. I like being with the best."

"I know what you mean. I really wanted an American outfit." Still, I was envious of his assignment to the airborne.

As we approached the head of the chow line, I felt green for another reason—the eggs. "Don't touch those," Mike advised. "They're duck eggs and chewy to begin with, but the hamburger grease mixed in will make you sick all day."

"What are you eating?"

"Sliders. Stick with the sliders every time." He reached around me for a tray.

"What the hell are sliders?"

"Hamburgers. You don't even have to chew 'em. Take a bite and they slide right down your throat. It's probably better not to chew them very much, anyway, you might actually taste 'em. And don't even ask about the meat!"

I did stick with the sliders, covered with mustard and ketchup, for every meal in the compound. My stomach never felt very secure, but I never threw up—and that was something. After a day and a half of greasy hamburgers my palate begged for variety.

The next several days were spent drawing jungle fatigues, jungle boots, attending orientation briefings, and watching the bulletin board every few hours for new orders. The army way was to allow enough time to recover from jet lag, stabilize your legs under you, and generally make you anxious to get the hell out of there to join a unit—any unit—before announcing your actual assignment. No matter where you were going, you would just be happy to be going somewhere—that was the army way, and it wasn't invented just for Vietnam.

My time was not so fully consumed that my mind didn't wander to other matters. My thoughts returned to Peggy. She had come into my life so unexpectedly that I sometimes wondered whether she was a dream I had conjured up to fill my loneliness. She had vanished just as quickly as she had appeared, but I knew she wasn't a dream because her perfume lingered on the shoulder of my uniform all the way to Saigon. The night before, I had pulled the dirty khaki shirt from my bag and sniffed the perfume. It was gone.

Her eyes had said so much to me and yet had defended the passage to her own heart. Tuesday was the day she was scheduled to fly into Saigon aboard another plane filled with arriving soldiers, and then return to the Philippines with a group returning home alive. I wondered about those who would be in metal boxes on cargo runs and others on stretchers aboard medical evacuation flights. But my heart ached to know whether Peggy had ever thought of me after that night at Clark. She was etched into my memory; I would find her someday, somewhere. I had to.

I needed a change of pace, and taste. Several experienced officers on second tours in Vietnam suggested taking a taxi to the Rex Hotel for dinner and drinks that evening. I was wonder-struck that there might actually be such amenities in a war zone's capital city. And the idea of taking a taxi into the same city we had sped through several nights before on a wild bus ride was a little unnerving. Nevertheless, my urge to find something digestible to eat was stronger than my doubts about the safety of the adventure, so I happily joined the party with a pocket full of newly converted Vietnamese piastres.

I was not disappointed. The Rex Hotel was an old French Quarter *grande dame*, showcasing an elegant foyer and a winding staircase that led to a popular rooftop restaurant, which had been fully Americanized. The bar was a popular spot to drink American beer or the French-owned beers, La Rue or 33, brewed right in Vietnam. Both the grand hotel and the beer were vestiges of the former French colonial period.

La Bière 33 was good, but La Rue was formaldehyde based. I really didn't want anything with formaldehyde in it. One of the old hands advised, "Bière 33 is the one beer to have, if you're having more than thirty-two!" I had more than that, but not that night. Ten years later, I ordered a beer in France on the Côte d'Azur and flashed back to that moment when the waiter delivered the familiar brand.

Mixed drinks were sold at the bar. Gin and tonic was most popular, inasmuch as it was rumored that the quinine helped in to prevent malaria. The rumors were good enough for me, so I opted for a heavy dose of preventive medicine.

Entrees were not French cuisine, but they were certainly superior to sliders. You could select your own steak from a cold display case, then grill it yourself on one of several open grills made from 55-gallon oil drums cut in half. While my steak sizzled, I watched lights from artillery bursting in the distance. Airstrikes were being inserted on the horizon, and I saw the thrilling trails of red tracer rounds spewing from U.S. Air Force C-47 cargo planes converted into warbirds named "Spooky." This was exciting, and exotic!

This was war as kings intended it to be waged.

A baked potato accompanied my steak, along with cole slaw, baked beans, and ice-cold beer. The rooftop cafe was covered with reporters, generals, U.S. State Department elders, wide-eyed first-timers like me, and most likely Viet Cong spies, all mingling as if we were of the same species.

I had discovered the romantic form of war that I always dreamed of but never anticipated finding. My mind ran away as I considered where this place really was. I wondered whether I might have traveled outside my own realm, but one thing I knew for certain: I was nowhere near my high school hometown of Thomasville, Georgia, or for that matter our temporary residence in Jacksonville, Florida.

Somehow everything seemed temporary now.

I wondered whether I would ever return to those places—or whether I even wanted to see them again.

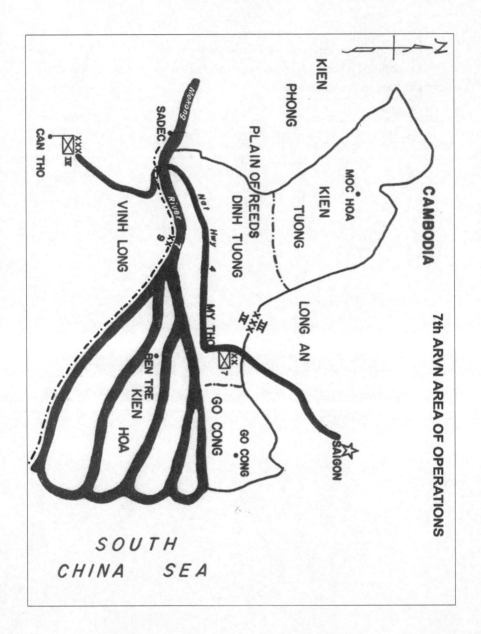

"In the Mekong Delta . . . one Vietnamese division commander told me that a year ago he wouldn't think of undertaking an operation in less than three-battalion strength. Now, he can move with a third of that force, indicating a sharp drop-off in Viet Cong capability and a marked improvement in Vietnamese Army capability. The Vietnamese Army has suffered from an uncertainty about our intent to stay with them."

—*U.S. News & World Reports,* September 11, 1968

Assignment: Mekong Delta

August 26–27, 1967

The *list* would appear soon. Everyone waited for the list; each of us was eager to find his name on it but dreaded the news announced by it. The list of new assignments was posted on the bulletin board near the water jug every day at midmorning. When your name appeared on the list, you shipped out the next day to your unit of assignment.

Several days of processing at Koepler Compound gave the new cannon fodder an opportunity to recover from jet lag and break in new jungle boots and uniforms. I hated the way I looked, smelled, and felt in new boots and dark-green jungle fatigues. Being new was bad enough, but being stigmatized with the appearance and smell of a new soldier in a combat zone was an insult. While everyone understood that you had to earn the old, worn appearance of an experienced Vietnam hand, I disliked broadcasting my tyro status. I would have gladly traded my new green uniform for a worn out old brown one from some departing soldier, but that just was not done. It was not the army way.

The first break in our morning lectures found me at the big glass water bottle for a cool drink. I tried to appear nonchalant as I glanced over the shoulders of those peering at a newly posted assignment list, and I spotted my own name there! I was on the list, but I lost sight of it before I could read my assignment. Casting nonchalance aside, I pushed my way through the less enthusiastic to get a better look.

I was dazed to actually read my own name typed on a paper announcing that I would be leaving this strange but safe compound in Saigon for the great unknown war zone. Some unknown place with strangers awaited the arrival of an FNG, or "fucking new guy." I also realized that there was a Viet Cong soldier waiting to kill me (perhaps the cleaning lady's cousin).

I read my assignment: the ARVN 7th Infantry Division Advisory Team—Team 75—in the IV Corps tactical zone. My stomach knotted as a panicky impulse seized me. I was going to the Mekong River Delta, the one place I never anticipated, and dreaded most of all.

I had spent my spare time in college preparing for this day by hiking in North Georgia's mountains. And while studying at the John F. Kennedy Special Warfare Center at Fort Bragg, I had always assumed I would be assigned somewhere in the mountainous jungle and therefore dozed through most of the orientations on the Mekong Delta. I recalled pictures of flooded rice paddies, large swollen rivers, and the inundated Plain of Reeds from a travelogue about an itinerary I never intended to take. My worst fear had been realized: this was primarily an ARVN tactical zone. Only the U.S. 9th Infantry Division's Mobile Riverine Force provided an U.S. presence there. "So," I supposed, "seven is my lucky number, and somebody has my number!"

My day to depart arrived with the next rising sun. I arose very early that morning, shaved in time for a final greasy slider, drew my M1 carbine. The Vietnamese, because of their small stature, carried M1 carbines, scaled down versions of the World War II M1 Garand rifle. U.S. soldiers normally carried standard M14 rifles or the newer M16s, but U.S. advisors were obliged to carry the same older weapon as their Vietnamese counterparts.

Both the M1 and M14 were too large and packed too much punch for the ARVN soldiers. I had carried the M1 in the Reserve Officer Training Corps (ROTC) for four years and was familiar with the rifle, its capabilities, and its feel. The smaller carbine was insignificant in comparison with the mighty M1; it had been designed as a self-defense weapon for officers, or as a second, lighter rifle for mortar and artillery gunners. The carbine was not a fighting man's weapon. Here its use was simply an accommodation to the smaller Vietnamese. We were clearly outgunned by the Soviet- and Chinese-made AK-47 assault rifles. I didn't like it.

But I was thoroughly excited about getting out of Saigon and discovering the real war story for myself. I packed a few belongings, and caught the wild bus back to the Tan San Nhut airfield.

The MACV flight scheduler told me to catch the helicopter that ran a daily shuttle between Saigon and Can Tho, the capital of the delta region. The chopper was making a special stop in My Tho just to drop me off on the way. I was one of two passengers aboard, the other being the normal courier on the once-a-day flight. I felt I was flying into isolation—where no one else would be.

The helicopter vibrated and bounced for forty-five minutes with hot air swirling through open doors. I anticipated miles of flooded rice paddies streaming by below, and I was not disappointed. Watery fields stretched endlessly. I was no stranger to farmland, but I had never seen crops growing in water before.

Eventually, I was deposited on a lonely helipad at the fringes of My Tho City, next to a cemetery. The earlier feeling of isolation returned like a strangling claw. Without an encouraging word the chopper lifted off, leaving me perplexed and standing with my carbine, a flight bag, a duffel bag, and a brown envelope of orders. I snapped off my carbine's safety and wondered which of the Vietnamese scurrying about were Viet Cong. I strained to see if any resembled the cleaning lady, but they all did. Five minutes later I was relieved to see a jeep speeding toward me, bouncing uncontrollably in potholes that punctured the road. The rattling vehicle left a cloud of dust in its wake, even though the road was still wet from a recent rain.

I climbed in and began the roughest ride I have ever experienced on a paved road. The jeep bounced so hard that I kept my teeth tightly clenched to avoid chipping them. No one dared talk in the jeep.

After a short ride that seemed much longer, I spotted a large, white two-story building flying U.S. and Vietnamese flags on parallel flagstaffs in front, the entire compound surrounded by a barbed-wire fence. Sandbag bunkers had been erected at the corners of the fence.

I learned that this was the Seminary, a Roman Catholic school leased in 1962 by the U.S. Army from a diocese exiled from North Vietnam and in need of funds. The U.S. advisory team was in need of a facility, so it was a match made in heaven. The stuccoed brick structure was of French colonial style, sporting a red tile roof. The building was roughly a four-sided trapezoid, with one side running parallel to the Rach Bao Dinh River and the opposite side adjacent to the access highway connecting My Tho with National Highway 4. Highway 4 ran from Saigon through Can Tho, joining the lower rice-growing regions to both capitals.

Advisory team administrative offices were in the front of the building, sleeping bays for eight people each were in the center, and the dining facility and bar were in the back. The dining hall was used for church on Sundays and movies in the evenings. The bar served one purpose, but only after noon. The courtyard was used for parking jeeps, landing helicopters, and playing volleyball. The roof was ideal for sunbathing, being closer to the sun and out of the line of fire. Sandbag bunkers along the barbed-wire fence supported the defense, the warlike purpose quite different from what the original tenants envisioned.

The Seminary served as headquarters for Advisory Team 75—a U.S. fortress in a foreign country. The ARVN 7th Division headquarters was situated in a former French Army caserne in My Tho City, about two miles away—far enough that the real war fighters and surrogates maintained a decent separation. My Tho City was the major population center for the northern river delta and the upper rim of the rice bowl that fed the country. It was a city of about fifty thousand people and the capital of Dinh Toung Province.

In 1962, Lt. Col. John Paul Vann began his saga as the original American legend in Vietnam in Dinh Toung Province, with the first air-mobile action that eventually enlarged the hostility into a U.S. war. At that time Vann was senior advisor to the ARVN 7th Division.

The 7th Division's area of operations consisted of four provinces: Go Cong, Kien Hoa, Kien Toung, and Dinh Toung. Geographical features made this terrain essential for both sides. Here were major communication

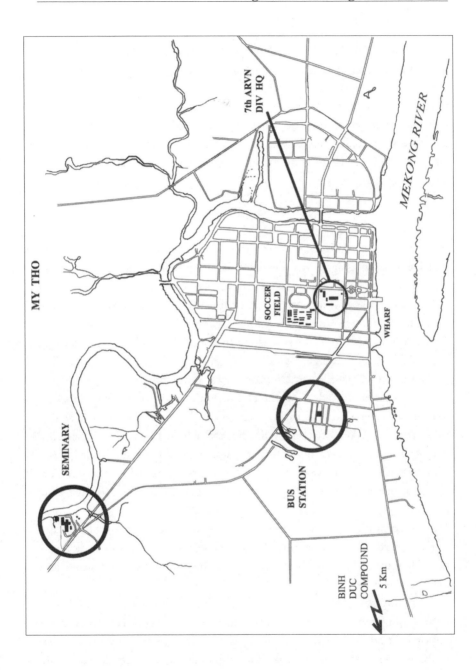

routes that included National Highway 4 connecting the Delta's rice bowl to the capital, Saigon; the Mekong River that connected Laos and Cambodia to the South China Sea; and 100 miles of coastline on the east and 130 miles of international border with Cambodia on the west. This network consisted of 490 kilometers of waterways navigable by ocean-going vessels and 735 kilometers of major highways. In addition, the flat region was highly navigable by infantry in all directions, provided the warriors did not mind getting their feet wet.

* * *

After two days of foot dragging, the adjutant, Major Wilkinson, told me that I would be assigned to the ARVN 7th Division's 2d Battalion, 11th Infantry Regiment as assistant battalion advisor. The battalion was stationed at Binh Duc, a sprawling compound of tin shacks that accommodated the division's training center and a regional military airfield. This battalion was part of a mobile strike force consisting of the 2d and 3d infantry battalions and the 32d ARVN Ranger Battalion. Together, the strike force operated in all four provinces of the 7th Division's area of operations.

I became energized as we traveled the last few kilometers of my long journey (this jeep ride to Binh Duc being a continuation of the roughest jeep ride of my life). We drove past the helipad where I had been deserted a couple of days earlier. I noticed that it was located between a canal and a cemetery where crypts were positioned above the ground, like those in New Orleans, because the water table was too high to bury the dead below ground.

We continued through coconut and banana trees until we turned at a sign on a dirt road that announced our final destination. I didn't think it was possible for the dirt road to be rougher than the paved road, but it was—and twice as dusty.

As I tumbled out of the wretched jeep, Capt. Bobby Hurst showed great enthusiasm when he met me. Bobby was from Florence, Alabama, and the senior U.S. advisor to the battalion. He spoke with the rapid clip of an Alabama fast-mover: sometimes I found that he had finished talking before I had started listening. His zeal was abundantly clear and contagious. Bobby had a reputation as a rising star in the army. He moved with short, jerky movements that matched his speech but he obviously knew what he was doing, and that was okay with me. I would adjust and learn to listen faster because my survival was associated with what this experienced officer had to offer. We would get along fine, and, besides, he was the boss—it was my responsibility to see that we did. As I looked Bobby over, I was reminded of the greenness of my uniform and the brownness of his. That distinction alone highlighted the chasm of experience between us. I had not yet stepped into a rice paddy to stain my green fatigues, but that would soon change.

Bobby introduced me to the rest of the team. Sergeant First Class Mendenhall, from somewhere in Florida, was the senior team sergeant; he was soon to be promoted to master sergeant. Mendenhall was an experienced soldier, not easily shaken. Staff Sergeant Rich, from South Carolina, would operate with me in the field. Rich was much younger, about my own age, but competent with more time in service than me. "Zeke" was our Vietnamese houseboy, and Major Bouie was the battalion commander.

I was shown a ramshackle sandbag bunker right outside our door, our last refuge in case of a serious attack. I saw the generator that provided intermittent electricity and the refrigerator, which was chilled by blocks of ice. A single bed and a metal wall locker were mine when we were here. One room in the building was filled with plastic furniture and primarily used by Vietnamese officers to play dominoes late into the night. The entire tour took less than five minutes. Finally, after traveling halfway around the world, I was fully oriented and ready for combat.

One last point on my orientation tour was a visit to the old French-style latrine behind our quarters. The place could be found in the dark by its smell. It was situated in a chest-high tin shelter and separated into four stalls. Inside each stall was a ceramic floor with two footpads separated by a hole between them. Nearby was a 55-gallon drum filled with dirty canal water. The pads were used for squatting, and the canal water was for flushing. The notion of using the contraption while trying not to breathe was nearly enough to make me stop eating at all, but not quite.

I settled in with the others for my first night in the *real* army. After a dinner of canned beef stew and French bread, I read a paperback western that Bobby had already finished—until I had to make the inevitable dash for the French latrine. No matter how rushed you were to make it in time, you had to remember to bring your own toilet paper.

Despite the grandness of the adventure, it all boils down to a series of little things. I had hoped there would be more to the war than this, but somehow I knew there would be *much* more.

"United States infantrymen rushed ashore from armored assault boats under heavy fire from a battalion of Viet Cong troops in the Mekong Delta. The enemy troops, crouching in rain-swept rice paddies, fired machine guns, automatic weapons, and recoilless rifles."

—*New York Times,* September 16, 1967

6

Rude Awakening

August 31 - September 15, 1967

At "oh-dark-thirty," we were jarred awake by the sounds of activity throughout Binh Duc compound. I heard Vietnamese voices everywhere, not panicked but in the tone of soldiers making hurried preparations to move, to launch an operation. As I rubbed heavy sleep from my eyes, Captain Hurst rushed from the bedroom in his skivvies to find out what the commotion was. In a moment he darted back and announced, "We're going on an operation. We'll get the details later, but we have to pack up and be ready to move."

"Do you want me to wake the NCOs?" I asked.

"They're already up."

I had packed many rucksacks in the dark during training, but this time was different—because this was an actual combat operation. Training had officially ended! That sudden realization sent a chill shrieking from my neck to my feet. What I had learned in all the endless drills and lectures was all I had to take with me from this point forward. There was no way to call time out. Time raced past while dawn refused to break.

Captain Hurst called out his mental checklist as he made his final preparations. That was reassuring to me because I checked my own intuitions against his list to ensure that I didn't commit a major error in my own preparations. I supposed he was doing this purposely and I appreciated his subtle but effective way of guiding me.

When we were satisfied with our packing, the four Americans walked together toward the battalion mess hall. I hoped to pick up a tray and walk through a line for coffee, eggs, bacon, grits and orange juice. Instead, we sat at a long table near Major Bouie, and a steward placed a bowl and pair of chopsticks before each of us. I watched as others scooped rice from a larger bowl into their smaller bowls, and I copied them. Then a steward passed along the table with a large pot, which was steaming hot and strongly aromatic. He dipped a ladle into the brew and drew a brown broth to spread atop our bowls of rice.

"Duck," said Captain Hurst.

Fortunately I had practiced with chopsticks, so I managed to scoop some duck and rice into my mouth. Either the duck and rice were seasoned inadequately or the dish was naturally bland. The rice especially needed salt. Breakfast fell short of eggs and bacon but was an equally long way from the sliders in Saigon; however, it was not bad, if you were hungry enough. I hadn't finished my bowl of rice and duck when Major Bouie stood and announced that the battalion would depart in fifteen minutes. Bouie left promptly, followed closely by the battalion staff. We lingered a few more minutes to stuff more breakfast into our mouths before we hurried to recover our rucksacks and rifles.

As we rushed out the door, an ARVN soldier handed each of us two small plastic bags, tied at the top. In the dim light, I couldn't make out what was in the bags, but one was about the size of a grapefruit and was rubbery; the other was smaller and squishy. As we left the building and the light improved, I could see that the bags were "doggy bags," or the ARVN version of a C-ration. The larger one was hard-packed, cooked white rice, and the other was leftover duck soup to pour over the rice later in the day. Afraid not to take either, I stuffed one bag in each of my shirt side pockets, not sure when I would see solid food again.

I realized that I didn't know where we were going, how long we would be gone, or what we would do while we were there. The same ominous uncertainty that had fallen on me in my unceremonious arrival at the helipad in My Tho returned. I felt hijacked.

I strained to throw my heavy rucksack over my back, lift the puny carbine, and walk out into the street with the others. My legs were unsteady beneath the unaccustomed burden. Meanwhile ARVN soldiers were already loading the 2 1/2-ton trucks ("deuce and a halfs") in a half-organized way. These trucks made up the junkiest fleet of transports I had ever seen.

"You and Rich take the same truck as the lead company commander. Mendenhall and I will follow Major Bouie," Hurst told me. It was the shortest operations order I had ever received, and I didn't feel very good about it. We ambled alongside the parked convoy of trucks until we saw Vietnamese 1st Lieutenant Vanh, the 2d Company commander, standing beside a truck near the head of the convoy.

I approached Vanh. "Sergeant Rich and I'll ride in back, if you need us. Do you know where we're going?" I asked.

Vahn looked right through me, not replying.

"Hey, sir. He doesn't understand English," interjected Rich.

All my language training escaped me. I wondered how we would communicate about simple matters, much less coordinate operations or fire support in an emergency. Vanh sat in the cab of the truck, and Sergeant Rich and I scrambled into the back with helping hands from obliging ARVN soldiers.

One truck was assigned per platoon, and with soldiers, rifles, packs, radios, and a few live chickens we were packed like living sardines in a can. There were no seats in the back of the truck bed, so everyone stood and held onto anything within reach, sometimes onto each other. I noticed that there were no sandbags in the bed of the truck either; I frequently prayed that we would not hit a land mine buried in the road.

As we rolled from the compound I still didn't know where we were going. I yanked a map from the side pocket on my fatigue pants to trace our route as we moved along. The trucks rocked and rolled considerably on well-worn springs, and the rough road made it necessary to use both hands to hold on. The breeze felt good in our faces, but I knew I'd be unable to find myself on the map in an emergency. The sun was already hot as blazes by 8:00 a.m. I wondered what it would be like when it really got hot.

On our way out of the compound, we passed several outposts of "ruff-puff," the Vietnamese Regional Forces (RF) and Popular Forces (PF), which were the equivalent of a militia. Under a collective term of territorial forces, the RF manned critical points like bridges, while the PF protected their hamlets and villages. Most of them were in the Mekong Delta, usually living with their families inside fortified outposts. They were a motley collection, but fond of waving as we passed in convoy. They always smiled because they knew the more operations we ran the less likely they were to be attacked. Actually, the ruff-puff would be a fairly easy target if the Viet Cong needed a quick victory, but the VC was generally loath to attack them because of their co-habitant families. The Viet Cong attempted to win the hearts and minds of the population—just as we did. This really was a popularity contest, after all.

After crossing a bridge over a wide canal, the trucks pulled to the side of the highway and rattled to a jerky stop. I expected the entire battalion to dismount and encircle the trucks in a protective perimeter. It did not. Instead, everyone stood there in the beds of the trucks like ducks in a shooting gallery. Meanwhile, Major Bouie and Captain Hurst disappeared into the ARVN 11th Regiment command post (CP) at Long Dinh. As he disappeared inside, Captain Hurst signaled me to follow him—almost as an afterthought. Rich and I jumped down from the truck and followed.

Inside, I met Maj. Cecil N. Neely, the 11th Regiment advisor. He shook our hands and graciously offered us some much-needed coffee, which was strong and very hot. I needed it after my early, rude awakening, even on a hot morning like this one. While we carefully sipped the steaming coffee, Neely explained that the VC had been blowing up bridges along Highway 4, and burying mines under the roadbed at night. The first vehicles on the road the next morning had set a mine off, blowing the vehicle to pieces along with the passengers, regardless of whether they were military or civilian. This practice tended to leave large holes in the highway, which had to be repaired, but not until the local population had been made aware of the success of the Viet Cong attack in the local area. Fear of these mines slowed the flow of rice to markets, which in turn had an adverse effect on the local economy. These activities had to be stopped. The briefing did nothing to reassure me about riding in the trucks.

A combined American-Vietnamese operation was commencing, generally along the highway, to protect the road itself and to push the VC back farther than ten kilometers in both directions. Mechanized infantry would patrol the highway in armored personnel carriers (APCs) supported by military police in wheeled French armored cars. Dismounted infantry would patrol the rice paddies, canals, and swamps ten kilometers on each side of the highway. Our mission was to find the VC troops and kill them, find and capture their mines, and gather information from the local population on VC locations and intentions. This operation was designed to disrupt the Viet Cong and regain the confidence of the population. The 2d Battalion was to patrol west of the district capital of Cai Lay.

Now I knew considerably more than I had when we'd left that morning, but I was still a bit vague about what my role would be on this mission. I could hear my mother asking the difficult question: "What will you be doing in Vietnam, son?"

We exchanged radio frequencies and were quickly gone from our exposed stationary positions in the back of the trucks, which lurched ahead to Cai Lay. We next halted in the center of the town. Major Bouie departed quickly to coordinate with the district chief, an ARVN lieutenant colonel. I was pleased to see the ARVN troops dismounting from the trucks, until I realized that they were not providing security, but instead, were buying cigarettes. They would purchase strong French cigarettes and touch a drop of green menthol onto the paper to give a cooling flavor; the cigarettes were instantly transformed into popular menthol-flavored Salems, minus filters.

As soon as Major Bouie returned the trucks jerked forward. Several ARVN soldiers sprinted to catch up, running to reach the rear of the trucks, and then were dragged on board. We surged ahead and continued to Binh Phu, a village composed of a series of small hamlets on a Mekong tributary just north of Highway 4. The noon sun seared us as we dismounted.

"You two stay close behind me for a couple of days," Bobby advised Sergeant Rich and me. I knew he was concerned about me on my first operation, and Rich was also relatively new. I appreciated his sentiment, but I resented being assigned to a nursemaid.

Admittedly, the going was tough at first. The trail we followed was dry and clear, but my legs felt weak and wobbly. We were carrying heavy loads on our backs, and I actually had to learn to walk all over again in the rough terrain of the rice paddies and canal lines. I felt everyone watching to see if I fell. I knew Hurst was watching my every move; his critical eyes burned my neck as much as the hot sun. I was determined not to falter.

The entire area was laced with small canals and streams. This was a populated region; local citizens had erected bamboo-pole bridges over most of the waterways to cross the canals and streams without getting their feet wet. Bamboo bridges were narrower than the sole of a jungle boot and sagged as we crossed, one at a time. ARVN soldiers rushed ahead of Americans at the bridges, because our greater weight might break the weak bamboo poles, forcing them to wade the murky, filthy water. Many bridges did indeed break under my weight.

After thirty minutes of stop-and-go movement, the entire column suddenly dove behind the cover of rice paddy dikes, trees, or thatched hutches. I heard the crackle of rifle fire a hundred meters ahead, and winced as bullets ripped through trees overhead.

Major Bouie turned to us and simply said, "sniper."

The shooter was a single Viet Cong sniper, intent on delaying our movement or just making a statement that we were not welcome.

As we pulled ourselves back up to our feet from behind the cover, Bobby Hurst came over to me and put his arm around my shoulder. "Congratulations," he said. "You have just earned the Combat Infantry Badge."

"This isn't enough combat to qualify for that!" I protested.

"Don't worry about it," he said. "You're lucky to get it out of the way now. Next time might not be so easy."

*   *   *

The rest of the afternoon amounted to a long walk in the sun without any more fire from the sniper. As dark approached, the battalion stopped in a village and established defenses for the night. The CP was in a thatched structure that appeared to be an empty rice barn. Hammocks were hung from wooden beams, and soon cooking fires began to emit the familiar aroma of fresh rice and duck. My appetite was raging, and the idea of rice and duck was more compelling now than it had been at breakfast. Finally, we were beckoned by Major Bouie to sit cross-legged around a straw mat on the floor. Night had fallen and darkness filled the barn; two small candles gave flickering light to our efforts to eat. Rice bowls were passed around, and we served ourselves with rice first and then chunky duck soup.

In the candlelight I was clumsy in picking up a large chunk of duck from my bowl with chopsticks. Hungry and not to be deterred, I grabbed the chunk with my fingers and raised it to my face. Candlelight glinted in his eye as I stared into the duck's blank face. I was considerably more startled than the duck, and I went to bed hungry that night.

My first day in combat had begun with a rude awakening way to early, a horrible truck ride, and a single sniper hoping to shoot someone and run away. It had ended with a long walk in the sun and a duck's head for dinner. I had a feeling that this was a preview of an entire year of my grand adventure. I wondered whether I should have joined the Peace Corps instead—or better yet, fled to Canada with Peggy. This war didn't seem to be all it was touted to be. If this was all there was, I wondered what the hippies were protesting.

* * *

On the second day, Hurst, having seen that I was at least physically competent to keep up with the ARVN soldiers, released Rich and me to walk with the leading company commander. Finally I was in my rightful place. Nevertheless it remained impossible to give any meaningful advice to the Vietnamese: their English was limited, and my Vietnamese was worse. I seldom knew the concept of our operations, the enemy situation, or our mission, except as I could surmise on my own or when Bobby received a quick brief from Major Neely over the radio.

I strove to keep up with our location by following our movements on my map. All members of the team did the same, and we double-checked with each other frequently. I needed to know our exact location in the event we required an airstrike, or artillery, medical evacuation, or to escape and evade capture if the battalion was overrun. The Vietnamese company commanders took their instructions directly from their battalion commander over an old U.S. Army PRC-10 radio, which needed manual tuning. At least, U.S. advisors had the newer PRC-25 with preset frequency selections.

* * *

The next eight days were much like the first. The battalion continued to sweep through hamlets to establish a government presence in the villages near National Highway 4. The highway bombers and snipers lived in the hamlets we were moving through, but our numbers were such that we were seldom challenged directly. Occasionally, the highway was blown despite our efforts and those of the mechanized infantry patrolling it. The engineers, who bivouacked nearby, usually repaired the road quickly, but a stray Lambretta or M113 APC striking a land mine was not so easily reassembled. Neither were the unfortunate passengers, and having witnessed that, I began to realize that simple luck was involved in surviving these random violent incidents. Death was not planned but was completely indiscriminate.

*   *   *

Eventually, we moved back to the highway and the same old beat-up trucks met us for a trip back to Binh Duc. As soon as we arrived at the compound, the other advisors dropped their rucksacks on the floor, grabbed clean sets of jungle fatigues and shaving kits, and piled into our jalopy jeep. It was apparent to me that they had practiced this drill many times before. We rattled our way over the washboard road to the Seminary. Bobby drove, I rode shotgun and the two NCOs smiled broadly in the rear seat, with their carbines stuck out each side.

A hot, soapy shower and shave restored me to someone I remembered. I had already lost a few pounds, and my jungle boots were blessed with that rough brown color that scraped the greenness from my feet, leaving me marked as a seasoned field advisor. We enjoyed a hot, solid American meal and a couple of cold beers in the club later for dessert. I had not been there long enough for mail to catch up with me, but I did have time to drop off a few letters at the mailroom. I had written them earlier and carried them around in my helmet liner until I could mail them.

Dear Mom and Dad,

I made it safely to Vietnam, as you can see. I've been on my first operation. Officially, I am an advisor, but I can't say that I have done any advising yet. I think my real job is simply liaison with the Vietnamese forces in the field. I really like the others on my

advisory team and the Vietnamese, also. I'll write as often as I can,
and send some pictures or slides. Please keep them for me.

I hoped the letters would tell them enough, but not too much, about
what I was experiencing. The thought of mail started my mind wandering
again, and my thoughts naturally turned to Peggy. How many times had she
been back to Vietnam? Where was she now? Had she met another soldier
who eclipsed her memory of me? I was afraid that I was already history to
her. How long before I would forget how she looked, or felt in my arms? I
wanted so much to see her again, talk to her, kiss her. I just wanted to know
that she was all right, and for her to know that I was, too.

* * *

Back at Binh Duc, time dragged. I was anxious to go back to the rice
paddies. We shared paperback books, wrote letters, played rummy and
dominoes with ARVN soldiers, and made trips to the U.S. Mobile Riverine
Force base at Dong Tam to scrounge anything useful we could get our
hands on. We usually carried trading materials with us to Dong Tam, such as
Viet Cong flags or North Vietnamese Army (NVA) military equipment in
exchange for sandbags, cement, or pierced steel planks to use in our bunker
construction. If flags were in short supply, the battalion tailor could generate
a few for a nominal price.

* * *

The highlight of this operational break was the arrival of "Slick," the
nickname Bobby assigned Captain Xuan, the new battalion executive
officer. Slick was slightly chubby with a round face, but he spoke excellent
English, having attended infantry training at Fort Benning, Georgia. He
knew and appreciated Americans and recognized our place in the unit,
which was enhanced significantly by his arrival. He was equally comfortable
with either his native countrymen or his adopted Americans.

Slick often invited the U.S. advisors to join ARVN officers to play
dominoes in the day room of our tin shack, including us socially in their
activities. We might was well play with them because we were unlikely to get
any sleep as long as the games raged on the other side of paper-thin walls. I

often sat up until the early hours playing with Slick and the company commanders.

Aside from Slick, I got along best with Lieutenant Kiem: it helped that Kiem's English-language skills were much better than either Lieutenant Vanh's or Lieutenant Thanh's. Kiem was a good-time guy who liked to joke and poke fun at anyone around him. We called him a cowboy. He was as outgoing in battle as he was in play. Kiem grew to be my best friend among the ARVN officers, other than my counterpart, Captain Xuan. When I was not with Slick, I sought out Kiem to take into the village for soup or iced coconut milk. We talked about the war, our families, and the United States. Kiem had an insatiable appetite for information on our country and clearly wanted to go to Fort Benning for training, following in Xuan's footsteps.

Slick made these relationships possible; he encouraged and supported our inclusion in everything. Our spirits were buoyed by the arrival of this affable soldier, and our relations with our allies improved considerably. Real friendships were being forged here.

Prospects for this war were improving, after all.

"Vietnam is for men with double vision. It is two kinds of combat against a two-faced enemy, and the combination is deadly. One fight pits the U.S. against North Vietnamese and main-force Viet Cong regular soldiers whose primary mission is to kill and maim the opposing armies. A second enemy, the clandestine Viet Cong guerrilla, wages the second fight. His uniform is the peasant black pajama, and his mission is a Communist innovation: to steal the people and territory away from the South Vietnamese government."

—*Time,* August 25, 1967

7

Storm Clouds Over the Double Y

September 16 - October 6, 1967

The purpose of a tornado siren is to warn those in its path of imminent danger. The interval between the siren's initial sounding and the all-clear signal is a dreadful time of waiting and watching for the consequences. Either you'll be swept to a horrible end or it will pass harmlessly by. Knowing is the difficult part—knowing it is coming, knowing the possibilities, and knowing there is nothing else you can do to prepare for it.

A new operation began much the same way as the first one—with an early morning alarm. This time we departed under cover of darkness, without breakfast. After trucking again to an area near the 11th Regiment CP at Long Dinh, we air-assaulted from a large, wet rice paddy codenamed LZ (landing zone) Springfield. We stood knee deep in warm water and mud and witnessed mass confusion. We strongly encouraged the Vietnamese soldiers to line up into ten-man sticks for a helicopter pickup, but without much success. We were vulnerable in our disorganization.

A heavy fog hung over the field like a shroud, delaying the choppers' lifting off due to lack of visibility. This was a fortunate turn for us because of our disarray in the pickup zone. We needed the extra time to organize the troops. Truck convoy movements were strictly a Vietnamese-run operation, but helicopter movements were the primary responsibility of U.S. advisors. My pathfinder training at Fort Benning had prepared me for airmobile operations, so I felt competent in every aspect from directing the helicopters to organizing the ARVN soldiers for their pickup. But I needed to train them to line up faster.

The overall assault was a combined operation using both U.S. and Vietnamese helicopters. The first flight to approach was made of U.S. Army Hueys. I was at the head of the column and popped a smoke grenade for identification by the flight leader while I spoke with him on the radio. The flight approached low and slow. A chopper touched down near each stick of Vietnamese soldiers while gunships circled overhead to provide protection. The troops got on board rapidly and I proudly watched them lift off for insertion into another LZ. I had done this many times in training, but this one was for real: this was how a textbook combat assault was supposed to begin.

Next, the Vietnamese Air Force (VNAF) H-34 helicopters approached in a staggered trail formation. Even though I could not communicate with them, I hoped they would follow the example of the U.S. pilots before them. Hope is not a course of action; the VNAF flight approached with too much air speed. As the lead chopper flared to land, the trailing choppers scattered like a covey of quail to avoid collisions. The result was H-34s all over the landing zone, facing in every direction of the compass. Needless to say, the infantry who had lined up so meticulously now scattered as well, some running from helicopters about to land on them and others running to board choppers that had landed a distance away. Trudging across the sodden rice field was difficult work, and the Vietnamese soldiers were visibly upset at their own air force cowboys for this display of ineptitude. The comparison was stark.

We encountered a half-hour delay for refueling after the second group had lifted off. Sergeant Rich and I took the third flight, which were VNAF helicopters that landed in the same distressed pattern as the second flight. After we lifted off, the helicopters took a circular route twelve kilometers north, over flooded rice paddies, and deposited us just south of converging canals know as the Double Y.

The Tong Doc Loc is a large navigable canal that runs from west to east on the southern terminus of the flooded Plain of Reeds. The canal joins with the Song My Tho, another navigable canal that runs generally south to connect with the Mekong River. The two canals approach from different directions, converge for a distance, and then separate to form the Double Y, clearly visible from the air.

Our mission was to search the area along the canals, and we spent several days accomplishing that. While we found signs of preparation, including underground bunkers, cache sites, and well-used trails, we found no ammunition, documents, or Viet Cong. We were soon lifted out in a reversal of our ragged approach and returned directly to the airfield at Binh Duc. The signs of so much activity along the canals disturbed me, and I wondered what it meant. I had a distinct feeling that I would soon see this area again, and that time someone might resist us.

*   *   *

Upon our return, we repeated our routine trip to the Seminary and our enjoyable personal recovery, including shower, shave, meal, beer, and mail. Back at Binh Duc, the rest of my team seemed content to enjoy the down time between operations to just relax and read.

Unlike the others I found free time a heavy burden. I wandered the battalion area in attempts to practice my language skills and learn what I could about the organization, status of supplies and equipment, defense, and training.

Although I could manage with the language while ordering a beer in the local market, my technical language was unsatisfactory. I prepared questions in Vietnamese ahead of time, carefully writing them out and practicing them. I asked great questions of the staff but, unfortunately, I couldn't understand their answers. This exercise was frustrating and may have explained why the other Americans spent their time in less stressful diversions. Nevertheless I would not accept defeat; I was determined to be more effective, to transform time from a burden to productivity.

Giving up detective work, I enrolled in the correspondence Infantry Officers Advanced Course. I was anxious to learn more and, now that I knew from experience how much I did not know, I was determined to close that gap. I could not wait until the war was over to learn how to fight. So I selected courses in supply, artillery, close air support, and company tactics.

I expanded my Vietnamese friends beyond Slick and Kiem to include Corporal Thanh, the battalion communications chief. Thanh was driven by his own demons. He was from Da Nang, in the northern portion of South Vietnam, and he spoke English. He had learned our language while working with his mother, selling soft drinks to U.S. soldiers along the road. The Viet Cong had murdered his father, in front of Thanh and his mother, for refusing to assist them. Thanh hated the Viet Cong with an intensity that was unseen in most other Vietnamese soldiers. He worked hard to keep his communications gear in shape and sprang into action if combat appeared imminent. He and I shared a devotion to our missions.

Thanh lived in a one-room wooden shack in the NCO housing area in our compound with his wife and three children. He regularly invited me to his home to meet his family, and one day I finally accepted. His children were happy to see an American guest, and I enjoyed meeting them. I believed I could help these enlisted families, especially the children, and I wrote my parents about it.

Dear Mom and Dad,

I live in a Training Center here in Vietnam. Today, I went with one of our Vietnamese enlisted soldiers to visit his family. They really are poor and have a hard time making it on army pay. I am going to try to get some supplies to help improve their living conditions. I was thinking that if the church group wanted to gather some canned goods or toys, I could help distribute them to the children and it would make a big difference in their lives in this war-torn country.

This was an opportunity that appealed to my parents. They contacted members of their church and soon boxes of clothing, toys, and treats arrived in the mail. I placed Corporal Thanh in charge of distribution, which

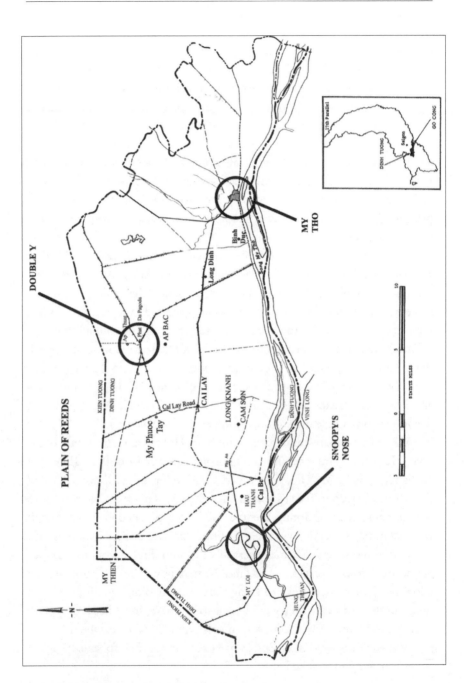

enhanced his status in the community and made me feel better, too. Maybe, I thought, I can make a difference here after all. I wondered if I should have become a foreign missionary or Peace Corps volunteer instead of a warrior.

Thanh explained how much good could be done with twenty bags of cement, so I set about getting it. I tried the U.S. Army-Navy base at Dong Tam but found that cement was seldom used for construction. I finally learned that most cement was distributed through the Agency for International Development (AID), an arm of the U.S. State Department, and placed directly into the hands of the province chiefs for community projects. Mine was a community project, so I made a courtesy call on the province chief.

The Dinh Toung province chief was an ARVN colonel who lived in palatial splendor in the largest residence in My Tho. I worked my way through his staff until I found myself sitting outside his office, and then I waited patiently for two hours before being escorted in to see him. In less than two minutes he heard my case, refused me, told me to mind my own business, then dispatched me by the back door. I had no recourse for appeal, but the little pedagogue had angered me. I refused to give up. Through other channels, I managed to acquire five bags of cement from Pacific Architects and Engineers in exchange for several homemade Viet Cong flags, which I decorated with a little duck blood to increase their value.

While I was on my humanitarian mission, Hurst was on a venture of his own. He met an American nurse, a hospital advisor from the AID at the civilian hospital in My Tho. We cleaned ourselves up as well as we could and drove our old jeep to Edna's apartment, which was comfortable compared with our austere living arrangements at Binh Duc. Situated in an old French colonial hotel, it sparkled with marble floors, large shuttered windows, and genuine furniture. Edna actually served wine with dinner while she told us about two little orphans, Oanh and Kim, whom she was thinking of adopting. Hurst invited her to bring them out to Binh Duc for a visit. I didn't understand why they would want to go there, but I kept my mouth shut. Maybe Hurst, a bachelor, was interested in Edna, or maybe not.

Midway through dinner Edna was talking about the orphans. "They're so special. When I get the papers. . . ."

She froze in mid-sentence; her eyes opened wider. "Was that what I think it was?"

I hadn't heard it before, but then I did. "Mortars. Sounds like one-twenties." We could clearly hear plunking as the rounds popped from the 120mm mortar tubes outside town.

"Got a bunker?" asked Bobby. "We only have half a minute."

"No!" Edna's face was pale.

"Under the table," Bobby ordered.

We crawled under the table, lying flat on the cool marble floor.

My mental clock told me we had a few more seconds before impact. I scrambled back out. "Anyone want your wine?" I asked as I grabbed my wineglass. Without waiting for a reply, I handed the other two glasses under the table, before sliding underneath.

We listened as the large mortars exploded in the city environs.

"I wonder if I could help them hit the province chief's house?" I wondered out loud. No one else fully appreciated my meaning or sincerity.

The attack ruined our pleasant evening. When the mortars ceased, we rushed back to Binh Duc to find the battalion preparing to move out on foot. For the rest of the month, we moved out of the compound every night to occupy security positions around the city. The one night we stayed at home the Viet Cong knew it. At 3:00 a.m. twenty-four 82mm mortars pounded us and we raced into our dilapidated bunker for safety. From our vantage point inside, we could inspect our own sandbag architecture and see the deficiencies. Flashes of exploding mortar rounds illuminated our faces through the gaps and holes in the sandbags, and the timbers shook around us. Sand trickled onto our heads and sifted down the backs of our shirts. Soon it was over, but we found several duds in the dirt road the next morning. We needed no further prompting to improve our protection.

*   *   *

As inexperienced as I was, I pondered our trip to the Double Y, and the activity we had witnessed there. Pieces of that puzzle were missing. I wondered what our intelligence officers concluded about the intentions of the Viet Cong in making elaborate preparations in a remote area and then departing.

When a storm approaches, sometimes I can feel it in my bones. I felt a storm now coming from the direction of the Double Y. We had been warned and we were in the interval between an alarm and a storm. I could not shake the feeling and soon we felt the cold breeze in our faces.

> Never before has America been so puzzled about a war effort. In no other conflict . . . has the dichotomy of decision between military and political considerations been so painfully evident.[2]

"Not since the bonus marchers stormed the Mall had there seemed such a clear and present danger to the Capital. The reason for the jittery saber rattling was the approach of a 40,000-man army of widely assorted U.S. resistance groups, descending on the Capital for a climactic weekend demonstration against the war in Vietnam."

—*Newsweek,* October 30, 1967

8

Trouble at the Double Y

October 7-9, 1967

The Double Y appeared to me in a nightmare. I had a premonition that we would return to that place on different terms from those in our first visit. Although I realized we were fortunate to have made the first trip to study the terrain and approach routes along the canal banks, it did nothing to alleviate my dread of returning. We had previewed the storage and fighting bunkers and knew what possibilities awaited us from the beginning. We had experienced a rare opportunity to walk the battlefield before the battle commenced. No excuses.

We were alerted in the evening with a warning order to be ready to roll early the next morning. Before dawn on October 7, we rose, packed, cleaned and oiled our carbines, and prepared to move. The same old rickety, racketling trucks awaited us, and we climbed aboard without fanfare. I detected a more serious tone in the preparations for battle than I had in our previous operations. Storm clouds were developing, darker and more ominous than ever before. A warning siren was shrieking in my mind.

Our trucks rolled past the usual landmarks, the Seminary and Long Dinh Bridge, before they stopped on Highway 4 near LZ Springfield. We quietly assembled into a rudimentary formation. No helicopters were scheduled for the assault; therefore, we would walk into the zone. Sergeant Rich and I followed the 3d Company near Lieutenant Vanh, the company commander. Normally he ignored me, but this time he wanted me to stay close by his side. This was not to be a walk in the sun.

We crossed a small canal running parallel to the road and dispersed as we crossed two kilometers of open rice fields. Ahead of us stretched an old dirt road, cut by trenches in several places, denying it to vehicles but passable as a high-speed avenue for infantry on foot. On my map I identified the road as National Road 221. From my history studies I knew that this was the same route used by the Vietnamese on January 2, 1963, in the infamous battle of Ap Bac. John Paul Vann had advised the ARVN 7th Division then. In a major battle leading to greater U.S. involvement in the war, Vann had turned a military debacle into an international spectacle at these very coordinates. His troops had met the 261st Battalion of the Viet Cong main force head to head at this spot, and lost. The lesson of history enveloped me as we trudged through the fields.

Today Lieutenant Vanh spread his company out as I had learned to do in basic infantry training (I had never seen the Vietnamese follow the book before). Infantrymen advanced slowly and carefully with rifles off their shoulders and carried at the ready. The serious intent in their cold stares and body language was evidence that they expected trouble: I believed that they knew more than I did about what lay ahead. Interrogation of villagers was equally intense. Although no one shared any information with the Americans, the air was electrified.

Third Company progressed cautiously through the hamlet of Ap Bac 2 and continued north to Ap Bac 1. We walked carefully but quickly throughout the day, crossing semidry rice paddies that were laid out like one of my mother's patchwork quilts. An hour and a half before darkness, we approached the final tree line before the Double Y. The company halted under the cover of trees one kilometer from the canal and waited while the rest of the battalion pulled itself on line facing the waterway. Stretched before us was open rice paddy up to the large trees along the canal line, parallel to our front. From our previous operation, we knew this canal line was covered with bunkers and ammunition cache sites, empty only a few weeks before. This time I believed Viet Cong were defending the bunkers.

In the center of the paddy before us sat a lone farmhouse surrounded by peasants gathering in their water buffalo for the evening. When our troops emerged from the trees an old woman screamed, and then yelled *Choi Oy!* "Oh my God!" at the top of her lungs. She continued to scream as she ran toward her house and the protective bunker inside. The entire scene immediately turned frantic. Her reaction to our appearance surprised me, but everyone who witnessed it knew exactly what it meant. She was directly between two armed infantry battalions destined to clash violently in this remote farmland.

Our infantry, arrayed on a broad front, marched forward across the open paddy directly toward the trees along the canal. We were totally exposed. (I recalled Pickett's charge during the battle of Gettysburg. We were Pickett's Confederate infantry moving against the dug-in Yankee infantry and artillery on Seminary Ridge.) This time the 514th Local Force Battalion was defending. We continued to move forward another hundred meters before an intense barrage of rifle fire erupted from the tree line, cutting through our ranks and stopping us in our tracks. The initial firing was more furious than I imagined possible.

Bullets thudded as they kicked mud and water around us. Others cracked near my head, forcing me to dive headfirst for cover behind a small dike in the exposed field. Sergeant Rich low-crawled beside me, and I could hear Bobby Hurst over Rich's radio as he called Major Neely for air support.

Hurst took a moment from the radio to yell, "Taylor, stay low, but move as far forward as you can to mark our front lines with smoke grenades. I have gunships en route."

"Roger!" I shouted over the noise. I waved to indicate I understood in case he could not hear me. I also wanted him to know where I was in the event air cover arrived.

I turned to Sergeant Rich and said, "Give me your radio and smoke grenades. I'll leave my pack here. Wait for me." Leaving him behind to cover my movements as much as possible, I crawled forward through the mud, trying to stay lower than the dikes.

By the time the gun ships were on station the radio was no longer working. I left it and moved ahead, staying behind the mud dikes as much as possible. I tossed smoke grenades ahead of me as mud and water continued to splatter from the strikes of bullets. I wondered whether what I was doing made any difference, but there was not much else I could do, so I continued to throw smoke grenades until I ran out. Darkness was closing in; smoke grenades would be useless soon, anyway.

I didn't dare try to get back to Sergeant Rich in the remaining light, so I settled into the muddy rice field to wait for the cover of darkness. I was near enough to the canal to see helicopter gunships receiving heavy ground fire. I had no communications, but Lieutenant Kiem's seriously wounded radioman lay near me, so I commandeered his PRC-10 set. Manually tuning this older, but working, radio, I connected to the battalion advisory frequency in time to hear Bobby Hurst give directions to the first flight of U.S. Air Force (USAF) F-4 Phantoms. He was speaking with the forward air controller, who had been able to get a fix on our position from my earlier smoke grenades. The F-4s dropped bombs and napalm until darkness made that impractical.

Air strikes blasted the canal line 500 meters to my front. The explosions of the 500-pound iron bombs were the most wonderful sounds I had ever heard. As the bombs crashed through the trees and exploded, they kicked up a spray of mud, dirt, and water that reached nearly to my position in the rice paddy. As napalm splashed into the trees, I heard the screams of burning men caught in the inferno. Fire turned darkness into light again and illuminated sights I did not want to see. Fortunately for the victims and me, that part was brief. Smoke mixed with the night to close the curtain on that awful scene.

As darkness fell over us VNAF Skyraiders relieved the Phantoms. I was pleasantly surprised by the skill of the Vietnamese pilots. The Skyraiders were fuel-efficient propeller-driven aircraft with a longer loiter time, enabling them to remain on station longer, as opposed to the Phantoms, which burned jet fuel at a phenomenal rate. Skyraiders flew slowly, but never very low. Their accuracy was amazing, and they carried a large payload of 250-pound iron bombs. When darkness was complete, the green tracers from Viet Cong rifles and machine guns streaked through the night toward the Skyraiders like fireworks. Some tracers were also spewed in our direction on the ground.

I overheard Bobby talking to the pilot of a USAF C-47 "Spooky" gunship that had joined the fight, replacing the bombers. The C-47 would be much more effective for close support in the darkness. As Spooky reported in, the Skyraiders sped homeward and a red stream of fire with its line of tracers, and awesome to see and hear, erupted immediately from its reliable minigun. Green tracers from the Viet Cong bunkers turned increasingly skyward. I used that opportunity to help ARVN medics drag our dead and wounded behind our front security lines. It was clear that we would remain in position all night, and we needed to consolidate our defenses.

*   *   *

In the mushy darkness I finally located Hurst, Rich, and Mendenhall at the edge of a pigpen near the lone farmhouse. Bobby was talking on the radio with the Spooky pilot. The pigpen smelled putrid, but that was the least of our concerns. I was glad Rich was with them because I didn't relish retracing my steps in the dark to where I had left him. My rucksack was in the rice field somewhere, but I was in no mood to search for it. Fortunately, someone lent me a dead soldier's poncho for cover during the long evening. I had been wet all day, and the poncho afforded some warmth in the chilly night.

We took turns talking on the radio to Spooky throughout the night. He concentrated continual fire into the canal line until daylight. We had attacked the 514th from the south, but no other forces had been deployed to trap that unit from any other direction. The 514th's escape routes along the canals remained wide open. I believed it unlikely the enemy would escape north into the Plain of Reeds, because the trail could be easily followed. But, the concealed trails on each side of the canals were protected routes not threatened by our fires. Relatively dry rice paddies offered other excellent high-speed escape routes east or west, but not north in the swampy plains, or where we were holding in the south.

I shivered through the night. Finally the first rays of sun in the east blessed us with their warmth. In the new light we initiated a coordinated search of the canal line. I expected the Viet Cong battalion to have escaped, but I fully anticipated finding at least twenty dead VC soldiers in defensive positions. The canal lines had been blasted all night and appeared devastated on the ground. Bomb holes covered the area, trees were splintered and shattered, and large tracts of vegetation were incinerated. I couldn't imagine anyone living through the devastation. Nevertheless, our search uncovered nothing—not one dead VC, no rifle, document, pack, or flag—nothing. I stood in awe of a unit that could recover every indication of its presence, in the pitch black of night, while under heavy fire from the sky and ground, and escape with no trace.

We had suffered eight dead soldiers and a dozen seriously wounded. Frankly we were lucky to have escaped with so few casualties. We had been totally exposed to the enemy rifle and machine gun fire during the initial outburst. Fortunately, the Viet Cong troops had fired too high in the initial outburst, and most of their bullets passed over our heads. Even so, most of our casualties had resulted from that first violent eruption. Our infantry did not maneuver under enemy fire; rather, it depended on air power to destroy the enemy force while returning fire from the cover of the paddy dikes.

Two U.S. Army helicopters were summoned to evacuate our wounded. As the first chopper lifted off, its propeller blast blew the ponchos off the bodies of the eight dead soldiers laid out on the ground side by side in their last military formation. The bodies were quickly covered again with ponchos and tied like holiday packages to be delivered home—prodigal sons returning home. Another chopper landed to remove the bodies. The detail of soldiers designated to load the precious cargo was too few and the pilot signaled us to hurry. Without any hesitation, I pitched in to help a small Vietnamese soldier lift one of the covered bodies. I was surprised at how heavy the small body had become and how its rigidity made it more awkward to handle.

As we struggled toward the helicopter the corpse began slipping from my grip. The poncho, wet from mud and blood, slid from my fingers. I grasped it to hang on, aghast as the body slid from the poncho and splashed headfirst into the mud of the rice paddy.

"Oh, my God!" I groaned in horror as I stared into the face of my friend, Lieutenant Kiem.

I had been a few meters behind him when the Viet Cong opened fire on our exposed ranks. In my own rush to cover I didn't know he had been hit. Then I remembered taking the radio from his wounded radio operator.

Seeing Kiem like that was a weight that demanded my strength. Perhaps I should have been closer to Kiem during the battle, but battle was the biggest gamble in life. Then, while carrying my friend, I had dropped him into the mud. Weak from shock and exertion, I could no longer lift him at all. Soldiers gathered to help recover the bodies loaded Kiem on the helicopter.

As they shoved him into the chopper I staggered in the mud alongside. The blast of the rotors kept his face uncovered by the poncho. I saw Kiem's open, lifeless eyes until the chopper lifted off. No, not just until then—still, forever. He returns to visit me every October. Kiem longed to go to the United States, and now he follows me here.

*   *   *

The rest of that day and the next we marched north into the Plain of Reeds, exactly the direction least likely for the 514th to have gone. I wondered whether that was precisely the reason we were going that way. Eagerness for battle had evaporated with the rising sun.

Indeed, we searched without finding anything except deep and fast-flowing streams concealed in a swamp of waist-deep alkaline water and bamboo reeds. Before the deepest streams we made poncho rafts to cross the swirling currents. Several times I pulled drowning soldiers from the water. I was never a great swimmer, but the distress on a drowning man's face is compelling. And all of them looked like Kiem to me then; in every drowning face I saw him staring back. These I pulled out of the flood. Poor Kiem. If only I could pull him out of the grave.

After a thoroughly wasted day, helicopters lifted us to Binh Duc to recover and lick our wounds. During the flight I felt empty. Bobby was right when I complained about the sniper that helped me earn my combat infantry qualification—I had indeed encountered enough violence to satisfy me. I found other aspects of combat even more difficult, like death, futility, indignity, fear, loss of a friend. What else awaited the unsuspecting?

> The black, black, dark black blood
> Puddles up and hardens and mixes with the mud,
> And returns to the earth, the humus of the earth,
> And the stumpy, splintered trees shiver in their mirth.

Quite odd to the trees that the soldier stands alone
In a barren, blazoned field with boot upon a bone.
The hand of his enemy underneath his foot
And a watch in his pocket burnt and filled with soot.

The watch in his pocket, he drags out by the chain.
Then he turns it over and reads the words again:
"To Kiem, my pal." A tear comes to his eye.
The soldier's heart is broken: he saw his comrade die.

—Richard Taylor

"Speaker John McCormack denounced Congressional critics of the Administration's war policy, charging that they were giving comfort to North Vietnam. Rolling the newspaper in his hand and pounding it on a table, the speaker declared: "If I was one of those, my conscience would disturb me the rest of my life."

—*New York Times,* October 12. 1967

9

Friendly Fire

October 10-16, 1967

Friends should never kill each other, but sometimes the tide of war rolls up unintended consequences. That's war.

Following the battle at the Double Y our team made the usual pilgrimage to the Seminary, but this time hot showers could not wash away the stains. The excitement of a significant battle paled next to my distress. I considered the operation inadequately planned and badly executed. Above all, I was saddened by our own losses and troubled by the loss of Kiem, and distraught over dropping him headfirst in the mud. I focused my attention on cleaning my equipment, reading Bobby's worn-out westerns, and completing the Infantry School's correspondence courses. Dwelling on doubts about the war was depressing; trivial pursuits were mentally healthier. That defensive technique had been drilled into me as a boy.

On the morning of October 11, we boarded the old deuce-and-a-half trucks for a short ride to the My Tho wharf. The Vietnamese Navy waited to transport us on a mission in the River Assault Group (RAG). The ancient fleet consisted of discarded U.S. Army landing craft; it was the indigenous version of the U.S. Mobile Riverine Force, or MRF. We were bound for Ben Tre in Kien Hoa Province, birthplace of the National Liberation Front and a hotbed of Viet Cong activity and propaganda.

The boats thumped the docks upon their arrival at Ben Tre, and jeeps picked up our advisory team for a brief meeting with the U.S. advisors of the ARVN 10th Infantry Regiment. I learned that the U.S. 9th Infantry Division was conducting a search-and-destroy operation and had requested that the ARVN 7th Division provide a blocking force. The 10th Regiment was already committed to another mission, so we were substituted. We marched from Ben Tre to form an anvil for the U.S. Army's hammer, a classic military operation: the U.S. forces were to maneuver against the Viet Cong and crush them against us.

We moved up the road several kilometers. I noticed that the peasants in Kien Hoa Province were far less friendly than those in Dinh Toung. Trenches had been dug to cut the paved road leading from town. Soldiers in our battalion apparently shared my assessment; their concerns were etched on their faces. I was sure they didn't like being used as an anvil any more than I did. If the enemy didn't smash into us, our friends might.

Our infantry left the main road and entered a forested area in a spread-out formation. The forest was a single canopy of hardwood trees about twelve to fifteen feet high. The ground was level and clear for easy movement and visibility. As we approached our designated blocking position, I was reassured by the distinct sounds of a U.S. Army helicopter passing overhead. When it circled around to return, I pressed the radio handset to my ear to hear if anyone was trying to contact us. I heard nothing, so I checked my radio by calling Bobby Hurst.

"Red Oak Owner Six, this is Red Oak Owner Five. Commo check. Over."

"Five, this is Six. I hear you loud and clear."

Lieutenant Vanh, the 2d Company commander, approached and asked through an interpreter if I could contact the helicopter. "No," I replied, "but I'll keep trying. Do you have a message?"

As we were talking the helicopter flew over again—low and fast. I could make out the faces of the crew fifty feet above me—especially the intense face of the door gunner, who was pointing his door-mounted M60 machine gun directly at us. My blood turned to ice. I jumped at the staccato burst from the muzzle as the machine gun fired into our ranks. Smoke flowed from the breach as bullets ripped through the thin canopy of hardwood trees. Hot 7.62mm shell cartridges dropped on us, as did limbs and leaves.

I yelled into the radio, "Cease fire! Cease firing! We're friendlies! Cease fire, you assholes! You're shooting us. Make him cease fire!"

No response.

The silence was horrible.

I heard the helicopter turn for a third pass then it came at us again with guns blazing. The radio was useless since we were not on the same frequency. I dropped it and pulled the maroon scarf from my neck, waving it wildly while yelling into the air. I ran to get under the helicopter so the door gunner could see me better.

"Stop firing, goddamn it! Cease firing! Cease fire!" I yelled at the top of my lungs.

A soldier in front of me dropped to the ground and I heard yelling all around. I threw a red smoke grenade and kept my eyes on the sky for the bastard to return. I prepared to return fire at the U.S. helicopter with my puny carbine. It did not return, but the damage was already done.

I ran to a small cluster of men gathering about the fallen Vietnamese soldier. I recognized him as Lieutenant Vanh's radio operator—the man I usually followed when we were moving. He had been hit twice in the chest. The sucking chest wound produced gurgling noises from his lungs and heavy bleeding from his chest, no doubt from a severed artery near his heart.

The medic was covered with blood but he had stopped working. He indicated with a shrug that there was nothing else he could do. Vanh requested a medical evacuation and I ordered Sergeant Rich to request one even though I knew it was already too late. The wounded soldier's face was pale white, and his eyes were clouding over as I tried to penetrate them with mine. I wanted to read his thoughts. I took his wrist to check his pulse but could not detect one. He looked up, lips moving, trying to speak, his eyes filled with fear. His strength was fading fast; the poor man knew his life would end in a few moments. I held his hand as life slipped away. I was horrified by it all and furious at the helicopter crew for firing into us.

Instant hostility radiated among my former ARVN friends, including Corporal Thanh, the battalion communications chief. His clenched jaw and bleary eyes told me that he was angry enough to kill. The radio operator had been one of his communicators, part of his team. My hard work in helping Thanh gather sandbags and goodies for kids was erased by one senseless act of "friendly fire."

Captain Xuan and Major Bouie rushed in and took charge of the situation. Bouie ordered soldiers to carry the dead and wounded back to the road for transport to Ben Tre. The column moved again, aimlessly.

I was angry as hell and frustrated that I couldn't stop the slaughter even by putting my own life at risk. I wanted to reverse the entire day and start it over. I'll never forget the faces of the M60 door gunner or the eyes of the terrified, dying radio operator. They are other phantoms that follow me still waiting for an opportunity to tell me something. What do they want to say? Why do they return with the same unspoken question: "Why?"

When I thought I had accepted the death of Lieutenant Kiem, the face of the radio operator staring into my eyes replaced it. This is the human cost of war.

An official investigation of the incident determined that the helicopter pilot had radioed the 10th Regiment CP and asked if any of their units was operating in the area. The reply had been negative: after all, we were not one of the 10th's units. The stupidity of it all appalled me. The U.S. Army had requested our participation; the local advisors had briefed us; yet no one knew we were there? I was consumed by an enigma too difficult to fathom. I wondered what Peggy had seen on the flight to Vietnam. What had she seen that scared her away? Had she seen the future? I was not sure I was ready for the future, either. More lay in waiting.

* * *

The rest of the operation was a blur, my thoughts blunted by the experiences. The U.S. 9th Division killed some VC, primarily from air operations, but not against our fragile anvil. We encountered a few snipers, hostile villagers, and unforgiving terrain.

The weather punished us further; water was growing scarce but the bounty of Kien Hoa sugar cane, bananas, and cucumbers moistened our parched lips as we walked in the merciless sun. Eventually, we made our way back to the docks to cross the Mekong for home, but not for long.

"General Giap, North Vietnam's Defense Minister, reported that his soldiers have taken a fearful pounding in their head-on collision with U.S. troops. To cope with superior firepower, Giap stressed the need for better training and indoctrination. But most importantly, he called for a major change in tactics, emphasizing small-scale guerrilla operations to erode U.S. determination to fight. Hang on for a long war."

—*Newsweek,* October 23, 1967

10

River Assault

October 18-23, 1967

This was no glorious crusade; the fratricide in Kien Hoa convinced me of that. Our efforts to win the war seemed futile and pointless. The excitement of combat was invigorating, but the thrill was followed by depression created by bungled opportunities, "friendly fire," accidents, and most of all, losing friends. A void appeared where purpose should have been.

We prepared to launch another major operation. The tempo of activities increased, providing less time to restore our bodies and minds between missions. I wondered why were we increasing our operational pace at such a rate. That old feeling of wandering about in the dark in search of the truth returned to nag me.

Our newest venture carried us to Go Cong Province, near the Rung Sat Special Zone. Operational security had become a major concern for us, especially when operating near Highway 4. An organized band of informants had established observation posts to signal our movements to the Viet Cong as soon as our trucks left the compound. This time, instead of going toward Highway 4, we returned to the Mekong River wharf at My Tho. There we boarded landing craft of the Vietnamese Navy's RAG. This time armed patrol boats escorted our ragged flotilla.

The RAG chugged down river toward the mouth of the wide, muddy Mekong River, the *Cuu Long* or Dragon's Mouth. At the broad river mouth silt and sludge were expelled into the South China Sea. Tides here were so strong that the waters changed direction at high tides, refusing the stream's deposits and forcing the river back inland.

Vibration, noise, and pungent diesel fumes spewing from tired engines of the World War II landing craft made it nearly impossible to sleep. The deck was so crowded that few could find enough space to stretch out, but that didn't stop anyone from trying. The noxious, gray cloud that wrapped around the boats made breathing the fumes unavoidable. In time a trance-like state soothed the mind and made general discomfort seem like a bad dream. Semisleeping soldiers were strewn about randomly, making it impossible to walk. The ghostly boats appeared to be an apparition ferrying a cargo of the dead through an early morning mist. I wondered whether this really was a journey of lost souls.

The convoy plowed down the river all night, the warriors shivering from the cold night air and dampened from the water. At dawn the mystic flotilla arrived at the river's mouth. We chugged from the muddy water into the waves of the South China Sea, flotsam to drift ashore. I imagined we might keep going until we sailed off the edge of the Earth. Instead the flotilla plodded ahead one kilometer, then swung in a large arc back toward land. The scene before us was not a white sandy beach; it was a tangled swampland where blacks, browns, and grays prevailed in a dark, foreboding panorama.

The landing craft formed an assault line and steamed for the beach. The timing of the river ride delivered us to this place at first light and high tide. Unfortunately a sandbar snarled our plan by stopping the entire formation

500 meters from shore. The landing craft reversed engines but were unable to back off the sandbar while fully loaded. High tide had already crested, so the sea had reached its highest level: We could not float off. Engines strained, puffing diesel smoke in torrents, but we were thoroughly grounded. Our only option was to step off into the dark water at a considerable distance from shore and walk inland. Having discharged their burdens, the boats could float away.

"Take off your rucksacks," Bobby wisely advised the Americans. "Hold them in one hand and your rifle in the other. If you lose your balance, the rucksack will go to the bottom. If you're wearing it you'll be inverted with your feet above you. Also unsnap your chinstraps."

That was sound advice, and we adhered to it without question. I noticed the Vietnamese soldiers were following our example.

Ramps went down in preparation for storming the beach. Captain Xuan demonstrated remarkable leadership and courage by being the first one off the boat. When he stepped off, he held his .45-caliber automatic pistol over his head. Slick was completely submerged into the muddy brine, with only his upraised pistol out of the water. When he surfaced his chin was barely above the water line, waves splashing in his face. It would have been comical, but the situation was far too serious for laughter—we were about to find ourselves in the same predicament.

We stepped off the ramp into the surf, one by one. After the initial shock, I discovered the footing on the bottom to be worse than it appeared from the surface. The ocean floor here was not hard sand, as I expected, but soft mud from the belching river. Goo sucked my boots deep down if I stood in one place. I was forced to keep walking, or I would be slowly sucked below the water's surface. Everyone around me made the same discovery. Fortunately no one was shooting at us. One sniper on the beach could have annihilated an entire battalion, like the bobbing ducks in a shooting gallery.

The coastline was a bitch. There was no beach at all, but instead a swamp that extended to the edge of the water. Mangrove roots extending straight out into the ocean, pushing out large, exposed tentacles to trip us and entangle our feet. Miraculously, the entire battalion made it ashore without losing a single man. We exhausted raiders sprawled out on the roots of mangrove trees, completely sapped, and we lay there undefended for an hour before resuming military activities.

*   *   *

Five days evaporated as we trudged through the swamp and tangled with snipers—who were apparently local guerillas, because we found no evidence of main force units there. (Traditional units were too intelligent to live in this dismal environment.) I was not sure why we were searching here in the first place. This operation reminded me of our expedition into the Plain of Reeds when we knew the enemy was not there. Anyone who lived here would have to be very stupid or have a very nasty disposition.

On our last day in the desolate marsh, we trudged to an actual beach to prepare for our departure. The beach we found was beautiful, white, and sandy, with two exquisite French colonial homes facing the coast. The South China Sea appeared quite different from this vantage point: it was a beautiful blue, enticing, and clear. But from the sea itself, looking toward shore, the same water appeared moldy brown, ugly, and forbidding. Evidently the changed perspective made all the difference.

The Vietnamese searched the two colonial beach houses and uncovered Viet Cong documents and two antitank mines, but no one was home. A helicopter arrived to recover the documents and deliver new ~ Major Bouie. As the helicopter hovered ~   ~, the downdraft of the propellers sent red tiles sailing from the roof and slung them in our direction like frisbees. One soldier, casually watching the disturbance with his helmet lying at his feet, was hit in the forehead by one of the flying tiles, which rendered him unconscious. Blood flowed from an open gash along his hairline—another casualty of idiotic action. The same chopper that sent the tiles flying through the air evacuated him.

After the sailing-tile incident, we stretched out in the warm sun enjoying an unexpected respite on a utopian white beach. We stayed there most of the day, drying our clothing and ourselves, relishing the beauty of the South China Sea and just waiting for our ship to come in.

The landing craft appeared late in the afternoon, at low tide. The boats stopped a full kilometer from the beach this time, twice the distance from which we had waded to land. Now we reversed our earlier plodding through the muddy bottom to the landing craft. The warm sun had baked us all day, making warm waters feel like ice to our skin. The water was only armpit deep this time, but the walk was much longer. Upon reaching the boats, we were thoroughly soaked and exhausted. We faced a long river ride in open craft. Once again diesel fumes, noise, vibrations, crowded decks, and a cold night breeze were our shipmates. Shivering dried our wet clothing but did nothing to warm us. I could hear the chattering of teeth above the loud throb of diesel engines.

We arrived at the My Tho wharf at four a.m. To our universal dismay, no trucks waited to ferry us to Binh Duc; we were forced to walk back to the compound and arrived as the first light of the sun broke over the horizon. The walk after the long ordeal dejected us, but no one seemed to expect anything to go according to schedule. After all, this was a war—sort of.

Life's a bitch—then you die.

—Anon.

11

Into Snoopy's Nose

October 24, 1967

We were being propelled headlong into trouble again. We could sense it, but when an operation order quickly followed we knew it. Our battalion was trucked back to the wharf for a nighttime trip up the Mekong River to Cai Be. The RAG pressed slowly ahead with diesel engines straining against the strong current. Two Viet Cong battalions, the 261st and 263d, of the 1st Main Force Regiment were known to be in the region we were entering. Both battalions were skilled and tenacious. The Vietnamese soldiers clearly were not thrilled with the prospects. Body language and dubious expressions spoke volumes about their serious concerns.

I asked Captain Xuan about the operation. He spit out the words, "Snoopy's Nose!" The reference was to a bend in a tributary that made a

280-degree loop resembling the comic-strip character Snoopy's nose. Everyone, Vietnamese and Americans, knew this hostile place by its lovable namesake.

The landing craft docked at Cai Be at 8:00 a.m., just as indigenous traffic into the town market peaked. A long night on the river had heightened our edginess to get on with the mission, yet we idled on the dock for an hour before trucks could get through the crowds in the market to the wharf. I was certain that reports of our presence had already been sent to our adversaries in Snoopy's Nose. Instigators in the market could well have deliberately extended our delay at the wharf, allowing spies to tally and identify our organization. A sense of danger settled over us.

Transportation finally arrived and we trucked north to an intersection with Highway 4. From the junction of Highway 4 and an old dirt road branching to the west, we walked into the unknown. Determination froze our faces into war masks.

This heavily populated region sprouted small hamlets about every kilometer. Our soldiers questioned the local peasants, who were nervous in our presence. Their attitude indicated that VC were nearby and probably had informants among them. Peasants were generally not partisan, favoring neither the ARVN troops nor the Viet Cong, but they were especially unnerved when both were nearby at the same time. That meant one thing: battle. And people would get hurt when the shooting started.

We proceeded one kilometer north from our dismount point and were engaged by snipers as we continued our approach march. Two soldiers were hit right away and were evacuated back to Highway 4. I calculated that the two soldiers' actually having been hit by snipers indicated that the shooters were disciplined main force soldiers, not nervous hamlet guerillas. Local force guerillas were more concerned with firing a few shots and escaping than actually hitting a target. Main-forces troops understood that it was easier to escape if the other side had wounded soldiers to delay it. So we paused to tend our wounded.

Major Neely interrupted the silence on the radio. "Red Oak Five, pop smoke. I'm inbound with passengers."

"Roger that. Smoke's out," I replied.

"I see violet smoke."

"Roger. You're cleared to land."

Neely did not say who the passengers were. I expected an artillery forward observer or someone else who could help in the battle ahead. I was surprised and disappointed as the passengers disembarked from the helicopter. One was an army specialist fourth class with a notebook and camera, an official army photographer from the press office in Can Tho; a Japanese photojournalist preparing a special report for Tokyo followed him. Both were unwelcome guests as far as I was concerned.

At the moment of their arrival, Vietnamese soldiers had detained several prisoners, and I could see they were treating them roughly during interrogation. I certainly did not want any incidents of abuse recorded on film, but the Japanese photographer seemed unconcerned with the rough handling. But the prisoners' treatment bothered me, and I wondered about his nonchalance. He seemed to be overlooking a story, so either his cultural background or the war had hardened his outlook. Frankly I didn't believe it was a newsworthy story, either, but the liberal U.S. press had conditioned me to expect the worst.

The photographer asked a series of questions in excellent English. In my first experience with a reporter, I tried to be honest, but I certainly volunteered no more than I was asked. The "spec four" was there to escort him and ensure that he had our full cooperation, also serving as a witness in the event that anything happened that might be disputed later.

Under duress the prisoners admitted that the 263d Main Force Battalion had been there. Snipers had covered the battalion's withdrawal into Snoopy's Nose. We packed up quickly and took off in hot pursuit of the escaping enemy unit. Our unwanted visitors tagged along behind me, cameras clicking. When we were on our feet, offering targets in the open fields, the sniper fire resumed and several soldiers were hit immediately. One was hit in his face, which was turned into a bloody mess. We stopped once more to evacuate our wounded. The Viet Cong tactic of delaying us with sniper fire worked: we slowed down while we used cover as much as possible. Each casualty that required a litter cost us five men—the victim plus four litter bearers. Walking wounded accompanied the litter details on foot.

I lay on the ground with the spec four and the Japanese photographer, talking about the operation while the evacuation was organized. The reporter was nonchalant about the firing around us, fueling my fears that he would stay with us for the rest of the day. I marveled at his attitude toward the imminent danger; either he was unaware of what lay ahead or he simply didn't care.

A medevac helicopter approached to recover the soldier with the face wound. Much to my relief the two visitors climbed aboard. As a more accurate reflection of our misguided priorities, I suspected that the helicopter had come for the journalists and that the wounded man luckily had caught a ride.

Thirty years later, I was viewing a photographic display of the works of international journalists killed in Vietnam, and found photographs that a Japanese journalist had taken just hours before he was killed. Studying his picture, I recognized him as my visitor. Some time after his visit with us, the photojournalist had been killed while covering another battle. A description of his death accompanied his photographs, confirming my assessment that he carried his cavalier attitude to his eventual end.

When the journalists were gone Captain Xuan impatiently signaled me to join him. Slick pointed toward a large six-foot-wide track recently trampled through a swampy field. The grass was about two feet high, with six inches of water on the surface of the ground. The grass was freshly bent, indicating the direction a large number of people had recently trekked.

"What is it?" I asked. "Did one of our companies go this way?" I thought I had missed something while tending to the journalists.

"VC," said Slick. "263d Main Force Battalion." His tone was solemn.

My heart froze for a couple of seconds, and I felt the blood leaving my face. We were literally right behind an enemy force of a size equal to our own.

"We're one hour behind them," Captain Xuan said, holding up one finger for emphasis. "They prepare defenses now to fight. Snoopy's Nose is just ahead. They are protected by the river on three sides, and we must go into his nose!" The implication of this news was suffocating.

Xuan said, "If you can get help from Americans—do it now, please!"

I could clearly hear sounds of digging in front of us and I called Bobby for help. "Red Oak Six, this is Red Oak Five. Over."

"This is Red Oak Six. Over."

"Six, my counterpart advises me we're in for a big one, and from what I see, he's right. Can you line up support now? It'll start pretty soon."

As I waited for his reply, I heard the first mortar round pop when it left the 82mm tube 200 meters away. Other shots quickly followed the first, and firing continued until rounds hit nearby, exploding into the tree line and muddy fields around us. Each explosion fell closer until the bursts coughed up mud that dropped on us as shell fragments whistled close overhead. The VC gunners walked mortar rounds toward us in a classic artillery technique.

I did not like the terrain we were in—an open field with a few two-foot-high dikes for protection. The 263d was dug into the banks of a tree-covered canal, well concealed and protected. Rows of trees on our flanks provided excellent cover for the enemy to maneuver around us. Our enemy had favorable terrain, time to prepare defenses, and numbers equal to our own. He had chosen the time and place for battle. The only advantage we had was firepower, but not even that materialized when we needed it most.

Reinforcements were requested by the ARVN, but no one expected them to arrive in time to make a difference. We were on our own, at least for the time being. This battle was to be us against them, using only what we had brought with us to the fight. And it did seem that we were going have a hell of a fight very soon!

Bobby had trouble arranging U.S. fire support. "No American artillery or air support is available," he informed me. "Tell Slick there's a large American operation underway and everything is committed already." Fire support was our best hope for victory in this engagement, and our only advantage. Now we had no advantage.

I passed the bad news to Xuan. "Can't you get artillery from Cai Be?" I asked.

Xuan reluctantly agreed to get the ARVN artillery cranked up, but I could see he wasn't happy about it.

After ten long minutes we heard ARVN artillery fire from the district capital of Cai Be. Within two minutes the artillery rounds burst, directly behind our own position. Viet Cong 60mm and 82mm mortar rounds were intimidating, but our own 105mm artillery shells were absolutely terrifying. The rounds could be heard whirring into our midst, then a second of silence, then the crack and blast of high-explosive energy. Zings from large shards of shrapnel sliced through the air like jagged knives, ready to slice off a head or an arm. Artillery rounds first exploded in the trees to our rear, near the battalion CP, and then made a trail across the open field toward our forward position. The artillery fire passed right through our ranks, halting before it reached the dug-in VC. Cries of wounded men and medics rose all around us. We were killing ourselves again.

Xuan was furious. "They will never fire for me again!" He spit the words in my direction.

"But, *Dai-Uy* [Captain]—we need them! This is the only support we have. Adjust and have them fire again," I urged.

"Never! I will never let them fire again, not even if the VC attack. You must get American artillery!" he demanded.

"Dai-Uy, we're trying, but there's a big operation somewhere else. No artillery is in position to fire for us."

"Convince them to move! This is an important operation, and we have a very dangerous enemy here. We need to attack now—before he attacks us!" I could see that Slick was afraid, and that didn't make me feel any better.

We had once again taken more casualties from our own fire than from the enemy fire directed at us. The VC obviously observed our plight and saved their ammunition.

Then a prayer was answered when a pair of Cobra gunships checked in. Bobby Hurst turned their control over to me, since I was at the closest point to the enemy-held river line; he was fifty meters farther back with Major Bouie. I eased over the dike into the open field and crawled a little closer to the river, stopping at the next dike. I wanted to get the helicopter fires directly on the 263d. As I lay in the open, trying to give direction to the gunships, I popped a purple smoke grenade to mark our front lines. Huge mistake! Not only did the gunship know exactly where I was, but so did the riflemen of the 263d.

Direct rifle and machine gun fire struck within inches of me. I couldn't discern exactly where the fire was coming from, but I suspected riflemen had used the cover of vegetation on our flanks to maneuver around us. I was apparently now their main target! I realized I was alone, between the enemy and my own soldiers; I also couldn't believe I was in such a stupid predicament. Rifle shots snapped overhead and thudded into the ground around me.

I vaulted over the dike to seek cover on the reverse side, but that didn't improve my situation either. The rounds were still striking all around and very close. Even a bad marksman would surely get lucky soon. The odds weren't in my favor. I had to do something to drastically change the situation, and fast.

I low-crawled toward a hedgerow that ran in a different direction but stopped when I realized that the rifle shots were still following me. I was giving the Viet Cong far too much time to get lucky. I knew that if I was hit, I was too far away from the others to expect any help. If shot, I would have to stay and continue to take hits. To help me, someone would have to expose himself to crawl to where I was, but I didn't even see how anyone else could help me, anyway. Even worse, I might be captured!

I was as as close to the enemy as to my own soldiers. It struck me like a bolt of lightning: the VC were trying to capture an American. That was why I had not been hit yet. The VC had maneuvered around my flank and had me pinned down with close rifle fire but never hit me. I remembered how their snipers were able to strike our soldiers with considerable accuracy only a few hours earlier. They were saving me for captivity.

It became very clear to me that I would rather die running than be taken prisoner. I stood up suddenly and ran, leaning low, toward the hedgerow in which the friendly front line was concealed. VC rifle fire followed me with bullets whizzing past on both sides and with increased intensity as I sprinted faster. Then I realized the Viet Cong were indeed trying to hit me. But I was escaping. Halfway to safety, my legs collapsed and I fell face-first into the mud: I just *knew* that I'd been hit.

I quickly checked myself and realized that my legs had become cramped from running in the mud. The VC were still firing, but finally the ARVN troops returned fire over my head. I quickly rubbed out the cramp, gathered my strength, struggled to my feet again, and ran as fast as I could, stooped over, for the additional twenty meters back to the hedgerow. I plopped down behind the dike and saw Captain Xuan casually lying on the ground. I lay beside him, breathing heavily.

Slick looked at me and smiled. "The gunships are working well!"

I didn't even try to answer. I didn't know if I would ever be able to get back on my feet again.

Cobra gunships did great work for a while on their own, hosing down the trees along the river with machine guns and rockets. Slowly I recovered.

I was informed by a radio call from the 11th Regiment that the U.S. 9th Division Mobile Riverine Force (MRF) had moved 105mm howitzers up the river on barges that were now anchored to the shore, ready to fire in our support. All the MRF needed was fire direction. I had never excelled in adjusting artillery fire in officer basic training, but this was a do-or-die situation. Regiment gave me the frequency to contact the artillery. I was glad I had studied the artillery correspondence courses while resting at Binh Duc.

With fresh memories of the ARVN 105s exploding on us, I looked at Captain Xuan. "Do you want me to bring American 105s on the Viet Cong position?"

"Yes, of course," he responded, much more confident than I felt.

"Remember what happened with the ARVN artillery?" I asked.

"I'll die before I have them fire again," he said. "You can do it!"

And so I did. I called in the first volleys, and they seemed to be generally in the target area. More important, the high-explosive rounds were not falling on us.

Captain Xuan's confidence was rising; he directed the cooks to move farther back and prepare rice. I knew we would spend the rest of the day directing fire into the river line instead of making an infantry assault, which was fine with me. My knees were still weak from my earlier exertion, so I was not sure I could even walk into Snoopy's Nose in my present condition, much less attack.

Just before nightfall Captain Xuan asked me to join him. We moved fifty meters to the rear, toward the battalion CP where I found Bobby and Master Sergeant Mendenhall. We all took turns eating C-rations and adjusting artillery fire. I was happy to have help with the artillery, and we spent most of the night pouring it into Snoopy's Nose.

By the next day the 263d Main Force Battalion was gone. The enemy, dug in along the river, had three avenues of escape. He could wait until night and cross the river directly behind them and continue north or follow the river east or west. Two additional battalions would have been required to completely seal off the Viet Cong positions until they could be destroyed. There had been sufficient time to bring in reinforcements in daylight to seal them off, but it was not done, for whatever reason, and another opportunity for success was lost. After all, it was not enough to find the enemy—victory meant defeating him on the battlefield.

With the 263d gone, we were left empty-handed. I was still puzzled by the same questions as before. Why were Viet Cong main force battalions engaging us so close to the populated areas? Why were they stockpiling large supplies of ammunition so close to the cities? Why did we consistently find them, engage them, and allow them to escape to fight again another day? Because of my narrow escape in Snoopy's Nose, I was puzzled about what the recent fights really meant. There had to be a larger purpose: everything happens within a grand design, a framework. Where was the pattern?

There obviously was one, but why couldn't I see it more clearly?

"It was the kind of news that surprised even insiders: Robert S. McNamara was departing the Pentagon after seven years to preside over the World Bank."

—*Newsweek*, December 11, 1967

12

Changes

November 1967

Our operational tempo rose to a fever pitch in October. The pace of operations literally ran us ragged, going from one operation directly into another. Continuous operations in all four provinces of the division's operational area became normal. In November, we finally returned to our base at the Binh Duc Training Center for a rare battalion change-of-command ceremony. I didn't know what Major Bouie's next assignment was, and frankly I didn't care. I had been rather disappointed in his leadership.

Captain Nguyen Van Tao succeeded him. I had similar doubts about Captain Tao as well. He seemed to consider himself an aristocrat. Information was leaked, probably intentionally, that he was connected to Vietnam's President Thieu through marriage. Tao's wife was a beautiful

Vietnamese woman from Cai Be, and she often drove a car to visit while we were in the Binh Duc center. Owning an automobile was a sure sign of prosperity in impoverished Vietnam. The change of command was accompanied by many other, more superficial, changes and some important adjustments as well.

Combat operations were transformed significantly under Tao. I suspected that Xuan influenced most of those, especially after he had risen to the challenge during the operation in Snoopy's Nose. All men in the battalion began wearing a maroon scarf, signaling our identity to friendly aircraft as well as to ourselves during maneuvers. After the initial snickering about the scarves morale actually improved.

In the field Captain Xuan assumed a more direct leadership role, as well, shifting additional influence to me as his U.S. counterpart. I typically accompanied Xuan behind the lead company instead of walking with the first company commander. This benefited us in several ways, not the least of which was improved communications due to Xuan's excellent English-language skills and proficiency in U.S. infantry tactics. Xuan became the combat leader, and that was a good thing.

One thing that made it good was that he appreciated the importance of supporting arms. As his U.S. fire support coordinator, I worked with him closely and effectively—and none too soon. Battalion search-and-destroy formation were modified to position two leading companies in parallel formation, instead of only one company leading in a single column following one man.

These changes alone more than doubled our potential as a maneuver force with better command and control, a broader front, and increased opportunities to employ U.S. firepower. These were significant advancements from our rice paddy view of the world.

Another important enhancement for us Americans was our each being assigned a *dao binh* in the British tradition of an officer's "batman." A *dao binh* was an ARVN soldier convicted of a nonviolent crime, such as desertion, and sentenced to work off his time by hard labor in the field. *Dao binhs* did not carry weapons, but they did carry our rucksacks. This helped considerably by reducing our heavy loads and, more important, it raised our prestige among the Vietnamese.

* * *

Our operational pace remained intense through November, but we made contact only with local guerilla bands instead of main force Viet Cong units. Snipers were emboldened, however, and became more aggressive in following, flanking, and stopping us with well-aimed shots. We continually evacuated soldiers wounded by well-placed fire from a considerable distance. We advisors became more apprehensive about our greater physical size and distinctive appearance compared with the smaller Vietnamese. We wanted to blend in to avoid being singled out by snipers, but that was obviously difficult.

We tried to live and eat as much like the Vietnamese as possible, but we didn't get enough nourishment from perpetual duck soup and rice to preserve our strength. With help in carrying the extra weight, we could still eat with the Vietnamese to build relationships and still augment our diet with tasty C-rations from our rucksacks. The additional solid food helped us regain our vigor and some of the weight we had lost.

*   *   *

The monsoon rains eventually tapered off, but the scarcity of clean rainwater for drinking and cooking accompanied the drying of the rice fields. Although the Mekong delta was still covered in shallow water, finding clean drinking water was a serious concern. We were constantly reminded of Coleridge's "Rime of the Ancient Mariner's:" "Water, water everywhere, and not a drop to drink." Rice paddy water was dark with manure and mud, and the running streams were alkaline and bitter. The stagnant water was also a breeding ground for mosquitoes and leeches. We added two iodine tablets plus a package of sweetened Kool-Aid to each one-quart canteen of water to camouflage the pungent taste. The water in our canteens stayed warm and tasted like sweet sludge.

The best drinking water was rain collected off thatched roofs into large ceramic jugs. Although tinted green from the bamboo thatch, it was clear and clean. Mosquito larvae sometimes twitched on the surface, but that water represented liquid gold in the parched delta. Unfortunately, an ARVN or VC battalion could wipe out an entire hamlet's water supply with one visit.

Some nights on operations during the dry season I went to sleep so thirsty I would hallucinate, usually dreaming about a large, ice-cold, frosty bottle of Coca-Cola. Other team members often related the same dreams, probably because we talked about them so often.

Mosquitoes were another nagging problem in the Delta. Generally, we slung small nylon hammocks for sleeping above the ground and we surrounded the hammock with a mosquito net. If we were near the enemy, we could not use the hammocks or netting, and the cannibal-like insects feasted on us. A thousand humming mosquitoes kept us awake all night, and multiple bites left our faces and hands swollen. Every day we gulped down a small white malaria pill with sludge water, and every Monday we forced ourselves to swallow a big orange malaria pill, knowing it would induce stomach cramps. An occasional glimpse of a Vietnamese soldier or civilian in agony with malaria dispelled any idea of skipping the pill.

An army moves on its stomach, but an army that scrounged off the land had more much difficulty in finding food in the dry season. Occasionally we killed a water buffalo to eat, but found it extremely tough; they were usually avoided because they were prized, almost sacred, possessions due to their utility as workhorses.

One day, just to get a bowl of soup, I accompanied a food detail into Cai Be. At the market I watched as the Vietnamese cooks bought caged rats to take back for dinner. I ordered an egg roll with my soup and selected only rice and vegetables at dinner.

However, after dinner I was invited to participate in a ceremony representing the drinking of the enemy's blood. A soldier held a duck in the air, slit its throat and allowed the fresh blood to flow into a dish of peanuts. The dish was passed around for each of us to drink. My stomach flip-flopped when I was handed the dish, but I remembered the rats and knew it could be worse. I managed to suffer through this ceremony like a diplomat, but I felt more like a weak-kneed warrior.

* * *

Through those times, I stayed in touch with my family while sparing them most of the details. I wrote my sister Janet, a student at Georgia Southern University, wondering at the same time where she stood with the campus protests:

November 14, 1967

Dear Janet,

This will be brief because I am very tired. I'm just lying here waiting for time to turn the generator off and kill the noise and lights. I didn't get much sleep the last several nights because of Charlie, but I'm going to sleep tonight, no matter what happens.

We just got back from a security mission in Cai Lay. Last night Charlie tried to hit the town but didn't make it. He put a flag up out in front of our position though. This morning, we sent a company out to get it. We did get it plus four prisoners. I'm sending the flag home when I get a chance. This week we have a big operation starting here in the Delta. You will probably read about it in the papers.

Thanks for the letters. I know I'm pretty bad about answering, but I just haven't had the opportunity lately.

Bob wrote me about his horse. I guess he is going to be a real cowboy. By the way, is the old car still running, or have you salvaged it yet?

I appreciate your writing. Keep it up and I'll write again when I have more time.

*   *   *

By the end of November we had been on continuous operations for several weeks, and prepared for an extraction by helicopters. The battalion assembled in a large, dry rice field and lined up with security around the perimeter. I felt that we were finally a professional fighting force.

When a flight of eight helicopters approached, a soldier near the head of the formation popped a smoke grenade and tossed it into dry grass. The wind ignited the grass, transforming the LZ into an inferno. We faced a wall of flame as the fire swept through the dry waist-high grass. The helicopters flew past without landing, while ARVN soldiers ran for their lives—live ammunition, grenades, rocket launchers, and mortar rounds dangling from their bodies. The well-organized extraction morphed to total chaos in a matter of seconds. Then a sniper added panic to the confusion by firing at us before he fled the scene himself.

The inferno raged for four hours until it burned out. When the battalion finally reassembled, we waited another two hours for the helicopters. The more things changed, the more they stayed the same.

The news of "Mac-the-Knife's" departure struck Washington with the force of a string of Claymore mines exploding along Pennsylvania Avenue. One friend remembered when McNamara expressed haunting fears that his counsel to two Presidents to pursue the war may have been ill advised.[1]

"President Johnson dropped in on United States troops in South Vietnam today to bring them a Christmas greeting and promise that the people at home "shall not fail you."

—*New York Times,* December 23, 1967

13

Sudden Death

December 1967

Christmas was approaching quickly, but the Grinch was active in Vietnam. In early December we embarked on another riverine operation into Kien Hoa Province. The 2d and 3d battalions of our regiment and the 32d Ranger Battalion combined into a mobile task force to find and destroy the VC 263d Main Force Battalion. This time we began with enough troops at our disposal to finish the job. The rich agricultural area offered a bounty of bananas, sugar cane, coconuts, cucumbers, and Viet Cong. We quickly made contact with the 263d, but the elusive enemy slipped away again, avoiding battle.

I detected a disagreeable attitude developing in our battalion, but could not discern the reason. As an example, Corporal Thanh got into an argument with the battalion commander's radio operator over communications procedures. Determined to have things his way, Thanh approached the soldier in a threatening way, and then a third soldier bayoneted Thanh in his thigh. The wound was serious enough, deep in the large muscle, but Captain Tao refused to allow a medic to tend to Thanh's wound. Instead, Tao directed the battalion to establish camp in a damp, heavily vegetated area infested with mosquitoes and had Thanh left in the open rice paddy, unattended. I walked into the paddy alone to bring my friend back into the perimeter, but he refused and remained alone all night. He was finally evacuated next day, his punishment concluded.

Another example of a sinking attitude occurred when a small patrol of soldiers was dispatched across a swamp to reconnoiter a river line on our flank. The company commander tried to give additional instructions, a frag order, to the patrol by radio but he could not contact the unit. In frustration, he grabbed an M79 grenade launcher and lobbed a grenade toward the patrol. It exploded in the mud twenty meters from them. His method worked. They were on the radio instantly! Although the grenade got their attention, it did little to reinforce their loyalty.

Witnessing increasing hostility, and desperation, the caustic atmosphere disturbed me, but I couldn't understand why it was. The old feeling that I was missing some important information returned to plague me. I wondered whether somehow Captain Tao's patrician nature was contributing to the tension. On the other hand the approaching holidays could have been causing the soldiers' preoccupation with family, home, and peace.

I suspected that something was amiss with the Viet Cong as well. Other indications, such as their avoiding contact supported that feeling. I was troubled that I could not assemble all the pieces of the puzzle in my mind. I felt storm clouds billowing in for a big blow. The old warning siren howled in my mind again, and it had been right before.

* * *

In mid-December, we launched a search-and-destroy operation to the Double Y. The last time there, we had walked through Ap Bac and run headlong into the 514th Local Force Battalion in a bloody battle. This time we were trucked to LZ Springfield and an air assault was launched near the confluence of the canals. The VC force was not there, but caretakers and security forces were present to protect the site.

In several small skirmishes we killed six VC security guards, captured two, and destroyed several bunkers. The big surprise, however, was in what we found: large stocks of arms and ammunition. Along the canal banks underground warehouses were jampacked with supplies of AK-47 ammunition, as well as 60mm, 82mm, and 120mm mortar rounds; antitank mines; Chinese "potato masher" hand grenades; and recoilless-rifle rounds.

It appeared that the VC forces were preparing for a massive assault. Large quantities of ammunition had recently been transported down the Ho Chi Minh Trail, through Cambodia and across the Plain of Reeds. We found documents, a Viet Cong flag with fringe around it, a large Communist Party flag, and Viet Cong and NVA medals. This was a significant discovery, and ARVN 11th Regiment headquarters rewarded the battalion with a quota of Vietnamese awards.

We watched in amazement as the piles of ammunition from underground grew. Captain Xuan called, "Lieutenant Taylor, I have some medals to present. I would like to present one to you. Which medal would you like?" he laughed, building our growing rapport.

"Thank you for your courtesy, *Dai-Uy*. But, the medals would mean more to your soldiers. I'd rather have the flags," I replied honestly, hoping Slick would not be offended.

"Then it's done! I'll present the Communist Party flag and the Viet Cong flag to you. Sergeant Rich, would you take a picture, please?" An impromptu ceremony was hastily organized. Afterward I stuffed the flags into my rucksack for souvenirs.

We spent several days uncovering and counting the loot. Then we rigged it for demolition. ARVN soldiers stacked large piles of munitions and placed C4 plastic explosives with blasting caps inside. WD-1 communications wire was unrolled as far as it would reach. The wires were attached to a hand-cranked generator to set off the charges.

The explosions were tremendous—far greater than those of 500-pound bombs. Large chunks of debris ripped through the farmhouse nearby, which had survived the first battle with the 514th Battalion. Large shards of metal and clumps of mud flew well over our heads and landed with thuds in the soft field behind us.

"Smaller piles!" admonished Xuan, laughing.

* * *

The following day we were still gathering VC ammunition from across the canal. Unknown to me, an old man, a woman, and a young girl were helping ferry the ammunition in their sampan. It is likely that their loyalties were closer to the Viet Cong than us, but they helped us nevertheless. That was the prudent thing to do because we were here and the Viet Cong was not. Our aerial observer, Swamp Fox, was circling slowly about two miles away in an L-19 single-engine airplane.

"Red Oak, This is Swamp Fox. Over." He checked in.

"Swamp Fox, this is Red Oak Five. Over."

"Red Oak, I see several VC in a sampan, trying to escape your operation with a large quantity of supplies. Over."

"Swamp Fox, do you have our position or do you need smoke? Over."

"I have you in sight. Request permission to engage. Over."

I hesitated. What could be wrong? I saw the L-19 slowly circling about two miles away. He had identified VC escaping with some of the supplies. He had a positive spot on our position and he had asked permission to engage the enemy. I had a gut feeling that something was not right, but I didn't know what. I usually made quick decisions but now I hesitated. It just didn't feel right.

"Red Oak, can I engage? They'll be gone if we don't do something now," he persisted.

I hesitated again; I couldn't figure out what information was missing. He knew our position, he was two miles away, and he saw VC escaping. What I knew made perfect sense, but I didn't know that the civilians were in the sampan a few meters away.

"Go ahead, Swamp Fox." I definitely did not want to allow any VC to escape.

A minute later I heard the engines of the L-19 screaming low and fast—*directly at us!* I had been in this position before with the helicopter in Kien Hoa. I grabbed the handset of the radio, gripping it so hard that it might have broken.

"Cease fire, Swamp Fox! Cease fire! You're directly over us! Cease fire!"

As I yelled, I heard the roar of four 2.75-inch rockets rip from the wings of the L-19 and saw them flame directly into the canal twenty meters away. I could not imagine why the L-19 had fired into our position, but I wanted it stopped.

A thunderous explosion erupted from the canal, sending water and debris spraying us on the canal bank when the rockets ignited the explosives in the sampan. Miraculously no ARVN soldiers on the banks were killed, but when I saw the old man and woman after they had been fished from the canal, both were dead. The girl, probably twenty years old, was missing a hand and her arm at her elbow. I was afraid she would die of shock and loss of blood before she could reach medical care.

Now my own hands were bloody with friendly fire. This was inexcusable to me. The aerial observer had had one picture of the situation, and I had another. Had I known the civilians were in the boat or that his target was so near us, I would have refused the fire mission. But I didn't know. Somehow that knowledge didn't make me feel any better.

This was not a war; it was fratricide, one big accident after another. If the Viet Cong went to sleep, we would eventually kill ourselves off. I already hated the war and the Viet Cong. Now I hated Swamp Fox and myself as well.

We remained in that dreadful place for two weeks, disposing of all the ammunition caches we could find. I came to accept the accident as one of many in war. Yet I reviewed events leading to the tragedy over and over, playing it back and stopping the script in my mind to study it, desperately trying to discover what went wrong. I chastised myself for not trusting my instincts while relying on someone else's view of reality. I wondered what Swamp Fox was thinking. But he hadn't seen it up close and personal, as I had.

*   *   *

Publicly, Army and Marine generals say they've found few faults with the M-16 rifle, but privately they admitted that Defense Secretary McNamara forced the weapon upon them.[2]

Eventually choppers picked us up and ferried us back to Binh Duc. When we arrived, the battalion began two weeks of refresher training in basic soldiering skills, which was certainly overdue. The U.S. 9th Infantry Division military assistance training team and the ARVN 7th Division training center cadre were on hand to assist.

We conducted a full range of qualification firing on rifles, including the M1 carbine and M14 rifle. The training was sorely needed, and when we finished we were ready for combat with fresh zeros on our carbines. On the day after Christmas Uncle Santa surprised us with new M16 rifles. Joy to the world! The entire battalion had just completed qualification firing on M1 carbines, including rezeroing, and on the next day new rifles were delivered.

More joy was coming. The Viet Cong disrupted our training to avenge their losses of ammunition at the Double Y. They pounded our base camp with 82mm mortars and sniped at us inside our compound in broad daylight.

We reacted with hot pursuit. As soldiers were handed new M16 rifles, which they had never fired, they were marched directly into the field in pursuit of the enemy, loading magazines as they marched. I was incredulous at the stupidity of the decisions—all of them. An infantry battalion qualified with M1 carbines now had them replaced with new M-16s that had never been test-fired—much less zeroed—and was being marched directly in pursuit of an enemy. Advisors spent the night crawling around the perimeter, instructing ARVN soldiers who spoke very little English on the operation of the rifle. It was absurd.

Malicious jokes weren't over. I was notified that the Johnny Grant show was coming to My Tho, and the division senior advisor selected me as an escort. I knew the beautiful actresses Diane McBain and Sherry Johnson and Playboy Bunny Sabrina Scharf were in the troupe. I *dreamed* of escorting them. Never mind! The next day I was informed that the 3d Battalion had been alerted for an operation and was short an officer, therefore. . . .

Instead of escorting the girls of my dreams, I escorted a bunch of ragged ARVN soldiers on river assault boats steaming back toward Kien Hoa. The region was laced with booby traps, and we lost soldiers as soon as we stepped ashore. Nasty little "toe poppers" were small boxes buried in the ground. Inside the boxes, the primer of a .30-caliber bullet rested on the tip of a nail. When stepped on, the nail activated the primer and the round went off, usually taking toes or part of a foot with it.

Merry Christmas to all!

> The war in the delta is between the South Vietnamese and the Viet Cong, and it is likely to remain so. Whoever controls the "Dragon's Mouth," where the three main branches of the Mekong reach the sea—will ultimately control the country. The government's influence extends precisely to those points where a soldier puts his foot on the ground.[3]

"From Tucson came a check for $11.03, the contribution of a Sunday school class. Another check came from a child, along with this note: "I would like to give up a Christmas present from my parents and send $5. It is very little for what the guys in Vietnam are doing for us."

—*New York Times,* December 23, 1967

14

East of the Sun

Early December 1967

As a result of successes in the Double Y, Viet Cong main forces had been pushed farther away from My Tho and prepared to defend their supplies. Government troops used the opportunity to operate in traditional zones farther away from the cities.

We soon found ourselves bouncing on the flatbeds of the rattletrap trucks along Highway 4 en route back to the Double Y for the umpteenth time. ARVN units were pushing into VC strongholds to take the initiative from the enemy before the Tet holidays. We were aware that active U.S. Army Special Forces operations were aimed at detecting and reducing the flow of supplies from the Plain of Reeds.

From LZ Springfield we trudged north through familiar Ap Bac hamlets and dry rice fields. While on the march, we received an urgent change of orders. A Civilian Irregular Defense Group (CIDG) company, under command of U.S. Army Green Berets, had run directly into a battalion L-shaped ambush and was in serious trouble. It requested assistance or reinforcements. The CIDG company was somewhere west of the Double Y, near My Phouc Tay, a Special Forces camp established to monitor and intercept infiltration routes from Cambodia through the Plain of Reeds. Green Berets recruited and trained their own local troops from the civilian population.

We marched quickly through dry paddies in the direction of the CIDG company to reinforce and relieve it, but we were careful not to rush into another ambush ourselves. I changed the radio frequency to the Special Forces advisory net as we marched, to establish contact with the endangered troops. As soon as I called, a soldier shouted into the radio that he was behind a rice paddy dike, pinned down by enemy fire.

"Marble Four, this is Red Oak Five. Over," I responded, keeping my voice calm to reassure him.

"This is Marble Four. Over!" He shouted into his handset. His voice was almost drowned out by background noise.

"Situation report?" I requested.

"We walked into an ambush! A VC battalion! Heavy casualties. We're under heavy fire. I don't know how long I can hold out." I heard his bleak assessment through crackling rifle fire in the background.

"I'm near the front of an ARVN company. We're approaching from your rear. The rest of the battalion is behind us. Tell your people not to shoot if they see us coming up. We're wearing green uniforms and maroon scarves." I wanted to prevent another friendly-fire incident, especially since he was rattled.

"I can't tell them anything! We're spread all over and we've been shot to hell. Everyone around me is dead, even the captain," he sobbed.

"Are you talking about the CIDG company commander?" I asked, hoping for clarification.

"No! Captain O'Malley. He was in front of me when he got hit. I crawled here before we were overrun. I left him, but I still see him," he sobbed again.

"Where are you now?" I asked.

"I don't know where the hell I am! I don't have a map or compass. Can you hear the shooting? They're shooting at me. Hurry up and get here! I can't hold out. I'm almost out of ammo, but I'm not shooting. Maybe they'll think I'm dead, too."

He was panicked, but I needed him to help us find them. "Give me some help! Can you see a reference point? Give me something to guide on."

"I'm flat on my back. The only thing I can see is the sun. I'm east of the sun. Just go east of the sun," he kept shouting over and over.

"You have to do better than that. Everyone in Vietnam is east of the sun. Help us find you," I pleaded.

We never linked up with the Special Forces soldier and his troops. His last report indicated that the Viet Cong had started to withdraw as we approached; they didn't want to engage a unit near the size of their own. The remnants of the Green Beret's ragged company pulled themselves together and got home to My Phuoc Tay.

Late in the afternoon we reached the ambush site. We marched west—into the sun—until we found Captain O'Malley. He was a young redheaded all-American boy who had been killed instantly in the first onslaught. The back of his head was blown off, but his face was undamaged and his eyes stared up into the sun. I gagged at the sight of his brains spread over the dry rice paddy. His surprised expression burned itself into my memory. I blinked my eyes to erase his stare, but it remained there even when I closed my eyes.

Other warriors from both sides were sprawled about the killing field joining O'Malley in his final morning report. I went from body to body, looking at each of the dead, trying to erase the image of him from my memory—without success.

Nothing worked.

Another prodigal son had registered for roll call.

*　　*　　*

Much farther east O'Malley appeared sooner than I expected. Almost exactly one year later, I was dining at the 82d Airborne Division commanding general's mess at Fort Bragg, North Carolina. Several young officers came through the serving line and settled at my table. As we gazed at one another, I was shocked by the appearance of one redheaded first lieutenant who took a seat adjacent to me. Even though I already knew the answer, I asked the young officer if he had an older brother. First Lieutenant O'Malley told me his brother had been killed in Vietnam.

I remained silent.

> Sweden granted asylum to seven more American GIs who said they deserted to escape war service in Vietnam.[2]

"B52 bombers winged over North Vietnam, climaxing a massive air bombardment of highways and military facilities. U.S. Command is also watching closely what appears to be an increase in North Vietnamese traffic down the Ho Chi Minh trail through Laos."

—*Atlanta Constitution,* December 7, 1967

15

Unfriendly Fire

January 1968

Christmas passed without any serious VC-initiated attacks. We delighted in the approaching Chinese New Year, or Tet. Fewer mortar attacks and rocket barrages, and less sniper fire than usual, marked a quiet phase in a crazy war.

Vietnamese and Americans alike marked their calendars down to the Tet cease fire, which was only a week away. Unexpectedly, though, we were alerted to move into a security position near Cai Lay. When we arrived we found the city quiet but jumpy. U.S. advisors in Cai Lay were going about their normal routine, but were edgy about an anticipated Vietcong attack.

Our first morning there we awoke to find Viet Cong flags erected overnight near our positions. We understood the message quite well: we were not welcome! Patrols swept the area removing the flags and searching for the perpetrators. The next morning the flags reappeared.

The battalion searched around Cai Lay for four days, fighting boredom and collecting VC flags and signs from trees. We literally camped around the psychological operations (psyops) center.

A fifteen-year-old Vietnamese boy adopted us, which was not unusual. Kids loved to hang around, begging for candy or C-rations. This lad tried repeatedly to start conversations with me, but I kept running him away. A ten-year-old boy soon joined him. Their persistence aroused the suspicions of some battalion staff officers, who detained them for questioning. The boys were separated from one another, and the younger one quickly confessed that they were collecting information for an old man who told them what to find out. The old man, who was swiftly rounded up, revealed that the three of them were working for the 261st Main Force Battalion, which was camped nearby and preparing to attack Cai Lay.

Under pressure the three VC spies reluctantly revealed the hiding place of several AK-47s and ammunition. ARVN soldiers joyfully recovered the weapons and brought them to the psyops center for examination by Lieutenant Than, the battalion S-2. Than was a competent intelligence officer, but I always suspected he knew more about the enemy than he was willing to share. He stood on the porch of the psyops office and examined the captured weapons, which were his responsibility. The mechanics of the Chinese-made assault rifles were familiar to all of us, making what happened next so surprising.

While Than examined the rifles on the porch, I stood in the front yard talking to several other officers—we were planning a trip into the village market for crab soup. The staccato rip of eight AK-47 rounds fired at extremely close range suddenly split the air. The burst was so close the sound alone could have knocked me down.

At the same instant that I flinched I felt a slam against my shoulder, spinning me around violently, tangling my legs. I hit the ground on my back and that second jolt knocked the breath from my lungs. Events seemed to be happening in slow motion. I saw smoke rising from the barrel of the rifle, startled faces of the other officers, sky spinning around above me, and then the faces of people looking down at me. As if looking through their eyes, I saw myself trying to get up, but my legs were twisted underneath and would not obey. I was embarrassed by my predicament and wondered how I could reverse the scene, play it back to the beginning, untangle it.

I heard Bobby say, "Medevac is on the way!"

I muttered, "Is anyone hurt?"

"You'll be all right. It doesn't look serious," Bobby replied.

Who was he talking to? Everyone was watching me; I felt ridiculous lying on the ground. This had to be a joke, and I was the only one who didn't get it.

I struggled to stand, only then beginning to realize that I was in shock.

"Stop! Don't move! They'll bring a stretcher," said Bobby.

"I'll be damned! No stretcher," I said. But my head felt light and my knees were weak as I managed to get halfway up. Hands reached for me, but I brushed them aside.

No one would wrap me in a poncho, I thought. I visualized Lieutenant Kiem sliding from my grasp, head first into the mud.

"I'll walk!" I could feel hands on me again, helping me to my feet. This time I allowed it; I was desperate to stand on my own feet.

The medevac helicopter landed near sector headquarters, and the Cai Lay advisors gathered to watch. I was upset by my situation, but there was nothing I could do even though I didn't want to be a spectacle.

As I walked to the chopper with the help of several others, I looked at my left shoulder to see the wound. I didn't see any bullet holes on the front of my shirt. Then, I looked over my shoulder and saw a jagged six-inch rip in my shirt and a little blood, but not much. I felt better already. My left arm and shoulder were numb, but I was not in pain, so I decided to enjoy the chopper ride. I was embarrassed, however, to be able to walk to a medical evacuation helicopter. I had seen too many people loaded feet first. And a seriously wounded 9th U.S. division soldier was already on board. The stop to pick me up had delayed his arrival at the hospital.

The chopper ride from Cai Lay to the 9th Division mobile army surgical hospital (M.A.S.H.) was brief. Upon arrival at the helipad I was forced to lie on a stretcher; inside the medics cut my shirt away with scissors and quickly cleaned and stitched my shoulder. It was almost too fast for all the trouble of getting there. I was quickly rolled into an air-conditioned Quonset hut. The cold air hit me hard, but a wool army blanket tucked under my chin was warm and relaxing. I couldn't believe how tired I felt as I warmed up and instantly fell asleep.

When I awoke I was staring into the face of the most beautiful woman I had ever seen. Lieutenant Brickhouse, an army nurse, was changing my intravenous feed. I was instantly in love with the wife of the emergency room surgeon, just like everyone else who met her. I had heard rumors of her existence, now I knew the rumors were true. I relished being under her occasional care for a few days, but my wound was too slight to merit much attention.

I thought I would enjoy the enforced vacation, until a commotion began in the bed next to mine. I turned to see a U.S. soldier covered with blood and mud, who was surrounded by a crew of medics working frantically to cut half a boot off the half of his foot that was still attached. He writhed as they worked. I wanted to run away.

I remained for four more days, until I was released on light duty. I was paroled on January 26, with an appointment to return on January 31 to have the stitches removed and my wound examined. Lieutenant Brickhouse admonished me to stay in a sterile environment to avoid infection. That didn't seem too difficult at the time. We were approaching the Tet cease-fire, so I could stay in the seminary and recover until I received a clean bill of health.

Bobby picked me up at the hospital. "Hey, how you doing, Lieutenant?" inquired my boss.

"I'm okay. Nurse Brickhouse took special care of me." I intend to invoke some envy.

"Some idiots have all the luck," he countered. "I'll take you to the Seminary to stay during the cease-fire. They have a medic and clean sheets there. I packed a change of clothes and your shaving kit, and they have your pay waiting for you as well as some mail. Need anything else?"

"My rifle." I said.

"It'll be okay at Binh Duc. You won't need it at the Seminary. Cease fire started."

"Well, I guess I'll be okay then."

"For your information, I'm going up-country to visit friends, some advisors I know. Rich is going to Vung Tao for in-country R&R [rest and recuperation]. I encouraged Mendenhall to join you at the Seminary, but he wants to hang around Binh Duc. He'll probably get bored, and you'll see him there, anyway. Most of the ARVNs are leaving for the holidays, too."

"Sounds like a plan."

We rode in silence until Bobby spoke again. "How do you feel about going back to the battalion . . . after this?"

I thought for a minute before answering. "Well, it's strange, but I want to go back. I've been through worse than this."

"You mean after getting shot?"

"Yeah."

"I can get you a staff job."

"Spend the rest of my time in Vietnam in the lap of luxury? No way! Really, I want to go back to the battalion."

I wondered how an experienced officer like Than could have had such a stupid accident. But I didn't dwell on that sore subject; was too familiar with stupid accidents already.

Bobby said, "Than has been punished."

I assumed he meant Than had received a fine or the ARVN equivalent of an Article 15, but I didn't pursue it further. I never saw Than again. I only hoped the accident had really been an accident, after all. I was just glad that the round that struck me had not been an inch higher or to the left. Otherwise I would likely not be writing this story.

> The Viet Cong announced that they would observe three-day truces at Christmas and New Year's and a seven-day cease-fire over the Vietnamese lunar new year, or Tet.[2]

Tet Offensive

★ Province capitals and other cities
☆ Military installations

Quang Tri
Hue
Phu Bai
Phu Loc
Da Nang
Hoi An
Tam Ky
Chu Lai
Bong Son
Kontum
Pleiku
An Khe
Qui Nhon
Hau Bon
Tuy Hoa
Ban Me Thuot
Nha Trang
Da Lat
Tay Ninh
Phu Cuong
Bien Hoa
Duc Hoa
Long Binh
Gia Dinh
Moc Hoa
Saigon
Phan Thiet
Chau Phu
My Tho
Phuoc Le
Vinh Long
Rach Gia
Ben Tre
Sa Dec
Can Tho
Phu Vinh
Soc Trang
Ca Mau

N
S

Kilometers
0   100

Miles
0   100

MAP 5

"At dawn on the first day of the Tet truce, Viet Cong forces, supported by large numbers of NVA troops, launch the largest and best-coordinated offensive of the war, driving into the center of South Vietnam's seven largest cities and attacking 30 provincial capitals from the Demilitarized Zone to the Mekong Delta."

—*The Vietnam War Day by Day*

16

Big Storm

January 30–31, 1968

I relaxed as well as I could at the Seminary, recovering from my unfortunate gunshot wound. Over an American-style breakfast, I overheard talk of the Viet Cong breaking the cease-fire during the night in Saigon and cities farther north. Apparently these were not very successful attacks, but any violations of the truce were disturbing. However, these infractions appeared to be minor, relatively small squalls in the land of big monsoons. While I was bothered by the violations, I could do nothing about them, so I spent most of my last day at the Seminary on the roof in sunning, reading, and listening to music on the Armed Forces Network (AFN).

After dinner and a long stopover in the watering hole, I made my way downstairs to find a place to sleep. Since I didn't normally live in the seminary I had no assigned bunk, but I found an empty one belonging to someone away on R&R. I claimed it, stripped, and crawled between the clean sheets.

I was sleeping soundly when the big storm broke. An explosion in my room lifted me off the mattress. A brilliant flash that ruined my night vision was immediately followed by a ripping blast. Wall plaster pelted me as I fell back on the bed. I hurriedly rolled off the bed to the sound of tinkling glass, as in windows breaking. In midair I hoped there was no glass on the floor. I rolled underneath my bed and stayed there, trying to decide what to do next. At least I was protected from falling building material where I was.

I knew instinctively that a rocket had penetrated the wall. The next noises were of men rushing from the room to battle stations. I didn't have a battle station because I was not normally assigned there. I had no rifle with me, no ammunition, helmet, or any other soldier things after my release from the hospital. I calculated that the attack would end in an hour; a ground attack was unlikely, but a mortar or rocket barrage was probable. A plan developed in my mind: stay out of the way. Rockets continued to hit other parts of the building, punctuating my decision.

I hated rockets, but I thought I was in the safest place possible for protection against them. I was more afraid of being shot by barstool warriors inside the building than the Viet Cong on the outside. I reached up and dragged the sheet and pillow off the bed and wrapped up for the duration. After all, Lieutenant Brickhouse had advised me to keep my stitches clean until I returned to Dong Tam to have them removed.

*　*　*

I dozed fitfully for a while through the rattle of small-arms fire. From my bunker under the bed I could see daylight breaking. I figured it was safe enough to roll out for breakfast, so I slipped on my trousers and sat on the edge of the bed to lace up my jungle boots. I strolled out of the room as I carefully slipped into a clean, starched fatigue shirt for my doctor's appointment. As I entered the hallway, I was surprised to find the walls still lined elbow to elbow with officers and noncommissioned officers in full battle dress, flak jackets and helmets, and holding rifles.

The officer-in-charge saw me and demanded, "Where have you been?"

"Trying to sleep," I replied. "What's going on?"

"We're under attack. Get your gear and stay on the porch."

"I don't have any gear. I just got out of the hospital, and I have to go to Dong Tam today to have stitches removed."

"Find some gear and get your ass back here. You aren't going anywhere."

Following orders, I wandered back to the bedroom and groped around in still-dark corners until I found an M1 carbine belonging to the person whose bed I had borrowed. I found two 30-round banana-clip magazines with the carbine, but that was all. I grabbed my jungle hat and returned to the porch. I felt conspicuous without the helmet and flak jacket that the others wore.

I listened to the discussions and I picked up bits and pieces of information as the others talked. I sorted rumors from fact. I heard a battle raging a few kilometers away in My Tho, so when I was told that the city had been attacked and captured by the VC, it confirmed what my eyes and ears were telling me. Although I could see and hear it, it was still unbelievable!

Unanswered questions struck me at once. How was I to get through My Tho to the M.A.S.H. at Dong Tam for my appointment? What was happening at Binh Duc? Where was Mendenhall? How was this whole thing even possible? What was I supposed to do now?

I knew that staying on the porch of the Seminary with staff members was not the answer; I needed to rejoin my fighting unit. I'd told Bobby that I wanted to stay with the battalion, and that was where I most wanted to be then. Although I hadn't forgotten the last moments I had with the battalion, one of its officers had put a hole in me. I stored that in the back of my mind.

Concern for Mendenhall was my most pressing concern. I left my post on the porch and headed for the communications center. In the radio room I asked, "Have you heard anything from Red Oak Six Alpha?"

"Yes, we have. He's with the ARVN and just reported they're getting ready to move. He's out there alone and that's a violation of MACV policy!" replied the officer in charge. "An officer has to join him in the field."

I stared at him, not able to believe what he was suggesting. Then I looked slowly around the room and asked, "Are there any volunteers to go out and prevent a policy violation?" Silence thundered.

I looked back toward the major and said, "I don't see any volunteers, so I guess I'll go. Can you arrange transportation?"

He looked at me skeptically. Neither of us could believe this conversation was taking place. We were actors in a comedy-horror show.

"Hand me the mike." I held out my hand for the radio handset. "I want to talk to Red Oak Six Alpha." The major passed me the microphone.

"Red Oak Six Alpha, this is Red Oak Five. Over."

"Five, where are you?"

"I'm at the big white building; you know the one. What's your situation?"

"We occupied the fish oil factory last night and took some fire, but mostly listened to the fight in the city. Now we're getting ready to move out—counterattack into My Tho."

"What route will you take?"

"Wait. I'll ask Slick. Tao is in Cai Be. Slick is in charge."

While I waited, I thought it would be a natural match; Slick was my normal counterpart anyway. He needed me to maintain contact with U.S. fire power, if there was any to be had. I knew I should link up with them as soon as possible.

"Five, this is Six Alpha. Over."

"This is Five."

"Slick said we'll walk right past your position, and he'd be honored if you'd join us."

"I'll be looking for you. How long?"

"We should be there in under an hour."

"See you soon. Out."

I rushed from the building to the supply room to search for any surplus battle gear. I found a web belt, two ammo pouches, two canteens, a first-aid pouch, and a steel pot. I kept the carbine and two magazines with sixty rounds, and hurried to the bedroom to adjust the belt and helmet. I remembered my small portable radio and my camera, stuffing them into an empty ammunition pouch. I was not equipped for the battle of the century, but when the war comes to you, you go to work with what you have.

I ran to the front gate and in the distance I saw two columns of ARVN soldiers advancing cautiously on both sides of the road in our direction. Mendenhall was easy to detect; he was head and shoulders taller than the others. I realized how easy Americans were to spot in a gaggle of Vietnamese. I swung open the front gate and walked out.

The Adjutant General's Corps major in charge of the main-gate bunker yelled, "Hey! You can't go out there!"

Without turning around, I shouted over my shoulder, "And who's going to stop me?"

I fell in and matched strides with Mendenhall. His briefing was short; we had talked on the radio only an hour before. "The ARVN are scared." That was all he said, but it was enough; so was I.

"What's the objective?" I asked.

"My Tho!" Mendenhall clipped his answers. I realized he was as nervous as me, maybe more.

The gravity of the situation settled over me. The tables were completely turned: we were now on the outside of this country, and the Viet Cong occupied a commanding position on the inside. The bad guys had taken over our city, and we had to fight to get back in. The world was turned upside down.

I needed more information. "Who is counterattacking with us?" I asked.

"Beats me." Mendenhall replied. "As far as I know we're it. Just us against a VC division."

"Division?"

"Yeah."

"I've never heard of a VC division!"

The column moved 500 meters beyond the Seminary before it left the paved road for dirt side streets in a residential area. I had not spoken with him yet, but I wondered whether Slick had detoured to the Seminary just to pick me up.

* * *

Two hundred meters onto the side road, machine gun fire broke out. The next burst was directly at us from fifty meters in front. Bullets passed so close that they *popped* as they went by; they ricocheted off buildings and the hard surface of parched ground. I saw everyone flat on the ground, just as I was. I examined my chest and shoulders to see if I had been hit. Vivid memories of being hit by that AK-47 a week earlier were still fresh. The sounds around me were exactly the same as then. It was as if being shot before was only a rehearsal for this, and I felt the bullet again in my mind.

I didn't find any blood so I assumed that I was all right. I remembered Bill Mauldin's cartoon from a more traditional war years earlier, where one GI said to another as they lay on their stomachs in the same fix we were in: "I'd get closer to the ground if these darn buttons weren't in the way!" I smiled at that. This situation would be funny if it wasn't so frightening.

As I looked myself over for punctures, I noticed the colorful insignia on my starched uniform: white name tag, black-and-gold U.S. Army label, silver-and-blue Combat Infantry Badge, silver airborne wings, red-and-gold Pathfinder Badge, gold infantry insignia, a silver first lieutenant's bar, and a red-and-gold MACV patch. I also wore a white T-shirt to keep my stitches clean. I resembled a Christmas tree—all lit up! I also noticed that the ARVN soldiers kept their distance from me, the prime target.

One platoon maneuvered around the enemy shooters, engaging them from another direction. When the VC shifted to return fire, I stood up and ran as fast as I could to a vacant building we had passed earlier. Others from the command group were already making their way there, as was Mendenhall. As soon as I was inside, I stripped off both of my shirts, threw the white T-shirt away and reversed the fatigue shirt so all the bright insignia were inside and out of sight. I was less conspicuous but keenly aware of how thin the shirt was. For the first time in the war I longed for a flak jacket.

Captain Xuan smiled and said, "I'm glad you could make it!"

By noon my stomach was growling. I realized I had missed the big American breakfast at the Seminary that morning. I had brought no rations with me and didn't have a rucksack to carry any. While Mendenhall had a pack, he had brought only one C-ration in it because he, too, expected to be back home for lunch. I realized that this action would not be over in time for dinner. Despite our thirst, Mendenhall and I carefully rationed the two canteens of water we each carried. (The sun was scorching by noon. I wanted to call time out and start the battle all over, better prepared.)

* * *

The close firing ceased and we moved again. The rest of the afternoon was spent in house-to-house fighting. The ARVN soldiers knew they should clear houses from the top down, but they had no way up, except from the bottom. As they tried to go up, the Viet Cong dropped grenades on them from above. Xuan kept me informed of the details of the skirmishes. I didn't like what I heard with my own ears nor the reports he gave me. I grew more concerned with each passing hour.

Each residential block we cleared, each building we took were major victories, but new obstacles stretched endlessly before us. As we approached the city enemy fire grew heavier and we took more casualties. Initially a large open field had protected our right flank, but it quickly merged into an urban wilderness as we drew nearer the city center, and it became perfect for snipers. We constantly ducked because the fighting was so close that we never knew who was firing at whom—shots erupted all around us. I detested our situation more by the minute but felt powerless to do anything. I was just being swept along by events.

Shadows grew longer as the protracted day sagged into afternoon. Large concentrations of VC were positioned in front and across the road to our left. Captain Xuan identified a single two-story dwelling with a large yard as a CP and established defenses around it. Hedges fifty meters from the house bordered it on two sides, and a shallow ditch with stagnant water cut across the other side. As we approached the house we passed an apartment building to our rear; it dominated our position across 100 meters of wide-open field. I didn't like the dominant building that overlooked us, but any position we took in the urban jungle presented inherent problems. This house appeared to be where we would make our stand—our Alamo.

The command group settled into the rooms on the first floor, established a defensive perimeter around the house, and tied the hedges and canals into our defense.

An old man and woman inside lit the house dimly with candles. A family altar stood in one corner with burning joss sticks and photos of deceased family members. The old man prayed at the altar every hour, lighting more joss sticks each time. Some of his family members had been injured in the fighting, but we couldn't help them. The most seriously wounded ARVN soldiers were also collected in the house, transforming it into an impromptu aid station, without much aid. Twelve seriously wounded men crowded the small room as moans rose from the civilians in the back room. The ablest of the wounded preferred to stay in place on the defensive perimeter.

As I surveyed the house and small perimeter, I realized how undersized our unit was. I had assumed before that the men were spread out into different sectors, but now I wondered. I asked Mendenhall about it.

"How many troops do you think we have?"

"We started with one hundred and fifty," he said.

"Hundred and fifty! Where is everyone?" I couldn't believe that number, only equivalent to a company, plus headquarters.

"They're in the same place Captain Tao and Captain Hurst are—Tet vacation, for the ceasefire."

"Why aren't we with them?" I wondered aloud.

"You're better off here, sir," he said. "At least you know who you're fighting with. Can you imagine being off somewhere else trying to figure out what to do? At least we know what we're doing," the veteran soldier advised.

I recalled my feeling of isolation at the Seminary. Truly I would rather be here. If we were to die in this place, it was better to be with people we knew. I had not seriously considered that until now, but I realized that dying in this small house was a distinct possibility.

I calculated in my head. If we started with 150 soldiers and had 12 seriously wounded here, that left us with 138. I had seen at least 12 more killed, leaving 126. It could be worse than that—but not better. We faced elements of a Viet Cong division. I didn't know how many VC were in a division, but the ratio in this fight was certainly unfavorable.

I wondered what I had stumbled into. I still had stitches in my left shoulder from being shot by a friendly, and now VC surrounded all of us. I wasn't sure whether we would be supported by fire power or reinforcements. Xuan looked distressed as he whispered into his radio. Afterward he assembled a small group of officers and addressed them in hushed tones. This could only be more bad news. I waited impatiently for some information, trying to establish eye contact with Slick.

Xuan slowly walked over very close to me. "The situation is bad," he whispered. "We started with one hundred and fifty soldiers, and now we face three hundred Viet Cong. There are many more in the city. We were ordered to counterattack but could only go this far before the enemy stopped us here. We are low on ammunition and have twenty-five wounded and thirteen killed. VC will counterattack us during the night since they know where we are. If you can get support from the Americans, please do so."

"I will," I said.

I reported his information to the war room at the Seminary. And I added, "I can confirm that information with my own eyes. We're out of food, water, and first-aid supplies. I'll need a radio battery soon; this one is approaching twenty-four hours' use."

The expected reply came. "I don't know how we'll get any supplies to you, since the enemy is between us." What a surprise!

"I realize that!" I fired back. "But we're the only thing between you and a lot more VC. This radio is the only way you'll know when they're coming!"

"We'll see what we can do tomorrow."

"Also, can you get me a fire-support frequency? We need fire support tonight. We have reports we'll be attacked."

"You have only one radio?"

"That's affirmative."

"I'll have fire support come up on this frequency, and we can monitor. We'll dedicate this frequency to you and switch other traffic to another freq."

"Roger that. Out." The exchange ended with a remarkable and unexpected show of support.

Intermittent fire continued through the night all around our perimeter. Headquarters called every hour for a situation report, if we didn't call first.

At 2:00 a.m. Xuan came to me again. "Many VC are moving around us and preparing to attack. They are crossing the road on our left. Can you get any fire support?"

I called headquarters immediately to relay what I had been told. "Get some fire support on the line," I pleaded.

"It may take a while," I was told. "Every asset is committed right now."

"How about the machine gun at the main gate?" I asked, remembering the jerk who had told me I couldn't leave.

"How can that help?" the major quizzed, clearly thinking I had lost my mind.

"Put it in the road and fire right down the highway with low grazing fire," I requested. "The VC are crossing the highway, and it might stop their reinforcements."

"We don't think that will help," came the reply.

"I don't give a damn what you think! If we're overrun, can you live with not having tried?"

"Roger. Out!" That was the response I wanted.

Soon I heard the machine gun firing in our general direction. I have no idea whether it helped or not, but at least it was something. Before that I'd nothing. It made us feel a little more in control of our fate. And bullets were cheap as long as they lasted.

* * *

Sporadic firing began around our perimeter as the VC probed us, but an all-out assault had not started. The VC reconnoitered our positions by fire. When we returned their fire, they identified our fighting positions and located our machine guns. We knew they were moving into position to attack, but we didn't know how many or when it would come.

A half-hour later, a U.S. Navy boat from the MRF checked in on my radio frequency. It was several kilometers away on the Mekong River, but I was gratified the Seminary had actually rounded up some support.

"What have you got?" I asked the boat's skipper.

"I'm on a monitor in the river. We have an 81mm mortar that can reach you. Our guns won't reach you from the river."

I called in a fire mission for the mortar and requested one round of smoke in an airburst. I remembered friendly fire incidents and didn't want another one.

I heard the smoke round pop nearby, but couldn't see it in the dark because buildings around us masked it. I knew it was not directly overhead and I didn't want to waste any more time. I adjusted the fires even though I couldn't observe their impact, judging by flash and sound only. After each volley I consulted Mendenhall before calling in a correction. I knew the mortar rounds weren't falling on us, prayed they weren't falling on civilians, and hoped they were falling on Viet Cong. It was not much support, but it was the best we had, and we were very grateful to have it.

I wasn't sure how effective the fires were, but I kept working it around our perimeter for two hours. We remained under constant rifle fire, but a ground assault never materialized. At 4:00 a.m., a rocket-propelled grenade struck the house. I heard screams in the back and discovered that the old man, one of the wounded soldiers, and the medic tending him had been killed.

Captain Xuan announced that we were getting out of the house immediately. Covered by the dark, we moved outside into the open yard. As we were relocating, our U.S. Navy patrol boat called to report.

"Red Oak, we have to check out. We're out of mortar ammo and have to return to Dong Tam for resupply. It'll be daylight soon. Good luck!"

"Thank you, Navy. I wish I could give you a damage report but I can't. I think you helped stop the major assault. I love you guys!"

"We like shooting for you. Call our number again sometime. Out."

* * *

It was still dark. Mendenhall and I lay on our bellies in the dew on the lawn. I crawled around to see where we were relative to Xuan and the command group. I didn't want to be too close but I wanted to be close enough. Daylight would break in an hour. We had no shovels, and the ground was as dry and hard as concrete. Mendenhall and I took turns monitoring the radio and scraping out a trench with our helmets. We had lived through that day.

We would have to see about the next one.

"Avoid any display of emotion during Tet and do not discuss subjects with the Vietnamese which breed emotion, arguments or insults."

- The MACV Observer, January 31, 1968[1]

17

Gates of Hell

February 1, 1968

Outside the house visibility improved as the sun inched higher, but I didn't like the view. Our vulnerability was quite apparent in the light of day. As Mendenhall and I scraped dirt with our helmets along with every one else, we grew more anxious as dawn broke over us. Darkness had afforded some protection, but under the rising sun we were completely exposed, visually uncovered and without protection. Digging was slow and tedious in the hard, dry ground without entrenching tools. Twenty-four hours had elapsed since we had last eaten and the imposed fast had weakened us. Worse, we were almost out of water and were sweating precious fluids from our bodies as we scrabbled at the hard surface.

Mendenhall and I wondered just how bad the overall situation really was. We knew it looked grim from where we were, and we had no promise of fire support, so we assumed that everyone must be engaged all over the country. When we took a breather from the hard work and worry, I remembered my small radio in my otherwise empty ammunition pouch. Real-time news might be the best ammunition we could have. I clicked the radio on and tuned to AFN, and we listened intently with the volume turned low. Slick asked me to turn it up so he could also hear the reports. No music was being played on the air, only battle reports from all over Vietnam. If we were not discouraged enough before, we were more depressed as we became aware how precarious the situation was throughout Vietnam.

We learned that a general offensive was underway all over the country. The enemy assaults were amplified by the large numbers of ARVN soldiers who had gone home for the holidays. While Saigon had virtually disarmed for the cease-fire, Hanoi had mobilized to attack with their greatest strength. Civilians also had traveled for the holidays, adding their numbers to the normal homeless, but exponentially increasing the numbers of refugees. With this bad news we felt more isolated than ever. Although we at least understood the dearth of support, it seemed that our survival rested in our own hands.

We were a motley little band of soldiers, desperately short of supplies, outnumbered and outgunned for the first time. Eroding our numbers were at least twenty-five dead, in addition to the wounded. Our losses were partially offset by a few wandering ARVN soldiers who wandered into our perimeter, looking for any unit to join. They would have been killed outright if singly by the VC who occupied My Tho, so they'd picked up the rifles of the dead and joined our fight.

Although our situation was bleak, I believed that if we recovered some of our soldiers and received a resupply, we could still be effective. On the other hand, there was little we could do other than hang on until our situation improved.

*   *   *

By the middle of the afternoon the sun had baked us. I kept thinking of hamburgers on a grill. The house, transformed from an aid station into a morgue, was filled with the smell of death. I went inside once to see about the wounded, but the smell made me dry-heave from my empty stomach. The sight was as awful as the smell. If the wounded could walk or crawl, they returned to the perimeter on their own rather than remain in the impromptu crypt.

Late in the day, we were joined by forty of our own soldiers who had managed to return to Binh Duc, where they recovered their weapons and ammunition before leaving on foot to join us. Their arrival lifted our spirits, and their numbers made up for our losses thus far.

Sergeant Mendenhall confiscated a straw sleeping mat from the house. We gathered short sticks and propped the mat over our trench for some protection from the brutal sun. Our scraped-out hole was only two feet deep and not quite long enough for us both to lie flat in it side by side. It was more a two-man fighting trench than a foxhole. Usually we sat in the hole, with our feet stretched out and our heads up to look around us. By this time, our body odor was so pungent that neither of us relished huddling together in the confined space, but at least the straw mat provided some shade.

Nearby an ARVN soldier was digging a deep foxhole for a Vietnamese lieutenant, using a shovel that had been found. The lieutenant walked to the soldier and exhorted him loudly to make the hole deeper. Mendenhall and I watched the exchange, wishing we had a shovel and someone to dig for us, too.

The digger was in the hole up to his chest and the lieutenant stood at the edge, encouraging him to dig deeper. During their exchange, a sniper in the apartment building overlooking us took advantage of the easy targets. He fired a burst of eight rounds from an AK-47 assault rifle. We witnessed bullets strike the Vietnamese officer and soldier ten meters from where we lay. The soldier in the hole was struck once in the head, killing him instantly. The lieutenant standing above ground was not so lucky. Three rounds struck him in the crotch, at the same level with the soldier's head. One round broke his hip, the second went through his intestines, and the third shot off his penis and testicles. The lieutenant fell to his knees, hesitated, and then toppled into the hole on top of the dead soldier.

After a brief pause to re-aim, the sniper's next three bullets ripped through the straw mat covering our trench. They didn't hit us, but Mendenhall hurled the mat aside with a single stroke, removing the beautiful target over our heads. Like turtles, we pulled our heads into the hole, but unfortunately the trench was not long enough, so both our feet were outside. Vietnamese riflemen directed a heavy volume of fire at the sniper, forcing him to duck into the building.

Mendenhall said, almost casually, "This is a hell of a predicament, sir."

"Well, you got any bright ideas?" I asked.

"We could make a run for the house," he suggested.

"No way! I've been there. There's more death there than here. It's sickening."

"I guess we'll just hang here and hope for the best."

"If I get shot, I'd rather die quickly like the soldier, rather than like the lieutenant," I offered.

"The lieutenant isn't dead, sir. Listen."

In the quiet, we heard moans wafting from the foxhole. They grew louder.

"Looks like we got two choices," said Mendenhall. "Both involve staying here and listening to the lieutenant."

"What are they?" I wanted to know.

"We can lie here with our feet exposed to the sniper, or drag our feet in and expose our heads."

"Mendenhall, as bad as you smell, I'm not sticking my head out just now. If something has to go, my dancing days are over."

"Me too . . . but if it gets worse, I might change my mind."

* * *

When the firing ceased an appalling silence hung in the air. For ten minutes all we heard were the agonized screams of the lieutenant in the hole. Finally he crawled hand over hand out of the hole, groaning loudly as he did. He was a bloody mess from his stomach to his knees, and his hands were bloody from holding his wounds. A medic approached him, spoke with him a moment, took one look at his wounds, and walked away.

The medic reported in Vietnamese to Captain Xuan. A loud exchange ensued between Xuan and the lieutenant in Vietnamese I could not understand, but I knew it was an important conversation from the desperation in their voices. All the soldiers who heard the exchange wore looks of resignation on their faces, but no one uttered a sound. The screams of the butchered lieutenant gradually changed to quiet sobbing.

The dreaded silence hung over us for an eternal moment. Captain Xuan's radio operator stood up with Xuan's .45-caliber pistol in his hand. He walked deliberately but slowly to the hole where the lieutenant lay in his own blood and held out the pistol to him. The officer slowly took the pistol in both his blooded hands. The radio operator turned quietly around and returned to sit by his radio. The lieutenant slid back into the hole with his dead soldier. Again there was silence. Then we heard one shot from inside the foxhole. The radio operator slowly got up again, walked to the hole, which had been dug for protection and was now a grave. He reached in and recovered the .45. He wiped it off carefully with his shirttail and returned it to Xuan.

The rest of the afternoon was hauntingly quiet, except for continuous news on my small radio and the rifle and machine gun fire a few blocks away. There were no feelings left in us; all emotions had been extinguished. We had again witnessed war's ugliest face. War was hell, and we had finally arrived at its gates. I didn't think life could get any worse than this.

Maybe death would come as a blessing, after all.

"The delta was the real world to the Vietnamese. Almost by definition that meant it was unreal to the Americans. . . . The delta was a uniquely South Vietnamese theater of action."

- Don Oberdorfer, *Tet*[1]

18

The Storm Unremitting

February 2-7, 1968

The sniper who killed the lieutenant and the soldier digging the foxhole was not satisfied. He represented our worst nightmare—and he would not go away. He had taken up residence in the apartment building overlooking our tenuous defense and was intent on making our existence a living hell. He moved from room to room, firing from a different window each time.

The news on my radio indicated that life in all the large cities was much the same as ours. I realized that all the soft-living rear-echelon guys were having a hard time, too. It seemed that everyone in Vietnam was struggling to survive. I was also aware that if Saigon fell completely, there would be no way out. From radio news accounts, I knew a lot more about what was happening in the battles for the ancient imperial capital of Hue, the Phu Tho Race Track and Chinese Cholon in Saigon, the Saigon River Y-Bridge, and the U.S. Embassy than I knew about the battle for My Tho. There were no American reporters where we were, and no one covered our war except for us.

However, I was able to piece together some of the situation in My Tho from my own observations, reports on the tactical net, and from what Xuan told me. This is what I knew:

The Viet Cong 9th Division, including the 1st Regiment with our old adversaries—the 261st and 263d Main Force battalions, augmented by other VC and NVA units—had infiltrated My Tho undetected during the relaxed security of the cease-fire. On the night of January 31, these units launched an all-out offensive coordinated with the general offensive throughout Vietnam. They expected the general population to rise up in support of their efforts, but they miscalculated apathy of the general population: the Vietnamese people really had no stomach for the war in their backyard.

The Viet Cong 9th Division had established its headquarters inside the bus station, near our position. The city's soccer field, one block from the ARVN 7th Division headquarters, was a major battleground, and it was under the control of the VC. My Tho's wharf was in VC hands; the helipad, where I had originally arrived in My Tho, and the adjoining cemetery were under VC control. The cemetery was also a battlefield. Our ARVN armored squadron had lost many of its M113 armored personnel carriers, along with their advisors, and had been under heavy attack, but the VC were keeping the squadron hemmed in. Viet Cong occupied the bridge over which the tracked vehicles had to cross the Rach Bao Dinh River to reach My Tho. The main traffic circle in My Tho, which controlled traffic in several directions, was also in VC hands.

The ARVN artillery battalion had been fighting for survival, using its howitzers in direct fire at point-blank range to keep the VC out of its compound, but it lost a main ammunition dump when Viet Cong sappers blew it up. As a result, the artillery battalion was desperately short of ammunition and unlikely to be able to fire in our support.

The U.S. 9th Infantry Division was fighting to help clear Ben Tre in Kien Hoa Province, which had been attacked a day later than My Tho. The capitol of Ben Tre was the birthplace of the National Liberation Front—an important political symbol to the Viet Cong. A U.S. Army major was quoted in the press as saying: "It became necessary to destroy the city in order to save it."

South Vietnamese President Nguyen Van Thieu was vacationing in My Tho for the Tet holidays, and I was sure the VC knew of Thieu's presence and would try to make My Tho a major battleground.

*   *   *

We had not eaten for three days and were in desperate need of ammunition, water, and medical supplies. We were so hungry and thirsty that I doubted our effectiveness if we were ordered to move. I became dizzy when I moved suddenly. At this point our hunger was beyond growling stomachs and hunger pangs—we were losing touch with reality, and maybe that was not a bad thing under the circumstances. Reality was too terrible to contemplate.

At long last, I was encouraged to see USAF F-4C Phantoms flying overhead. A U.S. L-19 with a forward air controller (FAC) aboard was also in the air. This was the same type of plane that Swamp Fox used for army fire coordination. I rejoiced at the first American fire support I had seen since the Navy river patrol boat the first night of the battle. I felt as though the cavalry was coming to our rescue.

On the radio, its battery miraculously still working, I heard the FAC informing the F-4s that a Viet Cong flag was flying on top of the bus station, only one kilometer from where we held our blocking position. (The bus station was the headquarters of the Viet Cong 9th Division.) I knew we were close to the station, so I called the FAC and informed him that I would pop a smoke grenade so he could identify our location. I didn't want his bombs dropped on us. I was glad I had taken the initiative when the FAC informed me that he'd not known we were there.

The sounds of jets scorching low toward their targets buoyed our spirits. They made their cannon and bomb runs screaming directly over us. When they released their bombs west of us, the fighters cut away to avoid heavy antiaircraft fire rising from the bus station.

The fins of bombs snapped open and we watched them float directly over our heads before they struck the bus station. We heard antiaircraft machine guns from the bus station engaging the fighters and the roar of the Phantoms as they flamed their jet engines. Brass shell casings from the 20mm cannon fell on us; we had to keep helmets on for protection from the falling debris, but we didn't care. We were in the best spirits we had been in for days. The bombs exploding only two city blocks from our position encouraged our beleaguered band. It seemed the tide had finally turned.

In the midst of the bombing, about a hundred refugees rushed up the dirt road, directly toward our position. Soldiers stood in the road to stop them because, sure enough, VC followed behind the fleeing civilians, using them for cover. There was no safe way to separate innocent civilians from enemy soldiers. The VC didn't fire on us, and our soldiers didn't engage them in the middle of the refugees. The path of the chattering refugees was turned 90 degrees, and they continued to flee the bombing by a route around our position, with escaping VC intermingled.

Our situation remained desperate, but I believed the balance had finally shifted in our favor. We were certainly helped by the inaction of the general population, which at least was not supporting the Viet Cong. Had it done otherwise, our battalion would have been lost.

*   *   *

A report on the advisory radio alerted me that the U.S. 9th Division had deployed an infantry battalion to the dock in My Tho. Its mission was to move inland toward our position, to provide us with some relief. We were to remain in a blocking position—as if we had any other option.

Already I felt that the hard resistance at our front had been softened by the Air Force attacks on the Viet Cong division headquarters. The stream of VC fleeing with civilian refugees seemed to confirm it. I believed we could move about more freely and search for the weakened enemy, but our mission was to stay in place. We were still critically low on supplies and were physically weak. All the same, I was anxious to get away from hell's gate before it swallowed us.

*   *   *

I was concerned that the FAC had not known our position. If he was unaware of our location, other fire-support elements might be also. I called the Seminary with our coordinates in the clear and requested they make it widely known. But communications broke down somewhere. At 11:00 a.m., as we baked in the sun, our tiny world erupted into explosions as 155mm artillery rounds burst inside our small perimeter. Our defensive circle was no larger than fifty meters in diameter, and six rounds exploded in that tight space, and more outside it. We were exposed, with no overhead cover.

Our undersized trench was scant protection, but it was all we had. Large steel shards whistled by us while clods of dirt pounded us. Our ears ached and rang from the blasts, which created such pressure inside my head that I thought it would split.

I knew it was U.S. artillery, since no one else had 155mm howitzers. A U.S. infantry battalion was approaching us and was likely clearing a path before them with the artillery. For a moment, I contemplated jumping into the deep hole with the dead lieutenant and his soldier, but I knew their decaying bodies would kill me if the artillery didn't. I had seen flies circling the grave: I imagined maggots crawling in a decapitated body.

We took only three casualties from the shelling. The low number of wounded amazed me, because the explosions were so intense. From then on I was skeptical of the killing power of artillery, although I was certainly afraid of it. The psychological impact was tremendous; I gained even greater respect for the Viet Cong who had escaped us so many times while being pounded by such vicious attacks.

*   *   *

We held our position until noon, when a company from the U.S. 9th Division linked up with us. I shook hands with Captain Matz, feeling relief at seeing Americans again. While we had to count each bullet, the Americans were armed to the hilt. As we stood and chatted casually with our fellows, the sniper in the apartment complex saw a target of opportunity and fired a round harmlessly into the ground at our feet. It was the greatest mistake of his life.

ARVN soldiers had never come close to hitting the sniper with their fire. But this time, a U.S. M79 grenadier calmly adjusted his leaf sight, took steady aim, and lobbed one grenade. We watched it slowly arc into the window where the sniper was peeping over the windowsill. He was extinguished in a burst of light when the grenade exploded. A cheer rose from our midst at the elimination of the constant threat, and in respect for the extraordinary marksmanship of the grenadier.

The U.S. 9th Infantry Division rifle company had released six captured VC to the ARVN right after our linkup. While we cheered the sniper's demise, an ARVN soldier fired into the prisoners and they fell backward into the small canal. I was as shocked as the other Americans, but nothing could be done. Ashamed and angered by this brutal, unlawful action, I wondered what we had been reduced to. Revenge for the unseemly death of the lieutenant and his soldier was neither sweet nor satisfying.

The U.S. infantry company moved on to complete the sweep through its assigned zone. We accepted a resupply of ammunition and a fresh battery for the radio at the road, and then we began clearing a path southward through the western edges of My Tho.

I was astounded by the devastation. The city had been bombed, shelled, shot, and burned into a ruin. Burned-out buses and cars were scattered in the road, and sometimes the passengers were still in them. One burned-out Lambretta taxi was still manned by a driver with the back of his head blown off and his body charred from the fire. In a macabre gesture, someone had placed sunglasses on him and stuck a cigarette in his mouth.

We could not escape the stench of burned and decaying human flesh. Seasoned soldiers walked around with one hand on their rifles, the other clutching scarves over mouths and noses to filter the air. Flies were prevalent throughout the city; I didn't want one fly to touch my skin. Bodies lay grotesquely beside the roads, where recovery crews were already going about the gruesome task of gathering them into trucks like road kill.

I shall never forget the smell—it haunts me still. I tried for weeks to wash out my nostrils with soap to expunge the smell from my memory. Nothing worked. When I remember it, I can still retrieve the horrible smell.

*   *   *

Later that day we arrived at Binh Duc. I had expected to find the training center destroyed, but it was relatively intact. The training center cadre had been mobilized to defend the base and the adjacent airfield. Apparently it had succeeded.

*   *   *

For the next three days, we ran daily patrols into designated sectors of My Tho and the surrounding urban areas to mop up and kill intransigent, hard-core Viet Cong. Some still hid in houses, and we were fired on in town for some time to come. But My Tho was basically in government forces' hands, if they could only maintain control.

The part played by the Vietnamese 2d battalion was minor in the grand scale of the Tet general offensive, but it loomed very large in my life. From a military perspective, we accomplished a desperate counterattack into one flank of a VC division, holding that side in place until larger forces compelled the VC to retreat. We had begun with 150 faint hearts and ended with about the same number, using replacements to compensate for our losses. For four days we'd had virtually no food, little water, and only the ammunition we carried in. We were unable to tend our wounded or bury our dead.

Myself, I'd witnessed things best unseen and unimagined. I experienced extremes of hunger, thirst, and fear in a situation I never expected to survive. My loyalty to the Vietnamese soldiers was strengthened after our trials, and my admiration for their courage and determination was bolstered. I was, however, extremely disappointed that all the warnings we received over the previous months had been ignored. We were so completely surprised by Hanoi's cunning move that although we defeated the enemy in battle, we would never recover. I wondered how our side could ever win such a war, and I wondered why the United States was fighting a war with no apparent intention of winning. I wondered what Peggy had seen in my face and in my eyes that had frightened her away. And what had she seen in the eyes of so many others before and after? I wondered whether I would ever be able to ask her.

> Efforts to assess the offensive's impact began well before the fighting ends. President Johnson announced that the Viet Cong suffered complete military defeat, an appraisal that General Westmoreland echoed in a statement declaring that allied forces killed more enemy troops over seven days than the United States had lost in the entire war. Militarily, Tet is decidedly a U.S. victory: psychologically and politically, largely thanks to the way it is reported, it is a disaster.[2]

of our rifles. We kept our jaws clenched to avoid chipping teeth and hung on for dear life.

The largest VC units moved from the city, but not very far away; local guerillas stayed behind to harass us and report our movements to the larger formations. This new disposition signified that we were regaining the initiative. The VC had anticipated a general uprising by the civilian population, which did not occur. Without the full support of the South Vietnamese people, the VC could not retain control of population centers nor set up provisional governments. They licked their wounds and planned the next phase. We were on the inside again, and they were on the outside, but hovering nearby and poised to strike.

ARVN and U.S. forces also sustained heavy losses in the battles of Tet. Our side was reluctant to leave the cities unprotected to initiate a major counteroffensive, but we could not leave the Viet Cong camped on our doorsteps indefinitely without taking action. A shift to offensive operations was inevitable.

I wrote home. I needed contact with the world I had left so long ago, but I omitted gruesome details in my letters. I had captured much of it on film, which I sent to my parents for safekeeping, shutting out the knowledge that they would review the photos and my accompanying narratives. A letter to my sister reflected my separation of the reality of my world from theirs:

February 16, 1968

Dear Janet,

How is everything going at Georgia Southern? I imagine it's pretty cold there right now. It's been windy here and gets chilly at night, but it's hot during the day.

The situation has been rather uncomfortable around here for a while now, but I hope it's beginning to get partially back to normal. It was real hairy while Charlie was in downtown My Tho, but he has moved back out to the country now so it has let some of the pressure off. I actually got to sleep in my own bed last night for a change.

Well, it's about time to go across town to the Seminary to get a good meal, so I'll have to close now. Be good and write if you have a chance.

*   *   *

> "The central issue is whether American troops can be used in a way consonant with this country's political objectives. And to achieve that goal, there is required a sweeping reappraisal of the whole Vietnam picture, including basic American strategy and the deployment of forces."
>
> —*Atlanta Constitution,* March 5, 1968

19

Mopping Up

February 1968

Active formations of Viet Cong were cleared from My T
rapidly reconstituted ARVN 11th Infantry Regiment and eleme
U.S. 9th Infantry Division. Snipers remained active, however, e
to take us on anywhere.

Any time we Americans departed the compound in our ju
traveled ready for hostile fire. Rifles faced outward, loaded an
safeties off. We drove at high speed, but our greatest fear
antitank mine was buried in the road and we would run ove
drove in the middle of the bumpy roadways—always of
shoulders. Sometimes our ride bounced so hard that the m

One hot morning in February, our team joined Vietnamese officers on the sandbag wall beside our tin shack, drinking coffee and watching airstrikes against a VC battalion two kilometers from our front door. Viet Cong gunners had launched a heavy mortar attack against us from that area the night before, and we enjoyed the payback.

Following an hour of air force aerobatics, a U.S. battalion dismounted from helicopters in an open rice paddy between our vantage point and the Viet Cong. Fighting started immediately. The VC withdrew quickly under pressure of U.S. firepower, and our troops swept on through. Our battalion was ordered to follow the Americans and occupy the area overnight to secure it.

As we approached the wood line, we made contact with enemy soldiers bypassed by the Americans. After a skirmish, we found a U.S. APC on the road; a rocket-propelled grenade had destroyed it in fighting the previous week. Alongside the APC lay a dead U.S. soldier face up toward heaven and eyes open. The soldier had been there for several days in the heat and sun. His bloated body smelled horrible, but we could do nothing for him, except report his location to the 9th Division liaison at headquarters. The division would send a recovery detail to return the unfortunate prodigal home. As we moved on, his image accompanied us.

We established an overnight defense in a forested area, which the airstrikes had pounded earlier. The next morning we searched for local guerillas in the nearby villages. They were not hard to find; they shot at us before escaping into the next village or tree line, only to shoot again when we caught up with them. Their mission was to delay us.

I had recently bought a new Canon half-frame camera to make 35-millimeter slides. Since I had ammunition in my ammo pouches now, I carried it in my shirt pocket. We were walking on a path parallel to a small canal when a sniper opened fire at close range. AK-47 rounds cut through the trees all around. Everyone of the command group dove into the canal together. When I climbed from the slimy water, my first thought was of my new camera. Of course, it was ruined—along with the film inside and two additional rolls I had used to take pictures of the ruins of My Tho. What a waste! The pictures documented a wasteland that had once been a prosperous city. An entire city was destroyed, and the unfortunate record was itself damaged. The whole war was a colossal waste.

* * *

We stayed near My Tho for the next few days. I followed the progress of mopping-up operations in other areas, including Saigon, and the battle still raging in Hue. My trusty radio served me well, and it occasionally offered music blended with the battle reports. I made sure I kept spare batteries on hand.

On February 12 the battalion boarded trucks and rolled north, following Highway 4 to Ben Tranh airfield. This was where John Paul Vann had launched his operation into Ap Bac six years earlier. From there we moved north on foot toward Long An Province. This was further north than we normally operated, and I gathered from the body language of soldiers that they expected trouble. We met stiff resistance each day, but after a skirmish of several hours the enemy would fall back.

Intelligence reports indicated that Viet Cong Military Region Two headquarters was in this area, along with the VC 1st Regiment. We were likely to meet our frequent adversaries, the 261st and 263d Main Force battalions. Classified reports indicated that a high ranking Viet Cong official—perhaps the commander of Military Region Two—had been killed during the Tet offensive. Even as an elaborate funeral was held, the VC was planning the next phase of the war.

As we passed through villages, we encountered punji pits for the first time. These were simply holes dug into footpaths with sharpened bamboo reeds, punji stakes, stuck in the bottom, points upward and then concealed. Punji stakes were dipped in feces; if one jabbed into the calf or foot, infection was instantaneous and could be fatal without fast medical care. We had not seen the crude devices in our area of operations, and an uneasy feeling accompanied us in the unfamiliar territory.

On Valentine's Day, my radio announced that the 3d Brigade of the 82d Airborne Division was to be part of the reinforcement package being sent to Vietnam in response to the general offensive. I was surprised; the 82d had always been part of our national strategic reserve. I wondered whether this meant that the United States was committed in a life-or-death struggle. Somehow, I couldn't believe our national survival was connected to the poor Asian nation.

Before noon we ran headlong into what we were looking for—enemy forces. Lots of them! We planned to maintain contact with them and work them over with artillery and airstrikes as we always did. This time the back door was to be closed by the ARVN 42d Ranger Battalion and the 3d Battalion of our regiment.

Plenty of air support was allocated for this high-priority operation. We literally stacked the aircraft in the sky, each waiting its turn to engage. We had VNAF Skyraiders, USAF F-4s and F-14s, and army helicopter gunships at our disposal. If there were any gaps in coverage, artillery was available to fill in.

Bobby Hurst and I took turns working with the artillery forward observers and FACs, while the Vietnamese engaged the VC at close range with rifle fire. Air strikes were close to our forward positions as we inched ahead, tightening the noose. I had only *dreamed* of so much dedicated fire support a few weeks earlier during the Tet attacks.

As darkness approached, we had closed to within 200 meters of the enemy and established a defensive perimeter around a thatched farmhouse. Aircraft had reported taking ground fire all day. As darkness closed, a Spooky C-47 gunship reported on station above us. It slowly circled over our area, and we were surprised to see green tracers streak toward it from every direction. Tracers even came from the path we had just cleared. No imagination was needed to see we were surrounded. Spooky was confused by the disposition of units.

"Red Oak, this is Spooky 41. Over."

"Spooky this is Red Oak 5. Over."

"I thought I had you pinpointed, but I'd like to verify your location again. Would you send up a flare?"

"Sure thing. Look for it in one minute." I found a pencil flare in my rucksack and triggered it into the air.

The flare burst overhead, and the pilot said simply, "Good job. You managed to get right in the middle of them!"

It appeared that the Viet Cong did not intend to conduct this battle according to our plan. Usually they fought when trapped and withdrew at night, but now seemed to believe that they had the upper hand and intended to seize the initiative. Their relative numbers likely encouraged them; there were enough of them to surround us. We were only a battalion of 500 soldiers, and they had us surrounded. There had to be at least two battalions, plus some local forces. In addition, the two battalions we again faced, the 261st and 263d, were always well trained and equipped. They would not fire at aircraft at night unless they had an advantage. I believed NVA troops were included in the numbers because they did not withdraw in the face of a fight. They intended to fight us under conditions favorable to them. The way they had fought and withdrew during previous days seemed to have been drawing us into this position. Most likely they planned to overrun us during the night; this observation was not lost on anyone.

The only time I had seen Vietnamese soldiers dig in was when we were pinned down during Tet. But serious digging began now, even construction of overhead cover. Special attention was given to crew-served machine guns; we prepared for a pitched battle at the farmhouse. We had faced these same units near the My Tho bus station two weeks earlier, and both sides were determined to complete unfinished business.

The attack began early in the evening with a furious rocket and mortar barrage, including a mix of 82mm and 120mm mortar rounds. The shells just kept coming. I was surprised that they had such an abundant supply of ammunition, given all that we had captured earlier at the Double Y canals and the heavy expenditures during the Tet offensive.

After the mortars and rockets opened up, an intense ground attack commenced. The attack was a coordinated effort more serious than any direct attack we had received before. Multiple prongs came from different directions. Well-versed military professionals, not local guerilla leaders, had planned this assault. These were the same techniques we taught to our battalion commanders at staff colleges. These Viet Cong units were likely commanded or advised by NVA officers trained in China or the Soviet Union. Not only were the ground attacks themselves well planned and coordinated, their fire support plan was coordinated with the attacks. While mortar rounds fell inside our perimeter, rockets simultaneously ripped through the farmhouse with earsplitting blasts. Close fighting broke out all around the defensive perimeter.

The sky erupted in light above our CP, blinding us for several moments. Debris fell on our heads. I knew we were in deep trouble again.

Spooky's voice spoke on the radio. "I know you have your hands full down there, but I can see where the bad guys are, so I'll just keep pumping fire in that direction. Just give me a call if you have anything."

"Roger that," Bobby shouted into the radio handset over the explosions and gunfire.

After a short pause Spooky added, "Just give me a call once in a while to let me know you're all right, buddy."

"Roger that," Bobby replied with less enthusiasm. Then he looked at me in a way that told me exactly what he was thinking: there was a good chance that we would not be around for long. We could hear the unspoken thought screaming in the pilot's voice.

Captain Xuan crawled over. He never crawled. "The 3d Company headquarters was destroyed by the rocket attack. VC are inside our positions," he said. "Be prepared to protect yourselves!" Our lines had been penetrated.

Americans scrambled into the earthen bunker in the old house, but I felt claustrophobic inside. The bunker offered some protection from rockets and mortars, but if the VC were inside our perimeter I wanted to be outside where I could see.

Spooky had night-vision goggles. "Red Oak, the bad guys are throwing something that looks like smoke. It could be gas."

Panic! We all had gas masks but never wore them except in training. The heavy rubber masks were hot and restricted visibility. Mine had been submerged in contaminated canal and paddy water, and I was certain the filters were clogged.

Bobby said, "Check your gas masks, but if push comes to shove, piss on a piece of cloth and hold it over your nose. The ammonia will work better against tear gas than these things." I didn't know if it was true or not, but I did know I had no intention of wearing a gas mask.

The attack continued through the night. Our defenses were penetrated several times, but each attack was contained. I decided to leave the bunker to see how Spooky was working, but mostly to see whether anything was happening nearby. In the flashes of light I saw heavy fighting a few meters from our position, hand-to-hand struggles between our soldiers and VC.

An M60 machine gun belonging to a dead soldier lay nearby. I crawled behind it and fired into dark figures approaching our position, aiming stakes making it easy to find the proper fields of fire. Our soldiers quickly shifted to fill the gap left by the penetration, and I readily relinquished the machine gun to a Vietnamese soldier.

Our backs were to the wall with no place to go—it was another fight for survival. The 42d Rangers and the 3d Battalion were under attack in their own defensive positions, but the sounds indicated that we were the main objective of the attack. I suspected the other battalions were being attacked to pin them down while they worked on us.

At 4:00 a.m. the Viet Cong made a last attempt effort to penetrate our defenses before dawn. They threw tear gas grenades and made another coordinated ground and mortar attack, but our lines held this time. By 5:00 a.m., daylight was breaking and the surface of the ground appeared to be blanketed with three feet of fog. As daylight broke, we could see it was not fog at all but smoke from the battle hovering over our fighting positions. In the dim daylight we could see VC recovering their dead. They used smoke grenades and started brush fires for smoke to conceal their work. Snipers kept us down while they went about their grisly task. For the most part, our soldiers left the enemy alone during that time, but at 7:00 a.m. the VC body recovery was still under way. Xuan ordered a limited counterattack to drive the last of the Vietcong away. In full daylight we walked about to survey the damages and losses.

The ARVN had suffered twelve killed and twenty seriously wounded. Damage to the farmhouse and surrounding trees was very heavy. Even after the long VC recovery operation, we recovered eight bodies that had not been dragged away. It was impossible to estimate how many of the enemy had been killed, but they were surely hurt severely, because we seldom found any bodies left at all after battle.

We believed, correctly, that we had won the battle: we were still there, and a larger enemy force had withdrawn. And it appeared that their casualties were greater than ours, therefore we'd won. The euphoria of victory eluded me. Survival was exhilarating, but I didn't feel much like a victory celebration.

> General Wheeler returned from his recent round of talks with General Westmoreland and reported that despite the heavy casualties incurred during the Tet Offensive, North Vietnamese and Vietcong forces still have the initiative: They are operating with relative freedom in the countryside, have pushed South Vietnamese forces back into a defensive posture around towns and cities, seriously undermined the pacification program in many areas, and forced General Westmoreland to place half his maneuver forces in the endangered northern provinces, thus stripping the rest of the country of adequate reserves and depriving the rest of the U.S. command of offensive capability.[2]

20

Rats of a Different Kind

March 1968

Intelligence reports informed us that we were being observed. We didn't need sophisticated equipment to figure that out. We were aware that our departures from our compound and our convoy movements were observed and reported to Viet Cong forces nearby. Initial reports that we were preparing to move could originate from anyone inside our compound or at the "ruff-puff" camp just outside the gate, or from civilians nearby. But we knew without a doubt that as soon as our trucks left the gates, road watchers would report our progress, giving the VC advance notice of our approach.

The spies captured in Cai Lay on the day I was wounded were typical—young boys or old men and women, not fighting-age men. They were a species of rat that wanted us killed. We had been lucky thus far, not being ambushed, but I knew we were vulnerable in truck convoys, especially with a battalion so lax in security.

Late in February the 3d Battalion, our sister unit, was sent into the Double Y to search for new caches there. I always considered the region our personal hunting grounds and resented someone else going in our place. We had shed our blood there, and drawn the blood of our enemy. It was hallowed ground to us, ours to defend.

Upon arrival at the Double Y, the 3d Battalion found the cache sites we had discovered earlier; they were completely repaired and refilled with ammunition and weapons. The battalion followed our procedure for destroying and removing the enemy's supplies. We knew the VC were tired of humping all that ammunition down the Ho Chi Minh Trail and through the Plain of Reeds to conceal it, only to have us come along time after time to blow it up.

This time the VC decided to deliver a message of their dissatisfaction. On its return to Binh Duc things changed dramatically for the 3d Battalion. The VC took action, using their spy network, for an assassination. As the truck convoy bounced home on Highway 4, a single man stepped from the side of the road directly in front of the truck carrying the ARVN battalion commander and U.S. senior advisor. In a reprisal assassination, the ARVN battalion commander was shot multiple times and killed, and the advisor was hit several times but was lucky enough to live. He was evacuated to the United States. Obviously the VC had plotted revenge while the 3d Battalion raided their supplies, and used their spies to trigger the ambush. I felt fortunate that another battalion had been sent in our place.

I also felt guilty.

* * *

VC ranks were decimated during their military failure in the Tet offensive and our combined counteroffensives. The Viet Cong was nearly destroyed as an effective fighting force and required augmentation from the North Vietnamese to reconstitute their units. Blood had been spilled all over a poor nation.

As March stormed in, monsoons followed with dark clouds and heavy rains. Monsoon rains seemed determined to wash away bad memories on both sides and bring in new supplies of clean water to replenish the land. Water was dumped from the heavens, washing away blood throughout the countryside and cities. Prevailing winds brought milder weather, along with fresh drinking water; both were welcomed by soldiers and peasants alike.

*   *   *

March was consumed with major operations using a combined task force of the ARVN 2d and 3d Infantry battalions and 32d Ranger Battalion, all under the control of the 11th Regiment. Aggressive Viet Cong activities reverted to pre-Tet tactics: make contact, delay, and withdraw under cover of darkness. We were mortared frequently in the evenings, so we knew they were still getting ammunition resupplies. Instead of staying in the Binh Duc compound, we spent nights on the ground in security positions and listening posts surrounding My Tho. The plan was simple: keep the VC farther away from the cities, out of mortar range.

*   *   *

Some nights we were fortunate to stay in our camp at Binh Duc. As monsoon deluges increased, rats of another kind moved inside our tin shelters from their underground burrows. A big rascal made a pilgrimage through my room after lights out, prowling along the two-by-four timber on the wall beside my bed. The beam was higher than my head and parallel to the top of my mosquito net. One night after finishing a well-worn paperback novel, I looked at the new place to stash it. I'd already decided to redirect the rat's travels, so I had stacked several used books on the ledge. Then, in the dim light, I watched from my bunk as the rat began his usual expedition along the two-by-four.

Scampering along his normal route, the rodent bumped headfirst into the books, stopped, and looked about. Then, to my horror, he stepped off the ledge onto the top of my mosquito net—right over my face! The net sagged under his weight until his churning claws almost touched my nose. He clambered along the netting to get to the foot of the bed. All the while I prayed the netting would hold. I was afraid to move, even to breathe. As soon as he passed over, I quickly rolled out of bed and removed the books to give the beast full right of passage. I didn't want a pet rat but I thought we could get along respectfully for a while. I didn't surrender, I just compromised to live in peace.

* * *

On another wet night, our advisory team crossed through the barbed wire fence to meet our American friends in our sister battalion. The noncommissioned officers of that battalion's team considered themselves card sharks and challenged our team to a poker game. Naturally we accepted the challenge. Our gracious, but confident hosts supplied plenty of beer and bourbon, accompanied by hors d'oeuvres of Spam and saltines. Within a couple of hours we were well into our game. One of the sergeants left to go to the latrine, and upon returning brought back a heavy case of C-rations.

"Come on. It's your deal."

"Hold your horses a minute. I want to cover this hole up." He slid the case of rations across the concrete floor against the wall.

"What for? You got rats, too?"

"Yeah. A big one comes in every night."

"Probably the same one that runs through our place." I imagined that my pet rat had been making the rounds.

"Deal!"

An hour later we heard the C-ration case scraping over the sandy concrete, and we turned as one. Before us the largest wharf rat I had ever seen materialized behind the sliding box. He strolled into the center of the floor, looked us over, and blinked in the bright glow of the electric light bulb over our heads. No one twitched a finger while he sauntered across the room and out the back door. I laid my cards on the table, finished my Jim Beam, and went home to my little rat. I left money on the table. Once you've seen one rat, you have not necessarily seen them all.

* * *

I had been in the field for eight months, which exceeded my obligatory six months of field time. I was ordered to report as an assistant G-3 operations officer in the tactical operations center in April, following overdue R&R at the end of March. I was to transfer my meager belongings from our camp to the Seminary before I left. Reluctantly I complied with my orders.

It seemed my days on the forward edges of life were drawing to an end. I knew I was fortunate to have survived the previous eight months. My nerves were battered, but nevertheless I was reluctant to leave the rats I knew for the unknown variety living in the Seminary. I should have been joyful at leaving combat for a vacation followed by a job away from enemy fire, but I was not. I didn't want to leave my friends in 2d battalion. And I was depressed from having lost my friend Kiem, by O'Malley's death, by the shot-up Vietnamese lieutenant in the foxhole during Tet—and by the war. The glorious adventure I'd imagined had become a losing proposition in every respect. I didn't see victory anywhere in sight, so I left for R&R, seeking only blessed relief.

> Fresh casualty figures show that number of Americans killed and wounded in Vietnam has now passed the total casualties in the Korean War.[2]

"Senator Richard B. Russell called for a change in U.S. military strategy that would remove restrictions on bombing North Vietnam cities and urged a naval blockade of that country's ports."

—*Atlanta Constitution,* March 13, 1968

21

Blessed Respite

March 1968

By the end of March I was nearly on the ropes—a prizefighter, punch drunk and not knowing it, wanting to keep fighting on. Death and destruction were not part of my consciousness, but the war ate at my guts like the foreign organisms inside. I was ready to forget R&R and simply fight on to the end, but Bobby recognized the signs and practically shoved me out the door. I had no idea where I would go and really didn't care. Bobby ordered me to see the personnel officer at the Seminary.

"Find out what's available and sign up for something. I don't care where you go, but you're going somewhere."

There was an opening for Hong Kong, so I took it.

I didn't know anything about Hong Kong but I caught a helicopter flight into Saigon, and a lift to the processing center at Camp Alpha. There I met two other officers, Wayne and Bill, who were also going to Hong Kong and had read some travel literature. While we talked my interest increased. They were well informed, so I agreed to hang out with them. I still didn't really want to be around people but I didn't know what else to do. I rationalized that I could shake them in Hong Kong once we arrived, if I still wanted to. My sole aspiration was to crash-land in an air-conditioned hotel room for a solid week of nothingness.

The next morning the three of us were bused to the civilian side of the air base, whence commercial flights departed. Wearing cheap civilian clothes from the military exchange, we boarded a Japan Air flight and settled into cushioned seats, perched side by side in a three-seat row. As the flight taxied into line for departure, blessed relief at leaving Vietnam washed over me. Clean sheets, cold beer, hot food, and a flush toilet would be just fine. I wasn't in search of any excitement; boring would be perfect.

The intercom crackled in the cabin. "Ladies and gentlemen, I'm sorry to inform you our departure is delayed. The tower is holding commercial flights for military air operations. The delay may be as long as an hour, but if we return to the gate we must reschedule our flight. Consequently we'll remain here with the engines running to keep the aircraft comfortable. I've asked the hostesses to serve refreshments. Thank you for your patience."

I was seated on the aisle; Wayne was in the middle. I whispered, "I can't even leave this stinking place."

Wayne, the optimist, grinned, "At least he opened the bar."

"Hey, you guys," Bill whispered from his seat near the window, "check out the cute chick across the aisle."

Sure enough, we saw a girl with short brown hair. She appeared to be about our age. She sat alone at the window seat on a short row across the aisle and one row up. She was scribbling in a book that appeared to be a diary. She looked American, but how could we tell? We stared unabashedly.

"I wonder if she's stopping in Hong Kong?" Wayne thought aloud.

"Would you like something to drink?" a Japanese stewardess in a kimono asked in perfect English as she parked the drink trolley in the aisle.

"I'll have a beer," I replied.

"Whisky and soda," said Wayne.

"White wine," decided Bill.

As the hostess prepared the drinks, rusty gears in our minds were grinding.

"Why don't you buy her a drink?" Bill whispered to me.

"Maybe she doesn't speak English." I groped for an excuse to avoid further human contact. I was not inclined to start another relationship on an airplane. I remembered my unfinished business with Peggy.

"I dare you!" challenged Wayne.

I could never turn down a dare. As the hostess handed me a beer and a glass, I summoned up my frayed nerve but settled for safety behind the stewardess.

"Would you offer that lady a drink, on us?" I requested as I handed her additional dollars.

She smiled faintly, bowed, pushed the cart a few feet, and leaned over to whisper to the girl. The girl closed her book on her tray and turned slowly to look in our direction. Her big brown doe eyes congealed my blood to chocolate milk.

"Thank you." She mouthed the words in our direction but delivered the message straight to our hearts.

We contemplated the next move as we sipped our drinks. Before we discussed what to do next, the plane rolled forward, relieving some of the tension. Soon we were in the air, leaving Vietnam behind and bearing for Hong Kong and unforeseen adventures.

She resumed writing as the airplane gained altitude, but when the seat belt sign bleeped off, she stowed her book in a backpack and slid into the empty aisle seat, nearer us. My excitement level rose.

"Are you soldiers?" she asked. I felt exposed as a jerk just hanging around with two other guys.

We introduced ourselves and explained that we were destined for R&R in Hong Kong for a week. Bonnie (for that was her name) told us she worked in a hospital in San Francisco and had saved her money for several years to finance her travels around the world, staying in youth hostels to stretch her limited funds. Her independence, courage, and initiative impressed me. She assured us that she would stay in Hong Kong for two or three days, and then go on to Tokyo.

"Youth hostels?" asked Bill. "Cheap, but not much fun. We're at the President. Why don't you stay there?"

"I can't afford it."

"You could stay with me," ventured Wayne.

"I don't think so! But thanks for the offer," she smiled, closing the subject.

"What if we chipped in to help pay for your room?" I ventured into territory that I should have avoided.

"No . . . I wouldn't feel right about that," Bonnie countered.

"Or two of us could double up, and you could have one of the rooms to yourself," I raised the ante. Once in the game I was determined to win.

"Please, buckle your seat belts," boomed a voice over the intercom. "We'll make a steep decent for landing in Hong Kong,"

"I'll think about it," she offered. "Let's talk after we land." The break allowed us to contemplate our changed situation.

We had each arrived at the same place in time with different goals. I wanted to be alone to recuperate and certainly didn't want any entangling relationships. Bonnie wanted to see as much of Hong Kong as possible on a limited budget. Wayne and Bill were looking for fun—and to them a bigger group meant more fun. They wanted relationships of all kinds. If the four of us stuck together, we would have to work out our differences, but I wasn't so sure I was willing, or able, to accommodate the others.

After scrambling to deplane the four of us lined up to pass through customs together. As we inched ahead, two Chinese policemen appeared out of nowhere. One requested in perfect English, politely but firmly, that the three men step out of line and follow him. We protested mildly but refrained from escalating the situation into an international incident. The policemen led us to separate interrogation rooms, leaving Bonnie alone. As we walked away, she called after us that she would wait after clearing customs.

It was evident the police suspected one or all of us of possession or smuggling drugs. We were questioned for half an hour and then led into separate rooms for a strip search, including the emptying and inventorying of our baggage. When every piece of clothing and baggage had been examined carefully, we were intrusively examined by medical-types wearing white coats and rubber gloves.

I was furious, humiliated, and disgusted by the entire episode. We had been viewed as white U.S. soldiers from Vietnam and singled out for the indignity. Never mind that we were officers. I decided to hate Hong Kong, but I was not sure whether to blame the Chinese or the British. My blessed relief had been stolen.

Richard Taylor

Author's Collection

Lieutenant Kiem (left) enjoys coffee while inspecting sandbags along a canal spanning one sector of the 2-11 Battalion's perimeter at Binh Duc Compound. *Author*

Battalion Commander Major Bouie (below) stands among a gaggle of radio operators and staff officers during a sweep operation in the Mekong Delta. *Author*

The author (above) chews the sweet juice from sugar cane in bountiful Kien Hoa Province while an amused Dao Binh looks on. A Communist Party flag (below) that is later presented to the author. From left to right: unidentified staff officer, Hurst, Tao, Xuan, and battalion doctor Bac Si. *Author*

Top: VC prisoners huddle near Snoopy's Nose with their arms loosely bound. *Bottom:* Female laborers for the VC are held for interrogation. *U. S. Army*

Lieutenant Kiem (left) enjoys coffee while inspecting sandbags along a canal spanning one sector of the 2-11 Battalion's perimeter at Binh Duc Compound. *Author*

Battalion Commander Major Bouie (below) stands among a gaggle of radio operators and staff officers during a sweep operation in the Mekong Delta. *Author*

Richard Taylor

Author's Collection

Captured ammunition blown in place near the Double Y farmhouse. *Author*

The author (above) at home in Binh Duc. *Author*

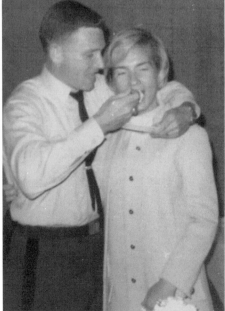

Sandy and Richard (right) sample wedding cake at Fort Benning's Golf Club following a life-time commitment at Kelly Hill Chapel. *Author*

Left: Returning to Vietnam from Columbus—the long farewell. *Author*

Below: Bravo Company field HQ on Hill 300 in War Zone D. Standing, left to right: Author Richard Taylor; PFC Wayne Czajka, artillery forward observer; Specialist Jim Johnson, battalion radio operator. Kneeling, left to right: Specialist Don Verruchi, company radio operator; Specialist Joe Sauble, artillery radio operator. *Author*

Above: Writing letters home from deep within War Zone D. *Author*

Below: Much needed respite from field operations at FB Green for Bravo troopers.
David Burnett, U.S. News & World Report

Above: Sp4 Steve Bohrer and his funny friend catch up on important news from home. *David Burnett, U.S. News & World Report. Below:* Lieutenant Colonel Tony Labrozzi ponders an excavated cache site with members of the platoon who discovered it. *David Burnett, U.S. News & World Report*

Lieutenant Colonel Tony Labrozzi consults a map in the field with a platoon leader.

David Burnett, U.S. News & World Report

Lieutenant Colonel Tony Labrozzi prepares his men for a mission in the field.
David Burnett, U.S. News & World Report

An Echo Company recon patrol prepares for a new patrol order in the field.

David Burnett, U.S. News & World Report

With the pin pulled, Labrozzi (above) prepares to mark an airstrike with a white phosphorous grenade. *David Burnett, U.S. News & World Report.* The division commander (below) inspects a cache site at LZ Mercer. The author is in center (back to camera), Labrozzi on the right (left side to camera), MG Putnam looks on (without hat), Lt. Dave Judge (far right in boony hat), Sgt. Rogers second from left facing camera. Mines, rocket propelled grenades and other supplies were pulled from beneath the ground. *U.S. Army*

Above: Relinquishing command to Captain Dana Gary. Labrozzi stands in the rear only a day before his own change of command. *Author*.

Below: Lieutenant Colonel Spry (left) takes command of 1-7th Cavalry. *U.S. Army*

Labrozzi practices "Charge!" with a cavalry bugle before relinquishing command at FB Green. Lieutenant Sweeny, in sunglasses, watches along with Captain Prosch, adjutant. *Tony Labrozzi*

Above: Living it up on Green. *Author*

Below: Playing cards at Green: Albert Vanderhaagen, Ron Vrabel, John Walters, and John Payne. *David Burnett, U.S. News & World Report*

True to her promise Bonnie had waited for our release. She was interested in our experiences with customs and was as upset as we were by our experience. By that time she seemed resolved to work out an arrangement with us for our stay in Hong Kong. An invisible bond had been established among us. At least she knew we were not carrying drugs. What she did not know was that one of us was a little off balance.

We crammed ourselves into a taxi for a breathtaking ride to the Hotel President, where the registration clerk informed us that no additional rooms were available. However, we were committed to keeping our band intact, so the three guys huddled and flipped coins for odd man out. The odd man kept a single room, and the other two were to share a room. Bonnie would get the third room for herself. Fortunately I won and got the single room. Wayne and Bill were similar—easygoing, happy, seeking good clean fun, undisturbed by the war in rear-echelon jobs. I was moody, disturbed, and somber; I just wanted to be alone in my room and brood for a week.

Bonnie was an adventurous spirit, who graced us by staying at our hotel at our expense with no strings attached. She became the organizing force who planned our activities, made the arrangements, and refused to allow me to become a recluse. She had already researched all the tourist attractions in Hong Kong, and dragged me reluctantly along when I preferred to stay behind. She informed us that we were all in this together and it would only work if we all stayed together. No one was alone.

I relented for the sake of the group, and her big brown eyes. Hong Kong became a dream come true. We picnicked on a hilltop overlooking Communist China, drank champagne, and toasted our enemy, and even "mooned" the communist guards at the border crossing, shocking our Chinese driver. We ate at the British China Fleet Club, took the ferry across the harbor, saw all the sights, and generally lost track of time and ourselves, forgetting that Vietnam even existed. Bonnie was perfectly safe with us, but we all fell in love with the angel in our midst. She had come out of nowhere bringing renewed hope.

It was a perfect world—too perfect to be true. When the final day approached, I realized that it all had to end and we had to return. Now I wished I had never come at all.

Bonnie left the hotel with us, and we shared a taxi to the airport. She was to board a flight to Tokyo, having cut her stay there short and juggled her itinerary to stay on with us. We boarded an Air France flight back to

Vietnam. Misty eyes prevailed when we exchanged addresses in the United States. Bonnie and I met again on several occasions, but that week in Hong Kong could never be reconstructed. If it had not been so real, and I had pictures to prove it, I would've sworn it was a dream.

> Former Vice President Richard M. Nixon pledged that if elected president he would "end the war" in Vietnam. He did not spell out how.[2]

"Students throughout the world cut classes as part of an anti-war strike organized by the Student Mobilization Committee to End the War in Vietnam."

—The Vietnam War Day by Day

22

Clock Winding Down

April–August 1968

"Ahhh!"

I settled into my very own soft bed at the Seminary with considerable ease. Even though I hated becoming a "staff rat," clean sheets and showers made the transition easier. I remembered all too well the night the general offensive began—would never forget it. I slept soundly and settled into my new job as an assistant G-3 operations officer. The G-3 advisor and several senior officers worked at the ARVN 7th Division tactical operations center seven days a week. Duty officers were rotated with one day on and two days off. The "day on" was twenty-four hours long plus time to orient replacements, which extended the "day on" to twenty-seven hours. The schedule required me to reset my internal clock, especially my sleeping habits, but it was manageable.

Duty officers prepared orders and maps for the next day's operations, kept in constant contact with field advisors, and coordinated with other units in the area, like the U.S. 9th Infantry Division and the U.S. Air Force.

* * *

I was working late one evening in the operations center when I noticed a stranger—the dirtiest American I had ever seen. His smell actually caught my attention first. I couldn't determine what clothes he wore, but he had long sandy hair and wore Ho Chi Minh sandals made from rubber tires. He was armed to the teeth; I had never seen one person carry so many weapons.

He was examining our situation map, and that propelled me to investigate. His appearance was so bizarre that what he said sounded completely credible.

I approached him warily. "Excuse me. May I help you?"

"I want to know about your operations," he informed me.

"I don't think you have a right to that information," I replied.

"I think I do."

"I'm Lieutenant Taylor, and I'm in charge here. Let's start at the beginning. How did you get in here in the first place?"

"I just walked in. No one had the balls to stop me!"

"Well, I have the balls to throw you out unless you give me some straight answers." By now I was backed up by security and I felt my authority.

"Okay, look." He relented. "I did just walk in, but I didn't think you'd let me in if I asked permission. So here I am, and I still need to know about operations."

"Who are you?" I insisted. "Do you have any identification?"

"Can we talk privately?" he asked.

I waved security back. "Okay."

"Look . . . I'm the advisor for the PRU. Do you know them?"

I knew the PRU was the Vietnamese Provincial Reconnaissance Unit, and I knew they worked with the CIA on special, highly classified projects. "Yes," I said.

"Have you heard of Phoenix?" he asked.

"Yes." I had heard of the Phoenix program, and I knew it involved assassination of Viet Cong cadre and spies hiding in villages, but I knew very little beyond that. I may have been curious but I didn't need to know.

"Okay. I'm a navy SEAL on special missions. I can't carry an ID. I'll be in some sensitive places. I just need to ensure I don't run into any friendly troops. It might be dangerous for both of us."

I eyed his load of armaments. He was a legally sanctioned assassin, but certainly no James Bond.

"Okay. I believe you." I did believe him but I didn't envy him. "Tell me the general locations you're interested in, and I'll tell you what we're doing there."

We had reached an understanding: I helped him with information, and he left as he entered. His odor lingered for a while. We heard gunfire in a village on the river later than night.

* * *

Occasionally we were on the receiving end of VC rockets or mortars. Usually little damage was done, but one night a sniper set up target practice directly across a canal from the mess hall in the Seminary. He fired a single round directly into the lens of our movie projector during the evening movie. As spectators slowly got up off the floor, someone started clapping. The movies were pretty bad, indeed, so maybe it was not a VC sniper after all but just one of our guys trying to spare us more movie torture.

* * *

At the beginning, settling into a new routine, the new job and new surroundings were exciting. By May the sparkle had worn off, and I was anxious to return to the battalion. The highlight of May was a visit to the ARVN 7th Division headquarters by Air Marshal and Vietnamese Vice-President Nguyen Cao Ky. In honor of his visit, the division arranged an elaborate display to showcase weapons and ammunition captured during the Double Y operations. Speeches, a parade, refreshments, awards, and copious brown-nosing were integral to the festivities. It added up to a genuine spectacle.

Bobby Hurst brought Master Sergeant Mendenhall, Sergeant First Class Rich, Captain Tao, and Captain Xuan along to see the sights. It was great to see them again, but I was uncomfortable: They were still on the front line while I was holding out in the rear. I missed the old unit more than ever. Staff assignments cannot replace being in a brotherhood of warriors in a struggle with the enemy and fighting for survival and victory. I missed the thrill of the contest and the experiences, but most of all the comradeship. Nevertheless, at the same time, and at a deeper level, I despaired at a war that I thought was going nowhere.

> In the space of seven days, the tides of history and the caprice of fate shook the U.S. with two mighty convulsions. First, Lyndon Johnson announced a bombing pause over most of North Vietnam, then said: "I shall not seek, and I will not accept, the nomination of my party for another term as your President." Finally, was the bullet ending the life of Martin Luther King.[2]

*   *   *

Late in May the division deployed a task force for an operation in Go Cong Province. I eagerly accompanied it to support operations from the forward CP, a great way to get out of My Tho for a while. We moved into a spacious villa and established a headquarters there. Operations lasted nine days. Battles needed to be commanded and controlled, but from a staff perspective it didn't compare with being on the cutting edge with real soldiers. I was more ready than ever to go back to the field, or go quietly home.

*   *   *

June crept up on me. An extra R&R space to Japan was available, so I used a week of ordinary leave to go—anything to break the crushing monotony. I appreciated Tokyo, though it would never compare with Hong Kong. In Japan, I visited friends from North Georgia College who were stationed at the U.S. headquarters at Camp Zama. Tommy and Glenda related a sad story of another classmate, Joe, who had visited them. He had told them he was going after the Medal of Honor, and now he was dead, killed in action. I thought the glittering Ginza would help me forget about Joe, but it didn't work.

*   *   *

As soon as I returned to My Tho, I was summoned into the G-3's office. The shift officer directed me to formally report to Major Coker, the

G-3 advisor. I immediately detected that everyone but me knew what was going on.

I marched into his office; the click of my boots on the marble floor reminded me of a condemned man walking to a firing squad. I wasn't disappointed.

"Lieutenant Taylor reporting as ordered!" I reported, with a hand salute.

I was not given permission to be at ease, so I stood uncomfortably at attention. From the corner of my eye, I saw the division advisor, a full colonel, standing in the background. His presence didn't reassure me about the benevolence of this inquisition.

"Lieutenant Taylor, I am very disturbed by the report I have just seen. What do you have to say for yourself?"

My mind jumped into overdrive as I strained to comprehend.

"I'm sorry, sir, I don't know what report you're talking about."

"Well, Lieutenant, just think about it for a minute. What have you been up to while you were away?"

Obviously I had enjoyed myself in Japan but certainly had done nothing illegal. And even if I had, he couldn't possibly know about it anyway. Furthermore, even if I had—and he did know about it—I certainly was not about to confess. So I stood silently, my thoughts scrambled.

"Lieutenant, why did you come into my office like this?"

That question confused me further. He seemed determined to nail me for some infraction but was changing the subject. I knew my face was pale while my hands trembled at my side. But I remained rigidly at attention.

"What do you mean, sir?" I inquired. I knew I had shaved. Maybe I needed a haircut, but it was not long overdue. My boots were shined, and my uniform was presentable. Immaculate uniforms never were a high priority in Vietnam, anyway.

"Taylor, you're out of uniform! Don't come into my office that way again," said the G-3. He reached for my collar and used a pocketknife to remove my cloth first lieutenant's bar.

An officer read an order, and the major pinned the silver "railroad tracks" of an army captain on my collar.

"Congratulations, Captain! We had you going for a minute, didn't we?"

"You sure did," I smiled through clenched teeth as I shook hands with the officers present, including the ARVN 7th Division commander. Apparently they had entered from the rear to enjoy the fun.

As I walked out of the palatial office, I was relieved that I was not in trouble, but being teased annoyed me. I pretended to be happy about the promotion but I was seething inside. It might be amusing to "staff rats," but I had no time for it in *my* army.

* * *

In July, I received orders to attend Ranger training before an assignment with the 82d Airborne Division at Fort Bragg. I was delighted with the orders; they were exactly what I'd requested. But I faced the ordeal of getting back into shape: the physical demands of Ranger training were different from survival in Vietnam. Adding to my difficulty was a class starting in September. I would be a "winter Ranger," and Vietnam's weather couldn't prepare me for that. I cut back on beer and potatoes, did push-ups and sit-ups while sunning myself on the roof of the Seminary, and occasionally drove to Binh Duc to run at the training center. Running was especially difficult in the heat and humidity, and ARVN soldiers thought I had lost my mind. Maybe I had.

* * *

While I prepared myself for the future, the war would not simply fade away. Time was still punctuated by foolish accidents that underscored our mortality. After visiting a friend, a captain, from advisor training at Fort Bragg I went to Binh Duc to run. When I returned, I was met with the news that he had been returning to his base in a jeep over a dangerous highway. While his noncommissioned officer was driving, the captain jacked a round into the chamber of his .45-caliber pistol. Intending to test the safety, he instead fired a round through his own hand into the chest of his sergeant. The sergeant died instantly, and my friend almost died in the resulting jeep wreck.

In another incident, we came under fire at the Seminary and the mortar crew prepared to return fire. It had rained all day, filling the mortar tube with water. When the mortar round was dropped into the tube for firing, it slid to the bottom, but the water in the tube allowed the round to be propelled only to the mouth of the tube, where it hung and protruded. A crew member caught the round in both hands before it could tip into the mortar pit. Cradling the live round in his arms, he sprinted through the hallway of the Seminary shouting, "Mortar, mortar, mortar!" until he reached the canal in back. He tossed the round into the canal, but it didn't explode. I had always been more afraid of Americans inside the Seminary than I had been of Viet Cong on the outside—for good reason.

Such was the life of staff rats, holed up waiting for something to happen to dramatically affect their lives. I wanted to be on the offensive, not just to react to events. But it wasn't that way any more. My closing days in Vietnam were stitched together by small but memorable incidents, like patches on a worn pair of jeans.

* * *

One patch occurred on a bright Sunday afternoon, when I had gone to the club to watch television. The bar was closed, but the club was quiet and relaxing. The TV sat against the back wall, opposite the bar. I was slumped in an easy chair watching "I Dream of Jeannie" on AFN television, when the wall was literally ripped apart by machine gun fire tearing through paneling in front of me. Bullets hammered into the bar behind me, shattering bottles of liquor and breaking a large glass mirror. It was all over by the time I hit the floor.

I got up off the floor and turned off the television. I wondered how it had survived the attack. I noticed that bullets had ripped through the walls on both sides of it and the chair where I was sitting but had punctured neither the television set nor me. I was grateful but puzzled. The club manager entered to survey the damage and take inventory. I asked for a drink, but he told me the bar would open later than usual.

The manager walked out on a side porch to an outside storage room. I heard him exclaim, "Oh shit!" I followed him out.

I smelled it before I saw it. Foamy, golden liquid flowed from the storeroom onto the floor, dripping onto the ground.

"Beer," I identified it instantly. "Saved by Bud!"

A tall stack of Budweiser cases was full of bullet holes, and beer flowed from the storeroom. I was overjoyed: Budweiser had actually saved my life! I never forgot my debt to that beer. I knew another hand was at work, too, someone watching over me, time and again.

* * *

My last operation in the field was as liaison officer to the U.S. 9th Division MRF in a combined operation on the Mekong River. After one night on the USS *Benewah,* I stayed for five days with "Hammering Hank" Emerson and the force on the river, but I had little to do. I was actually bored in combat. My tour of Vietnam had begun with rude awakenings and nightmares and ended with lazy dreams of home. Home! Where and what was home? I contemplated home, and wondered what it would be like going back. I was not sure I wanted to leave Vietnam—but of course I would.

* * *

It was finally time to go. The day I had awaited for so long was just another hot and humid day in Vietnam. I flew to Can Tho for out-processing. Most of the day was required to out-process everything I had in-processed previously, and I remained there overnight. No planes were flying the next day, so I rode in a jeep all the way to Saigon. We reached the long steel-girder bridge at Ben Luc, which was broken in the center, half-resting in the river. We crossed the river slowly on a floating bridge maintained by army engineers. When we were across I thought about burning bridges behind me. It was a quiet trip with a silent courier driving, but I didn't feel like talking anyway. During the solitude I reflected on the year I had just spent.

As we drove into Saigon in the open jeep, crossing the Y-Bridge, I marveled at many of the places I had followed so closely through the reporting on AFN during the Tet offensive. I was touring a historic battlefield but I was part of that saga. It was unlike any other war I had studied—strange indeed.

I stayed two days at Camp Alpha waiting for a flight. My khaki uniform seemed larger than it was a year before: I had worn no ribbons when I arrived, but wore two rows and a Combat Infantry Badge upon departure. As I thought about the long flight ahead, I missed Peggy. I had forgotten her for a time, but now memories of her flooded back. Somehow I knew she would be on my flight—she had to be, to complete the circle. I wanted to look into her eyes and tell her she was wrong about me. I had survived: I made it safely back despite the odds. Maybe we could begin a real relationship. Peggy would cry again, and ask me to forgive her for not meeting me in the terminal in the Philippines. I would take her into my arms and kiss her, and tell her it was all right. We would fly off together into the setting sun.

Only in my dreams!

I was back where I had started a year ago. Or was I? Peggy was not on the flight. I looked and waited for her to appear each time the crew changed, but she was never there. I peered around corners, stood and watched every flight crew member I saw, and even asked a flight attendant if she knew her. I never saw Peggy again but I will never forget her, either. Somehow I knew I could never return to where I had started my long journey; it was impossible to go back. I had lost my innocence in Vietnam, and what did I have in return? Medals? My life? Shattered illusions? Only experiences, images, and occasional visits from comrades left in the rice fields in the Mekong Delta. Returning prodigals, phantoms of the past, appear unexpectedly and ask the unanswered question: "Why?"

> U.S. sources contend that the present quiet may merely be the calm before the storm. Arms discoveries show that the Viet Cong now control more territory around Saigon than ever before. And they point to the blowing up of the Ben Luc Bridge, connecting Saigon with the Mekong Delta, an act they believe may have been carried out to prevent the South Vietnamese capital from being reinforced during an attack.[3]

"General William C. Westmoreland asked for 206,000 more American troops for Vietnam and the request touched off a divisive internal debate within high levels of the Johnson Administration."

—*New York Times,* March 10, 1968

23

Revival

August 1968–July 1970

War still raged in Vietnam, but I needed a revival, a long, sabbatical to find myself again. The interval between combat tours served to refresh my spirit and substantially change my future. I carried with me from Vietnam in 1968 a sense of personal victory—not necessarily of victory in battle, but victory in merely having survived and prevailed, in establishing that human spirit transcends war. Resigned to the inevitability of war, I despaired that our tactical objectives in Vietnam and our national goals at home were not aligned.

My orders directed, and I eagerly accepted, training as an army Ranger. I prepared myself for the intense, vigorous training and discovered unanticipated weaknesses, which I had believed to be strengths. My feet, weakened from being submerged in water during my tour in the flooded

Mekong River Delta, were quite sensitive to cold. I reached deep within for power to persevere, while taking special care of my tender feet. Despite my efforts my feet were frostbitten in Florida, but I left my hospital bed without being discharged, to finish training and earn the coveted Ranger tab. I was as proud of that accomplishment as anything else I had achieved. Rangers were the most aggressive and effective of soldiers. I yearned to be a member of that elite group and later would have the opportunity to help establish the first of the new Ranger battalions.

*   *   *

Following Ranger training I proudly reported to the 82d Airborne Division. With combat experience and Ranger qualification under my belt I expected a company command. I was chagrined when I was offered assignments at division headquarters as protocol officer or special projects officer. I absolutely refused both. After being bounced around for three days, I reluctantly agreed to go to G-3 operations to accept responsibility for the division's training ammunition program.

The biggest problem was managing training ammunition forecasts. Battalions requested ammunition for anticipated training, but conflicting demands invariably prevented them from using all of it. Consequently far more ammunition was shipped to Fort Bragg than was used, and at considerable cost. I tried to convince units to forecast more realistically but failed to make any headway. So I arbitrarily reduced their orders based on my own assessment. I knew I could replace any shortfall from the unused forecasts of other units. I saved the division and taxpayers millions of dollars—more money for the war effort.

My heroics were soon discovered, but they didn't garner the praise I expected. The corps commander actually commended the 82d for its successes in managing the recurring problem. When the division commander sought to find out how that had happened, he discovered that a young captain had done it on his own initiative. Instead of giving me a pat on the back, he locked my heels on the carpet in front of his desk and chewed me out for exceeding my authority. The peacetime army and I had issues to deal with. I was uncomfortable in the new reality, which was even more unsettling than the unreality of Vietnam. Which was real?

However, Fort Bragg offered needed change and restored my spirit. I was where I wanted to be—in the "shit-hot" 82d Airborne Division, jumping out of airplanes and hanging out with macho men. The spirit of the airborne raised my spirits above a troubled world and gently returned me to earth by parachute.

Two friends joined me: Nick, a crazy Special Forces captain, and Dave, another captain in the 82d Airborne. We rented a house in Fayetteville, and each rode his own Triumph motorcycle.

Fayetteville was home to many women who enjoyed good times with guys with money to blow. We believed we were on top of the world, and perhaps we were. As young, single men with few expenses and no obligations, we had money and time to spend, and we knew how to spend them both in style. Vietnam was half a world away, but shoved down deep, somewhere in our minds. We were lucky to have seen it, and now we had this to hang on to.

Life was fine in "Fayette-Nam." However, an occasional loud noise caused me to drop reflexively to the ground, publicly embarrassing myself. I could not fully escape images of my year in Vietnam. They would suddenly coalesce as apparitions of the people I had met along the way—like Lieutenant O'Malley in the commander's mess. When I had a bad night of "think back too much," I struggled with my personal torments. Practically every soldier knew he was going back to "the Nam." After Ranger training and a few months in the 82d, I was mentally and physically adjusted and prepared to return. I was determined to go to a U.S. Army division, one with plenty of support, especially artillery and helicopters. I talked with other officers with experience in various divisions, gathering their impressions. I decided the 1st Cavalry Division was my choice.

* * *

U.S. Defense Department sources disclose that the Army and Marines will be sending about 24,000 men back to Vietnam for involuntary second tours in a move made necessary by the length of the war, high turnover of personnel resulting from the one year tour of duty, and a tight supply of experienced officers.[2]

Orders arrived suddenly. I was disappointed when my return to Vietnam was delayed by orders for the infantry officers' advanced course at Fort Benning. I had mixed feelings about returning to academics, Ranger school was as intellectual as I wanted to get under the circumstances. I had already studied much of the advanced curriculum through self-study at Binh

Duc. The war might end before I got back to complete unresolved issues, and not only the war, but my part in it. I was afraid the war would dribble to an end before I had finished soldiering. I wanted fulfillment, but getting my ticket punched at the Home of the Infantry was also important. It was a rite of passage for command, and I was convinced that it was the only route to the company command I sought. So I loaded everything I owned in my car, lashed my motorcycle onto a U-Haul trailer, and reluctantly drove to Georgia.

The course lasted nine months. The class was filled with transient officers, most en route from or to Vietnam, and many coming from and going back after graduation. I was in the group that was both coming and going. Some of us took our training seriously; others used the time to relax and try to get families, minds, and lives back together; some did a little of each. Others marked calendars to grow a baby in nine months. I intended to stay in good physical condition, keep my ghosts from Vietnam at bay, enjoy my respite, and learn something that might help me later. Nothing else mattered much. I had an excellent vision of where I wanted to go with my military career and was unconcerned about my personal future. I didn't anticipate the one thing that would completely change my life and my plans.

* * *

President Johnson announced agreement with North Vietnam to begin preliminary peace talks in Paris. But, the President added, "There are many, many hazards and difficulties ahead."[3]

* * *

While holding onto life and advancing my career, I met someone. She was the kind of someone who, once you find her, you know you are no longer complete without her by your side. I had not planned for it, and my future was put in a new light. It struck so unexpectedly that I nearly made a mess of all of it. I had intended to concentrate on my career, lead U.S. soldiers in battle, and claim victory over the haunted battlefield of my psyche. I did not expect to fall in love. Neither of us expected it, but we were powerless to stop it. We tumbled into it together, complicating both our lives in ways we had not imagined.

It all began when my friend Dave from Fort Bragg joined me at Fort Benning for a later class. We each had separate apartments in Columbus, and since Dave had the larger apartment it was logical that I move in with him and use his spare bedroom.

One afternoon after class, I laced my jungle boots and jogged in an old rock quarry along the Chattahoochee River. After running, I found myself waiting near the front window for the blond in the apartment two doors away to come home from work. Sandy arrived in her old Volkswagen Beetle, which limped into the parking lot on nearly its last mile. A single mother, she dragged her groceries and lovely daughter, Paige, inside. She worked hard at the post hospital during the day and used evenings to prepare for the next day's work. The scene drew me back to my window day after day.

One day I saw Paige riding her bike and I invited her to split a Popsicle with me. Sandy was suspicious of my attentions to Paige, and I was afraid she thought I might be a pervert. My world was actually much simpler. Paige was a lovely little girl who reminded me of the lost urchins I had seen in Vietnam. Children deserved better than that.

I asked Sandy out repeatedly. She turned me down each time, explaining that she didn't want to get involved with anyone. She had suffered through several bad relationships and was not prepared for another one. I imagined that my prospects didn't look very promising to her, either. I refused to accept her logic or her rejection, and I persisted until she accepted after my third try.

I made reservations for a steak dinner at the Coco Supper Club on Victory Drive. We both knew the Coco had great steaks and good service, and we dressed up for the occasion. We talked as we ate.

"I'm so hungry."

"The steak is really good." Pointless conversation.

"Mine is so good I'll be indebted to you." Sandy implied she would return the favor by cooking a meal for me.

The way she said it threw me off balance. I replied, "I won't let you return the favor. I want you to be indebted to me!"

She blushed, stunned by my audacity. I was also surprised by my utterance and wondered what to say next.

After an awkward pause, she pressed me. "And what do you mean, you want me to be indebted to you?"

I felt my face flush; my heart throbbed; beads of sweat formed on my upper lip. I didn't know exactly what I had meant, but I knew I meant what I said. We were amused and embarrassed simultaneously by the position we were in. We had arrived at a clear juncture in our relationship.

Sandy sensed we were on the verge of an important discussion, but I was in over my head. I laughed it off but I had already tipped my hand. Plans for my life had taken a sudden detour, and I didn't know where it might lead.

I couldn't imagine a day without seeing Sandy, and I couldn't see her enough. We just couldn't seem to get close enough.

Finding ways to spend more time with her, I bought two old bicycles from a used bike shop. We rode together to an Italian restaurant for spaghetti, or sometimes walked or ran together after work. Running was a new experience for her, but I was determined to get her into an exercise program. It was a great way to spend more time together. Somehow it justified my physical education major in college: I was transformed into the coach I had always aspired to be.

I knew Sandy needed me to express my feelings, hopes, and dreams. I sensed her fear that I would disappear, as soldiers often do. I wanted to understand her questions better but I didn't know the answers. I was content for us to watch television together, enjoy Irish coffee and doughnuts on Sunday mornings, but most of all, just hold her. I never wanted to let go, but we knew that day was approaching.

*   *   *

Sandy wrote about that time in her own words:

> My cousin Jan had come to live with me, deposited on my doorstep in Columbus straight from Saudi Arabia. It would be nice to have someone help with the rent and we would have fun. Fun had been absent from my life for a while.
>
> My life was different from Jan's. I was divorced, supporting a three-year old child without a clue how to do it. My life was dull; I was living in black and white, on the fringe of a more colorful world, wherein Jan dwelled.
>
> She was cute, fun, and my ticket into the colorful world. She bought striped lawn chairs! In her world, people dressed in bright clothes, leisurely sunned themselves, and socialized around a grill sipping sweet drinks and making droll, witty conversation. This was a world where people did not work all weekend, the world I had dreamed of from the periphery.
>
> I continued on with my life—daycare, work, daycare, home— weekends on call at the hospital. We were on separate tracks. Hers

included tanning, shopping, and hanging out with a rock band while mine was head down and straight-ahead.

So, when I woke to find Jan missing, I was not surprised, but rather, dismayed. (Jan was heading to Texas in her Mustang.) She left with the rent due. The colorful life I had purchased by selling my furniture abruptly vanished. My technicolored world evolved into a whirling nightmare.

I was grateful for the simple existence I managed to carve out for us. I worked weekends and took in roommates to pay the rent and occasionally used the only thing Jan had left—lawn chairs—to sit in the sun.

One day after work, I limped home in my old blue Volkswagen; when I saw an all-American type with light hair, blue eyes, a sprinkling of freckles and athletic build, I took notice. He asked me over to watch a football game. I declined. Later, he came to borrow a bowl for chips, and asked me out once more. I declined again. The third time I finally accepted, running out of excuses.

I remember the words I could not believe he had uttered: "I want you to be indebted to me!" We fell in love on that first date and, as they say, the rest is history.

*   *   *

The dreaded day arrived. My class assembled in the auditorium at Fort Benning's Infantry Hall for graduation. After the speeches and hoopla, I tucked my diploma away and Sandy and I ran away to Florida alone. The closer we grew, the more nervous I became. She made me feel warm and comfortable, I didn't know how I could live without her. I pulled back; I had to clear my head and harden my heart.

We returned to Columbus quietly, issues concerning our future together unresolved. Sandy left for work, and I packed my belongings to stash for another year. We said farewell. But why was I leaving? I was running away from a relationship I wanted more than anything else. But I no longer controlled my future, the army did, and it was time to deal with that.

I left while Sandy was at work. I roamed about visiting family and old friends and preparing to return to Vietnam. I tried to escape the meaning of "I want you to be indebted to me." I tried but I couldn't shake it. I returned to Columbus for an honest discussion about us: who were we, where we were going, and the almost insurmountable problems we faced. We knew we had issues to confront, but we decided to tackle them together.

Sandy and I were married at the Kelly Hill Chapel on Fort Benning three weeks before I left for the war zone. I finally understood how significant commitment is. For the first time I was fully committed to someone, not an idea or a cause, but bound to another person.

* * *

President Nixon, in a nationally televised speech, announced he is sending U.S. combat forces into Cambodia to destroy Communist sanctuaries and supply bases.[4]

* * *

These were stressful hours for us and we lived each day as though it were our last. We struggled with our new relationship, facing a year's separation. Many of our friends' days had been shortened by the war; announcement of each death surprised us. As the end of life was brought to the forefront, life itself assumed larger meaning. We were determined to live each day as if it were numbered, like a priceless possession.

The period between combat tours was a bridge. I had someone to come home to, and Sandy had someone to wait for. But, our union didn't simplify our lives. I had not prepared myself for this psychologically, and my old career goals now conflicted with my new life goals. We were realistic about the difficulty ahead for both of us, but we were determined to hold our lives together somehow.

My first year in Vietnam had been a year of big battles. I had been a green lieutenant with limited experience and training. In the second period I was a different person altogether—more experienced, better trained, and changed by what I had experienced. It was also a different war. I would return to the war married and with a child due while I was overseas. I had chosen the army, but I didn't know where a family fit into that plan.

We faced our challenge to build something from that fragment of time. Sandy accepted a husband whose commitment was suspect: I would leave in the first month of our marriage, but she would have to cope with questions of whether I would ever return. In my turmoil I had not articulated my deep feelings sufficiently, and that would plague us for years to come, an effigy of a time some would say is best forgotten but can never be.

The year ahead would prove the most difficult either of us had faced, or ever would again.

"This week, American forces are to complete their withdrawal from Cambodia. "Cambodia is a mess," one official commented, "but South Vietnam is still the main event."

—*Newsweek*, July 6, 1968

24

Returning

July 1970

The clock ticked away our final moments together in Sandy's apartment in Columbus. Silently we drove my Chevy to the Muscogee County Airport. The more things changed, the more they remained the same. Everything about this trip to the airport was different from my first one, but in a sense, everything was the same. This time I drove, but the car still was not air-conditioned, and the temperature was again above a hundred degrees. My khaki shirt stuck to my back as it had during the drive to the Jacksonville airport three years earlier. I carried a single canvas flight bag, a tie-down manila folder with my orders and records inside, and a lump in my throat.

I had placed a small notebook with handwritten instructions to Sandy in the glove compartment of the car. It included solutions to every problem I could foresee—problems with the car, the apartment, the army—but nothing about how to cope with the loneliest year of our lives. I knew of course that if I could foresee the problem, it probably wouldn't be one; I hadn't imagined the gaping hole in our hearts.

I had to leave, but parting was more difficult than I thought possible. Sandy would stay home alone and pregnant. Essentially I was escaping my responsibilities as a husband and father. I felt like a coward, not a hero. When I had volunteered a year earlier I had not planned on being married when I returned. I knew I was lucky to have survived my first tour, and perhaps I was pushing my luck too far this time.

I showed Sandy the notebook, knowing it was inadequate for her immense needs but hoping she would find comfort in knowing I had at least considered them. The notebook probably comforted me more than her; I tried to provide a thread to hold to when things became difficult. But she would have to be self-reliant to survive the year.

She handed me a small package, more precious than the book I had given her. Her present represented faith in the future, trust in something stronger than either of us, and her love. Inside the box, I found a silver Saint Christopher's medal on a chain to protect a traveler on his journey. I was touched by it. I had always found it difficult to express my personal feelings, but I wore the medal every day I was away, next to my heart and alongside my dog tags.

The drive to the airport was difficult, simultaneously too short and too long. During our gut-wrenching farewell Sandy's thoughts were her own and I was afraid to ask. I had already redirected mine to Vietnam.

I knew that once I was in a military unit I would be okay. I didn't know how Sandy would cope with her isolation, and I felt awful about that. The army would keep me busy and give me a weapon, a place to sleep, food, and a purpose. I would be absorbed in a mission, justified in forgetting my responsibilities at home. Sandy would have to deal with her world alone.

We kissed at the runway gate. We regretted the way things were, already longing for each other before we parted and dreading the future. Her kiss burned my lips as I pushed away from her grasp to walk, unsteadily, toward the ramp to the airplane. It was the longest walk of my life.

* * *

Following tortuous army processing in Oakland, the plane landed in Honolulu at 8:00 A.M. We had time in Honolulu to wander about the terminal and stretch our legs before continuing our journey. Upon returning to the gate, our group was assembled for an announcement by the flight captain. "Gentlemen, we have a problem. We'll be delayed in Honolulu due to weather," announced the captain. "I know the weather here is beautiful, but a hurricane is lashing the Philippines, and Clark Air Force Base is closed. Trees have been thrown across the runway, the tower is closed and communications are out."

A faint cheer rose as the surprising news sank in. Unlike the others, I didn't want a delay. I wanted to get to my destination as soon as possible.

"We don't know how long this will be, but we'll make you as comfortable as possible. Buses are coming to take us to a Holiday Inn. You'll have to register with two people in each room, so buddy up. Pan Am will cover the rooms and meals at the hotel. You're not restricted, but if you leave the hotel, all expenses will be yours. Check with the front desk daily for flight information. You're responsible for making the flight. If you miss it, that's between you and the army. Any questions?"

There were many questions, but cheering drowned them out.

Our brief delay stretched into three days. My roommate, a captain named Jim, convinced me to go in with him to rent a yellow Mustang convertible. These stranded days counted toward part of our year, and Diamond Head was much nicer than Monkey Mountain.

Thinking Sandy would be worried, I phoned her each day from Honolulu to update her on my situation. I praised the beauty of Hawaii, too much, setting the stage for our anticipated reunion.

When I called her on the third day her patience had been tested: "Don't call me again until you get to Vietnam!"

On cue, departure instructions followed. I was relieved to be en route again. If I harbored guilt about leaving, I certainly felt it in Honolulu. Hawaii was halfway between heaven and hell. That episode foretold the future in ways I could not then realize.

* * *

We stopped at Wake Island and in the Philippines. I was more confident in myself this trip. Peggy had helped me through the first one, but I couldn't think about her anymore. She was now a mysterious ghost of a memory, who had appeared when I needed her and then disappeared. That was another time, a different life.

I was fully committed now, torn between my love for Sandy and my desire to fulfill my soldier's promise. While I had not anticipated balancing a family with soldiering, I soon discovered that family and career would always be in conflict. I managed both, but I never found complete synergy between them. Family usually took the back seat, while the army drove.

*   *   *

The Pan Am jet landed in Vietnam on the Fourth of July. I celebrated at the replacement detachment by filling out forms and waiting for an assignment. Jet lag roused me at 4:00 A.M. I wanted to walk around to clear my head, but I already had blisters on my feet from new jungle boots. I still hated the look and smell of new clothes in a combat zone. My uniform and boots were stiff, smelly, and too green. I was already experienced and didn't like the label of newness.

I was also bored. Long Binh offered little except sleep, food, and beer. A Vietnamese band entertained transient officers at the club, but I wasn't interested. My only two concerns were writing a letter to Sandy and getting a command in the 1st Cavalry Division.

At 7:00 A.M. on July 7 I joined other replacements at the First Team Orientation Center, where I met John Dodson from my Ranger School class. John had commanded a company in the 1st Battalion, 12th Cavalry, in Cambodia, and was waiting to go home. He related stories of the Cambodia incursion.

John Whitley, several classes behind me at North Georgia College, was also waiting to leave. Whitley had been flying an L-19 out of Go Cong with the ARVN 7th Division. He had been a Swamp Fox pilot in the Delta and delivered a discouraging report that "the 7th ARVN Division had really gone to rags." I was sad to hear that.

*   *   *

First impressions of the 1st Cavalry were encouraging. It was a professional fighting outfit and its training reflected it.

The first night at the First Team Officers' Club I ran into Capt. John Fuller and Maj. Bob Reitz. It felt like a family reunion, and I knew I belonged. Both were from my class at Fort Benning. We had heard the same rumors and expected to be assigned to the 7th Cavalry, two battalions of which had taken heavy casualties in Cambodia. That was fine with me; I was eager to join a battle-tested unit anyway.

The next day we assembled in bleachers as we normally did for training. A solemn-faced noncommissioned officer informed us that the division's commanding general, Major General Casey, had crashed in his helicopter and all aboard were lost without a trace. General Casey, admired in the division and a rising star in the army, was a caring and effective division commander. Although I did not know him personally, I knew his reputation and sensed the heavy loss. Casey's death delivered another message to each of us: We were all vulnerable, and expendable.

Later, I bumped into Capt. Robert Powell, also from North Georgia College. Bob commanded A Company, 2d Battalion, 7th Cavalry, "Cold Steel Alpha." I admired Bob; his strong sense of purpose had been an inspiration in college, and I was glad he was a successful commander in the division. If I could emulate him, I would also succeed in my command.

Lieutenant Colonel Ed Trobaugh, a no-nonsense guy, commanded the 2d Battalion, and Bob dragged me over to meet him. Our paths—Trobaugh's and mine—would cross in the future, at Fort Benning and in the 82d Airborne during the Grenada invasion, as well as a few months later in Vietnam.

* * *

Finally, on July 9, I received my orders to the 1st Battalion, 7th Cavalry Regiment. I was happy and skipped class to write home. Orders meant that we would ship out to U.S. fighting outfits. The war would start again for me the following day.

Dearest Sandy,

Last night I tossed and turned and had trouble sleeping. I kept thinking about you and prayed that you are okay. I know this is going to be a difficult year for you, but please be strong. I find my strength in you and I am counting on you to help me over the rough days ahead.

"Despite the outcome, the Battle of the Little Big Horn distinguished the 7th Cavalry in setting a pattern for fighting men in courage and devotion to their country beyond the call of duty."

— *Pacific Stars and Stripes*, 1970

25

Garry Owen

July 10–14, 1970

"Garry Owen" is an old Irish quickstep, traced back to the early 1860s. The "garden of Owen" was a boisterous beer rendezvous in Limerick, where rowdy boys gathered to play, fight, and drink. Garryowen was sung as an Irish Regiment drinking song and was picked up by a 7th Cavalry trooper. General George Armstrong Custer heard the tune and started humming it in 1867. The tune became so common in the 7th Cavalry that it served as the regiment's nickname, as well as its official song when words were added. "Garry Owen" was the last tune played for Custer's men as they rode out from the Powder River to the Little Big Horn.

> We know fear when stern duty
> Calls us far from home,
> Our country's flag shall safely o'er us wave,

No matter where we roam.
"'Tis the gallant 7th Cavalry
It matters not where we are going"
Such you'll surely say as we march away;
And our band plays Garry Owen.

In the Fighting Seventh's the place for me,
It's the cream of all the Cavalry;
No other regiment can claim
Its pride, honor, glory and undying fame.

* * *

I walked into the division personnel office at Bien Hoa as if I owned it. A major handed me a stack of orders and walked to a map of Vietnam taped to the wall.

Pointing to the map, the major said, "The 1st of the 7th just pulled out of Cambodia." He tapped a pin in the map near the Cambodian border. "They're at Quan Loi now. Here it is."

"How do I get there?" I asked.

"I'll get you a ride to the airfield. Show them your orders and get on the manifest for the first thing flying to Quan Loi."

"What's my job?" I asked the question that wouldn't go away.

"That's up to the battalion commander. You'll meet Colonel Labrozzi there."

"When can I go?"

"Be here with your gear in an hour. I'll arrange a jeep for you."

That was it. By noon I was on a C-130 Hercules bound from Bien Hoa to Quan Loi.

We landed on a red clay airstrip covered with pierced steel planking, which didn't stop red dust from swirling in the backdraft of the propellers. The rear ramp dropped, and everyone scrambled off with an urgency not seen at Bien Hoa. The C-130 turned around immediately and lifted off with troops who scrambled on as quickly as we disembarked. A blast of wind from the departing aircraft covered us with red dust so thick I had to cover my eyes and nose with my hands.

When the air cleared I sensed something was wrong. Looking around, I saw the fire base was nearly deserted. I walked into the operations shack to find out how to get to my unit.

"I'm here for the 1st of the 7th Cavalry," I announced to the sergeant behind the counter made from artillery boxes.

"Well, you're off to a lousy start, sir," he replied.

"What do you mean by that, sergeant?"

"Who sent you here, sir?" he asked.

"G-1 in Bien Hoa. My orders are for the 1st of the 7th at Quan Loi. Where are they?"

"Well, if you came in on that C-130 a few minutes ago, the last of your unit got on it headed for Phouc Vinh."

"Phouc Vinh? I guess I need to catch up with them. You have anything else going that way?" I didn't know where Phouc Vinh was, and I was angry at G-1 for sending me to the wrong place, wasting time. I was also pissed at the sergeant for making cracks about my plight.

"You're in luck, I guess. See that C-7 coming in?" He nodded towards a Caribou on short final. "He'll take off soon as he lands—heading for Phouc Vinh. He's carrying ARVN, though. When you get there just go to flight ops. They'll call your unit."

"Do I need to put my name on the manifest?" I asked.

"Shit no, sir. You're in the zone now. We don't do Mickey Mouse."

I grabbed my gear and hurried out to where the Caribou was turning around. When the ramp dropped a mob of Vietnamese soldiers clambered aboard, grabbing the available seats. Some had live chickens and vegetables lashed to the outside of their rucksacks, reminding me of countless rice-and-duck meals in the Mekong Delta. I was last on, and all the seats were filled. I noticed I was also the only American except for the pilots and crew chief. I didn't mind that but I was concerned about my destination. I didn't want to fly all over scenic Vietnam, just get to my outfit as soon as possible. I settled on the floor near the back ramp.

The pilot spoke over the intercom. "We'll take off for Phouc Vinh in one minute. If you're not going there, get off now. If you are, hang on. We're taking off fast!"

I was relieved to have confirmed that we were actually going to Phouc Vinh. I hoped my unit was really there, after all.

The C-7 has a narrow body and large wings and tail. It is not very fast, but it can take off in a steep climb. It was apparent that was what the pilot intended as the engines revved and he pushed the C-7 down the runway at top speed. He raised the rear ramp as he made a near-vertical takeoff.

Everything not strapped in or hung on came flying or sliding past me to rest on the bottom section of the ramp. I clung to a loose cargo strap to avoid sliding into the random pile.

The ground directly below was visible through the open top clamshell as the nose of the plane pointed up. Finally, the pilot leveled off, but a high-pitched whine from the engines penetrated my ears. I found C-ration toilet paper in my pocket, rolled it up, and stuck it in my ears as a buffer; that took care of the noise.

In an act of kindness, the crew chief left the top half of the clamshell ramp open. It was hot inside, and the Vietnamese emitted a pungent odor, having been out in the field for an extended period. It was the familiar smell from my past that reminded me where I had been and where I was headed now.

* * *

We landed at Phouc Vinh at 3:00 P.M. A clerk in the operations shack cranked a field phone to call the battalion for me. After he talked into the phone a moment he informed me, "Someone will come for you. Don't go anywhere." A jeep arrived soon and the driver threw my bag into the back while I settled in front for the short ride.

The normal disarray of a unit just arriving covered the camp. Tin shacks and sandbag bunkers were permanent, but the people were temporary, and these troopers obviously had just arrived. We stopped in front of one of the shacks. A hand-painted wooden sign reading "S-1" was nailed over the door. An officer walked out to meet me.

"Come in out of the sun, Captain," he said. "Got a copy of your orders?"

"Yep." I yanked a copy off the top of a stack.

"I need five copies. I guess personnel sent you to Quan Loi?"

I counted off four more sheets of paper. "Yeah. I'm glad I finally caught up with you."

"Want a beer?" he asked. "The water's no good."

I selected a Budweiser from the ice chest. "Bud saved my butt at the Seminary; it might work here," I thought aloud. The personnel officer didn't seem interested, and I didn't much want to explain it anyway.

"We just came out of Cambodia," he briefed me. "Took lots of casualties over there. We have a new battalion commander. What do you want to do?"

"Command a rifle company."

"You and everybody else. You'll have to wait a while. Several companies will change commanders in a few months, but most of them are new after the other guys got shot up in Cambodia. How about Headquarters Company?"

The mention of Headquarters Company sent chills down my back, despite the heat. "I don't want headquarters; I want a rifle company. I'd take it if that's the only way to get a line company, but you know how it goes. Sometimes you get stuck and can't get out. Or somebody says, 'You've already had a command, you can't have another.' Bummer!"

"I'll tell the old man. He makes the decisions on officers, but I know he's thinking headquarters. When we leave Phouc Vinh, the headquarters commandant will build the new fire base. So you'd be out at the fire base, at least. It's an important job. You'd be close to the action and could prove yourself to the old man."

"Well, I want to discuss it with him first," I replied, disappointed.

A runner burst into the shack, shouting to the S-1, "Fight in the street! Might want to get down there."

"Come with me," the S-1 called. "Bring your stuff, and we'll look for a place for you to bunk after we see what's going on."

I felt like an orphan, carrying my canvas zipper-bag and folder of orders in a combat zone. We approached a gaggle of men surrounding two people—one black, one white—who were shouting at each other. Neither was wearing a shirt, so I couldn't identify either by name or rank. I couldn't make out what they were yelling either, but it was ugly. It quickly grew worse.

The black soldier swung and landed an uppercut on the chin of the white man. The tall white guy fell backward and landed flat on his back in a cloud of dust outside the throng. That started a rumble between other blacks and whites. The fight ended quickly when the black man grabbed an M16 rifle and sprinted to a sandbagged bunker, where he fired several shots in the air. Everyone froze in his tracks. Military police screeched to a halt in their gun jeeps, mounted machine guns loaded and ready. A standoff followed: several hours of negotiation were to be required to dislodge the armed black soldier from the bunker. We didn't wait for it.

The S-1 had a few private words with the white officer who had been flattened by the blow. I couldn't hear their discussion. Following the excitement the S-1 and I resumed our stroll among the shacks, looking for an empty bed in officer country.

"What was that all about?" I asked.

We ducked inside a shack with a tin roof and sandbags stacked along the sides. He indicated a bunk with a dingy, rolled-up mattress.

"You can bunk here," he told me. "Get a clean sheet and pillowcase from supply. You can get all your field gear there, too. Just give the supply sergeant a copy of your orders." I dropped my heavy load on the bedsprings, reserving my spot.

The S-1 continued: "I don't know what started the fracas outside, but we've had racial troubles since we left Cambodia. Tempers are high; everyone's on edge. They're okay in the field, but as soon as they get to the fire base and start jiving and drinking and smoking pot—that spells trouble."

"What'll happen to the black soldier?" I asked.

"Labrozzi will decide, maybe court martial, article 15 . . . depends."

"Who was the white guy?"

"Bravo Company commander," he said, watching for a reaction from me. "Still ready for this shit?"

* * *

I attended the evening briefing in the tactical operations center and learned the battalion had been pulled from the field to reorganize, receive replacements, and serve as "palace guard" at the division's forward headquarters. The base, near the village of Phouc Vinh, was named Camp Gorvad after a battalion commander, Lieut. Col. Peter Gorvad, killed in action. Comforting thought. The camp stood like a massive roadblock protecting Saigon from the Cambodian "fish hook" border. On a map, the fish hook appeared to be trying to puncture the old rubber plantations and defoliated forests north of Saigon, piercing toward the heart of the III Corps Tactical Zone.

The battalion evening briefing prepared the battalion commander for the base commander's briefing. Lieutenant Colonel Labrozzi was a veteran several times over and wore the patch of the 187th Regimental Combat Team from Korea on his right shoulder. He was more seasoned than I expected, was lean and fit, and had a high energy level. He also had a sharp tongue and a temper to match. I found out that Anthony Labrozzi was known as "Mad Anthony" or the "Mad Italian," but never to his face. I suspected he was aware of the nicknames and was determined to live up to them. Mad Anthony chaired the battalion briefing—and he *was* mad as hell! Everyone who delivered a brief received a bite of his temper in return. I learned some colorful new words at the evening briefing, strong enough to make a new cavalryman blush.

By 9:00 P.M. the earlier disturbance had escalated into a battle within the fire base. Grenades and rifle fire were exchanged inside the perimeter by factions of Bravo Company, maybe others. Most of the attacks seemed directed at the company headquarters.

I hung around the battalion operations center after the briefing. I didn't relish walking into the fray, and I wanted to understand what the palace guard's mission was. By staying, I also hoped to find an opportunity to discuss my future with the commander. I didn't have to wait long. Labrozzi stamped in and grabbed my arm.

"Come into my office. I'm investigating this incident and I want you as a witness," he said, dashing any hopes that we could sit and discuss my career plans.

I stood against the wall while he interviewed numerous soldiers, black and white, on both sides of the fight. He talked and listened to them as individuals and in small groups. Sometimes he listened quietly, and sometimes he shouted and cursed. Occasionally he appeared to lose his sanity, but I suspected that Mad Anthony knew exactly what he was doing all the time. He skillfully mixed temper with pretense to achieve the effects he wanted. He was masterful as he investigated from every angle with remarkable stamina until 1:00 A.M. And he kept his patience. I wondered how I would hold up under his unrelenting pressure.

When everyone had departed he turned his cold gray eyes on me. First silence, then a question: "Do you know what happened here?"

"I don't understand all the issues involved, but I do know what happened."

"What do you want?" he asked.

"I want a line company."

"You're getting headquarters. Get some sleep. I'll tell you what I want you to do later."

The interview was over. I was disappointed. I stumbled around in the dark for an hour until I finally found the bed with my gear on it. I was thirsty and drank a couple of warm beers; then, using a flashlight for illumination, I wrote Sandy about how discouraged I was. I was upset over the Headquarters Company assignment, but the ruckus I had witnessed bothered me more: I suspected the fight was a symptom of deeper problems. I realized this was not the same war I fought in 1967 and 1968.

That was when I started my journal as well. When I drew my field gear at supply, I had asked for something to write in, a notebook. The supply sergeant handed me a green ledger from a shelf. It was larger than I wanted, but it seemed large enough to keep notes for a year at least. After I wrote home, I started to catch up on what had happened over the last week and ended with my thoughts that night. My letters and musings often became intertwined, like woven thatch on the side of an Asian hut.

Bob Powell had related something to me at Bien Hoa that I remembered. "This war is a lost cause," he said. "My goal is to be aggressive, but not to let anyone get killed." That remark from the finest soldier I knew had been disconcerting when he said it, but now I understood his meaning. Loneliness fell over me. I missed Sandy, and I wanted her to hold me in her arms and tell me everything was all right.

* * *

As I understood Labrozzi's plan, on July 12 I would assume command of Headquarters Company, the home to the cooks, clerks, and staff, the "ash and trash" of the battalion. The "fun" part would be building a fire base under the constant vigilance of The Mad Italian. The only ray of sunshine was that if I succeeded, and didn't kill Labrozzi or myself in the interim, I would be in line for Delta Company in two months. That was the gospel according to the S-1. (I knew he wouldn't deliberately lie—but sometimes the truth changed.) I didn't know how soon change would come.

I arose early on July 12, prepared to take my bitter pill of Headquarters Company command. When I walked onto the stage the script had been rewritten according to the author, Mad Anthony.

We didn't rehearse the change of command ceremony. Labrozzi said, "If you've been in the army more than a day, you don't need to practice this!"

I saw the line of troopers on the red clay of the company street. Labrozzi recited three sentences and the first sergeant handed him a company guidon. I noticed that the departing company commander was missing. Labrozzi placed the guidon in my hands.

I stared in disbelief at what I saw. The red and white cavalry guidon read "B-1-7." It was the guidon for Bravo, not Headquarters Company. I was thrilled and confused at the same time; I had not been forewarned of any changes. I only spoke four sentences because I was nearly speechless. I was also afraid if I said too much, Labrozzi might realize he had given me the wrong company.

"I'm proud to have the opportunity to soldier with such a fine unit and join you in accomplishing our assigned missions. I look forward to meeting each of you in the next few days. All company policies and practices remain in effect until further notice! First Sergeant, dismiss the company!"

After the ceremony, Labrozzi shook my hand formally and said, "Complete your inventory and be ready to go to the field in three days." Then he marched off. That was all the information I needed to take action, but I still had a few questions.

I located the S-1, standing nearby. "What just happened here?" I asked.

"He changed his mind this morning, after his investigation. He reassigned the Bravo Company commander and gave the company to you. Hope you can keep it!"

* * *

The people in Bravo Company, especially the first sergeant, impressed me from the beginning. First Sergeant Francisco Royas was a soft-spoken Hawaiian who could do anything—superman in my book! Paramount was the morale of the company. We started the company inventory immediately, and it was so well organized that we finished most of it the first day.

The executive officer (XO) was 1st Lt. Tom Consedine, experienced both as a platoon leader and XO. He would quietly do whatever was necessary to meet the needs of the unit. I was pleased with my first impressions of all the staff—clerks, armorer, supply. I believed that if I gave responsible orders and won the men's acceptance and respect, we would be fine. The past was the past; the future began that day.

Each evening I was ordered to send several squads outside the perimeter on night security patrols. We planned and made preparations to conduct an air assault while simultaneously conducting security patrols around the base camp. I sat under the dim lightbulb powered by the camp generator and wrote in a letter:

"I am really thrilled to have command of a company of the line, but I can also feel the awesome responsibility for the lives and safety of these men settling on my shoulders."

Activity normally started at 6:00 A.M. and continued all day until midnight. There was no time to reflect. Planning was done on the run; every minute was filled with activity. This was Labrozzi's style and this was the tempo of the battalion. This was the real cavalry, by God!

I completed the equipment inventory and met the troops over the next couple of days, reported the results to Labrozzi, and received the warning order to conduct an operation fifteen kilometers southeast of Camp Gorvad.

The combat assault would be in a wooded area across the Song Be River and along a district boundary. We didn't expect to find anything that close to the base, but one never knew about these things. This would be Bravo's first company-size operation since leaving Quan Loi. The company had a barbeque in the afternoon and watched a movie in a driving monsoon rain. No one minded getting wet, but the rain fell with such force that no one could hear the sound of the movie, and the screen could hardly be seen through the downpour. Yet the men sat there watching the movie anyway, and having a great time with water running down their noses.

The next morning, we had chapel services and another unrehearsed company formation in the muddy street to present Combat Infantry Badges to fourteen veterans of the Cambodia operation. Again I wrote home: "At that moment, I was especially glad to have the CIB already on my chest and a combat patch on my right shoulder. I'm gaining confidence, and I hope the soldiers will soon have confidence in me. I still feel I'm on probation. At least I have time to prove myself to them."

I would take these seasoned veterans into the field for the first time the next day. This was important, no matter what happened. I had to prove

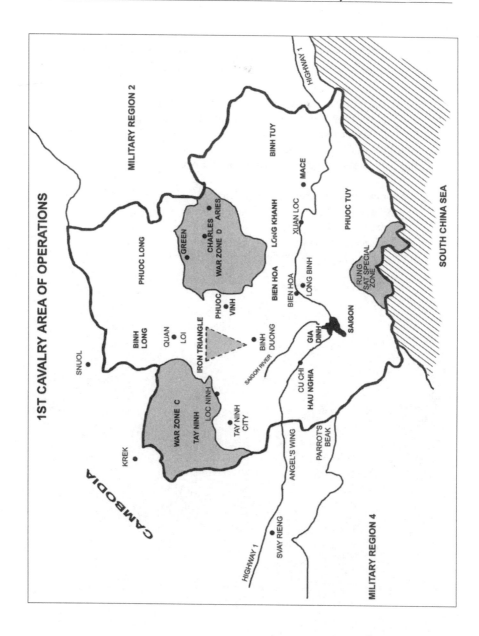

myself to them, and I would take a measure of their skills at the same time. I knew this would be a test that I couldn't afford to fail.

All through the valley the gooks were moving, Sergeant Flynn.
I could hear their AK's cracking, Sergeant Flynn.
Oh I heard their AK's cracking
And I heard their rounds a-smacking
But they knew not yet the spirit of Garry Owen.

Garry Owen, Garry Owen, Garry Owen.
In this valley of the Ia Drang all along
There are better days to be
For the Seventh Cavalry
When we charge again for dear old Garry Owen.

An end of the war would be good, not bad, for business.
War is, as we would say in business, a low-yield operation.

— Louis B. Lundberg, Chairman, Bank of America

Then hurrah for our brave commanders!
Who led us into the fight.
We'll do or die in our country's cause,
And battle for the right.
And when the war is o'er,
And to our home we're goin'
Just watch your step, with our heads erect,
When our band plays Garry Owen.

— "Garry Owen"

26

Combat Assault

July 14–19, 1970

Despite meticulous planning, combat assaults, once launched, become a dangerous flood of frantic activity, seldom proceeding according to plans. Infantrymen sit on the floor of helicopters with legs hanging out, wind in their faces, noise of rotors whopping in their ears, and accompanying gunships firing into the LZ. On final approach, door gunners on board open fire with machine guns. The small world of an infantryman is transformed into noise, turbulence, and confusion—then swallowed by the ominous silence of the jungle.

*   *   *

Our combat assault was launched from the helipad at Camp Gorvad on July 14, a steamy Southeast Asian afternoon. The company was well rehearsed in loading the helicopters—unlike the Vietnamese soldiers I had led. As we got under way, I was anxious yet confident.

Our operational area was fifteen kilometers south of Camp Gorvad. Defoliated brush had been reforested with young trees about twelve feet high. Heavy underbrush made foot travel off the trails difficult, and the trees had not yet re-formed a canopy for shade.

Our LZ was covered by low brush, secondary growth, over defoliated jungle. An easily discerned trail ran through the zone; it was actually a footpath on an overgrown dirt road. I spotted the trail from the air and could see that it had been heavily used. It was probably a hamlet-to-market trail. From the map, I knew the road followed a distract boundary. Viet Cong forces used heavily trafficked routes to cover their own tracks. The well-used trail became the center of our attention.

As each chopper landed, troopers jumped off and formed a close perimeter around the chopper. As the helicopters flew away, soldiers pushed out to expand the perimeter. I was impressed with how effortlessly they conducted this phase of the operation.

We needed to investigate the trail, but I didn't want to disturb it by walking on it. I ordered the lead platoon to chop through thick brush as it moved east on a line a hundred meters south of the trail and parallel to it. I knew our movement would be quieter on the road, but another plan was forming.

Thick brush hindered our movement, slowed us, and created unwanted noise as we cut a new trail with machetes. I believed that VC might use the dirt trail during the night. By leaving it undisturbed, we might surprise an unwary enemy. I hoped our thrashing in the brush south of the main trail would create a diversion and allow us to establish an ambush undetected.

I consulted First Sergeant Royas. "Top, I'm thinking about leaving half the company here. They could set up an ambush on the trail at dark. We'll just keep whacking through this stuff. What do you think?"

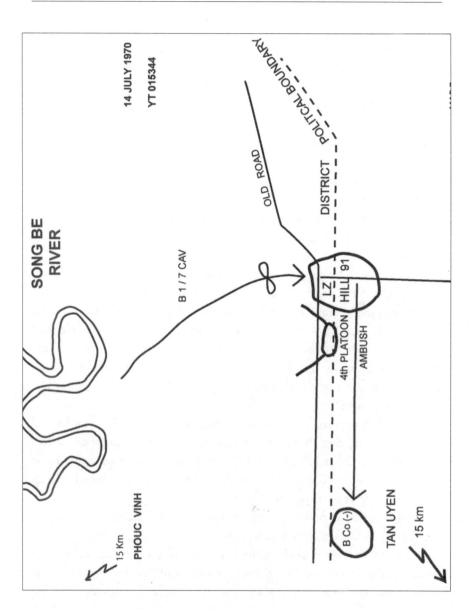

He nodded agreement. "Why not just leave 4th Platoon? They're already in the rear. They could set up a mechanical ambush and cover it with fire."

The 4th Platoon would normally be the mortar platoon, commanded by a lieutenant, but in an air cavalry battalion the mortars of all the companies were consolidated into E Company, and the 4th platoons converted to additional rifle platoons. Sergeant Dwayne Rogers, my junior platoon leader, led our 4th Platoon. This was the leanest platoon, manned by only twenty-three troopers.

"They're too small and don't have an officer."

"Don't worry, sir. They're in good hands. Too large an ambush will be too noisy, anyway. It's better to keep the noise over here."

I agreed with his points, although I was still a bit unsure about Rogers. "Okay, let's do it. I want to see Rogers to talk about it."

When I got to know Rogers better, he told me how he had been a truck driver in a logistics unit when his convoy was ambushed. He had distinguished himself by using a machine gun to counterfire into the ambush, breaking it up. When he was decorated he requested to be transferred to the infantry. He said, "If I had to fight anyway, I wanted to be in a fighting outfit."

When Sergeant Rogers reported to me, I told him simply, "Stay behind when we start moving. When we're two hundred meters ahead, send a patrol out to observe the trail. Figure out the best site for an ambush. Set up at dusk. Be in position when we stop for the night. Report every hour but keep it brief. Let me know if you need help."

Sergeant Rogers nodded his understanding and was already briefing his platoon on his plan when we moved.

The 4th Platoon established an automatic, or mechanical, ambush on the trail and covered it by fire from several meters off the trail. An automatic ambush included one or more Claymore antipersonnel mines set up to fire across a trail. A tripwire activated the mine. When the tripwire was touched, the wire pulled a plastic C-ration spoon from a metal clamp, which closed and thus completed an electrical circuit from a radio battery. The charge detonated a blasting cap in the Claymore. Claymores had been designed for manual detonation by a small hand generator, a clacker, which set off the blasting cap inside C4 explosive. The tripwire was the product of U.S. soldiers' ingenuity.

Setting up such ambushes was dangerous, but the greatest danger was in retrieval. Occasionally the person who had installed the wire became disoriented and accidentally walked into his own camouflaged trap. A Claymore mine was lethal to anyone on the wrong side of it; each mine was labeled "This Side Toward Enemy."

Bravo Company, minus 4th Platoon, crashed through the brush until it was too dark to see. I wanted to give 4th as much time and noise as possible. If anyone unfriendly was monitoring our progress, I wanted to distract him from the ambush site by our noise.

I spread the rest of the company out into an elliptical perimeter in the heavy brush to wait out the night. I directed that another ambush be established on the trail we had cut in case we were followed. I didn't permit cooking fires, so cold C-rations and warm drinking water were the sole menu for dinner.

I felt smug as I wrapped up in my poncho liner for protection from the cool night air. I would pull radio duty first, then Royas would take over while I slept. My first day in the field with Bravo had been satisfying. I detected no signs of disputes among the men, and my decisions had been accepted without question. I was pleased with the suggestion Royas made about 4th platoon and congratulated myself for accepting it. I was gaining control of the company in the field, but I knew I was still on probation with the combat veterans until we'd had our first fight. That was okay; these were combat soldiers who had their lives on the line. I hoped they would be skeptical of *any* newcomer.

Fresh air and quiet were a welcome change from the noise, dust, clutter, and constant activity on a fire base. When Royas took radio duty I dozed lightly. I would wake in an hour to monitor the battalion headquarters net, and to keep an ear tuned to 4th Platoon. I didn't expect any trouble, but that is when it usually comes.

* * *

I was in a half-awake state when a sharp explosion ripped the air. A flash of light briefly lit the dark sky. I glanced at the luminous face of my watch. It was 10:30 P.M., still early. The blast was several hundred meters away, but everyone was instantly alert and ready to react. Royas confirmed that it was the automatic ambush set up by 4th Platoon.

The radio squawked, and the soft voice of Sergeant Rogers whispered into my ear. "Six, this is Four. Over."

"This is Six. What you got?" I whispered.

"We got something in our ambush; we hear screaming. It could be pigs. Or it could be VC."

"Four, I want you to check it out. We need to know if it's VC. I don't think pigs are out at night; they're too valuable."

"Might be wild pigs."

"Can you get close enough to see?" I asked.

"Six, I don't think we should move right now. If they have a security force, they'll be trying to find us."

I didn't like leaving the ambush scene unattended all night. If those were only pigs, I needed to know, but I was convinced they were people. If civilians had been caught in the ambush, we needed to call for a medevac, but civilians were unlikely because a curfew was imposed after dark. I was certain we had hit VC on the trail, but I didn't know how many there were or why they were there. We might save a prisoner for interrogation if we acted quickly. If we left them alone and there were others, all weapons and documents would be removed. My experiences with VC in the Mekong Delta had taught me that. On the other hand, if any other security forces were nearby, my U.S. soldiers would be in danger.

If I'd been on the scene, I would have had to go for a look. But I was 200 meters away, the night was pitch black, and any movement would be noisy. I had assigned this mission to a young sergeant. I faced an important decision: I was inclined to go with my best judgment and order him to check the ambush site, but I also believed I should support the leader with the mission. The man on the ground is supreme; that was a principle I would adhere to during my entire command.

"Four, this is Six. Stay alert and get on top of it at first light. We'll go north to the trail at the same time. Ensure there aren't any more Claymores out."

"Roger, Six."

Half an hour later, Rogers reported again. "Six, this is Four. Everything is quiet."

"Four, this is Six. Roger. Good job. Out."

I calculated the bodies would be dragged away by morning and we would find another blood trail leading nowhere. Having made my decision, I had to report it to Battalion. I had already made a command decision to allow the leader on the ambush site to wait until daylight to investigate. If I reported the ambush to Battalion now, Labrozzi would make the same judgment I had, that the ambush should be checked immediately. If he gave me that order, my own order would be countermanded, or I would have to disobey him, or we would argue all night and I would likely be relieved of command. I decided to sit on the report until we had more information. If pigs had tripped the ambush, they were not worth getting sacked for. I had made my first tactical decision in favor of a subordinate leader, and I was determined to stand by it.

*   *   *

When the first rays of light peeked through, the company was ready to move. I intended to move north, cross the dirt trail, and walk parallel to the trail back to link up with 4th Platoon at the ambush site.

We were still moving toward the main trail when the radio crackled. "Six, this is Four. Over."

"Four, this is Six. What is it?"

"We have three VC bodies, three 9mm pistols, one M16 rifle, and three packs," he reported.

My heartbeat quickened. That was significant—three 9mm pistols were very significant! They were not merely Viet Cong; they were important Vietcong.

Now I had a report for battalion: "Rider Six Alpha, this is Gator Six. Over." I dreaded the reaction. When is good news bad news? I knew my delay in reporting would be questioned. I hoped the good news would overshadow the late report.

"Gator Six, this is Rider Six Alpha," acknowledged the tactical operations center.

"Rider Six Alpha, situation report follows. Automatic ambush activated at 2230 hours last night on hot east-west trail. First-light reconnaissance found three Viet Cong bodies. Results are three 9mm pistols, one M16 rifle, and three packs captured. Over."

The company continued to move to link up with 4th Platoon. Ten minutes later the battalion radio net cackled with the voice of the Mad Italian. "Good report, Gator Six. Why didn't you report sooner?"

"Rider Six, this is Gator Six. I wanted to know what we had. We were in no danger, and we couldn't check it out until now."

"You should have checked it out last night!" followed the expected admonishment.

"I'm on the ground and I decided to wait until light. I didn't want to be second-guessed on it." I stood my ground. I heard no more from Labrozzi on that subject, but he gave me fair warning that it wasn't over.

"Garry Owen Five is en route to pick up the goodies in a light chopper. Be ready to explain to him. Can he land there?"

"He can land on the road at the landing zone where we were inserted. I'll meet him there. Thanks for the warning."

We linked up with 4th Platoon troopers; they had already gathered the packs and weapons. Sergeant Rogers gave me a tour of the ambush site, including the bodies. My analysis of the kill zone indicated the three VC were passing through on the dirt trail. The one with the rifle was in front for security. The other two followed. Apparently they had been traveling alone. The packs contained the usual food, clothes, and medical supplies, but they were filled with documents, which was a further indication these were important VC.

I took one platoon and hurried down the trail to the landing zone as Garry Owen Five approached in his light helicopter. Garry Owen Five was Col. Morris J. Brady, the division artillery commander, who was in charge of the division forward CP. He knew his stuff and he commanded in much the same style as Labrozzi: kick ass and take names. I knew he had my name and probably intended to kick my ass.

"Gator Six, this is Garry Owen Five, I'm approaching your location. Over."

"Garry Owen Five, this is Gator Six. I'm at a landing zone with the goodies. I have one platoon for security, so you can land. I'm popping smoke."

"We have your smoke, Gator Six." Colonel Brady replied.

The chopper landed, and the captured weapons and packs were loaded for a quick departure. Brady stared at me, then yelled over the noise of the chopper. "Congratulations on a good operation. No complaints there—but you should've reported the ambush last night. What were you thinking?"

"I was thinking I was in command and made a command decision. And I still think it was a good one, sir." I stood my ground.

"I disagree with you, Captain. I'm responsible for the security of this fire base, and we needed this information sooner. Next time, check out the ambush and report right away." I knew he had a point, and I even agreed with it, but I had made my decision to support Rogers on the scene. We both had principles to protect. Nevertheless, I did not believe it wise to argue with him.

"Yes, sir." I saluted.

The chopper flew away and we returned to the ambush site in time to hear Labrozzi report that he was en route in another light helicopter. He was bringing a photographer to take pictures of the dead VC. Someone believed they were important enough to identify. This was serious intelligence gathering.

As I returned to the ambush site, Labrozzi was on final approach. His pilot squeezed onto the trail next to the ambush, and Labrozzi stepped out of his chopper. While the photographer took close-up pictures of the Viet Cong faces, Labrozzi talked to the men of 4th Platoon, congratulating them on their success. I was glad he didn't raise the reporting issue with them. The buck stopped with me on that one. The decision had been mine alone and I had made it clear that I didn't intend to argue about it. The good news of our success had helped me this time.

Labrozzi noticed First Sergeant Royas in the field and flipped into his Mad Italian routine. He believed first sergeants were his personal representatives from each company and belonged in camp except when visiting the troops on resupply missions.

"Why is your first sergeant in the field?" He shot the question at me.

I answered, "Another command decision." I stifled a smile; I knew it wouldn't work this time.

"You're making a lot of those in your first week, Captain Taylor."

"Yes sir. That's what the army pays me for." I knew I was sticking my neck out.

"Well, think about your decisions from now on . . . and talk to me."

I guessed I had finally driven my point home, but I had crossed swords with both of my higher commanders in the process. Labrozzi seemed to appreciate having a real commander in charge of Bravo Company. I believed the troopers knew I had supported them under pressure. First Sergeant Royas reinforced my thinking by saying he felt he could probably support the company better from the fire base, anyway—meaning that he was confident that I could command the company alone. All of those messages were important to me. I had stood my ground and won. I felt good.

After Labrozzi left I heard the command radio crackle once more.

"Gator Six, this is Garry Owen Five. Over." I wondered whether Colonel Brady had decided to take another bite out of me.

"Garry Owen Five, this is Gator Six. Over." I prepared for the worst.

"Six, I came back to let you know this action was important. Congratulations, and thank your men for me."

"Roger. Out." I was confounded. He seemed to be saying something in code.

I didn't discover what it was until a month later, when Labrozzi slipped the intelligence summary into my hands. "Souvenir!" he said. It stated that the dead VC included the colonel who was chief of staff of Military Region 3. A battalion commander and a political officer had accompanied him. Their documents included maps and the details of a VC spy ring inside Camp Gorvad. Several spies were rounded up the same day. I was not told then that the VC had placed a price on my head for these kills. When I found out I was proud to have pushed them to that extent. Unfortunately others would pay the price.

* * *

By the time the excitement quieted down, it was nearly noon. We had been distracted for far too long, and if the dead VC were important people we needed to be especially careful. I reiterated that information to my platoon leaders as a warning, though I didn't think they needed reminding. I sensed they were as anxious as I was to get away from outside attention.

I decided to sweep north of the trail. Several kilometers to the northwest, a patrol found a small underground bunker complex that had been used by the three VC for rest before their demise. White parachute silk lined the earth walls to keep the sleeping bunker clean. A trooper spotted an ammunition can buried nearby. He pulled it up using a rope and grappling hook in case it was booby-trapped. The can was stuffed with more documents, which Labrozzi was more than happy to see recovered. This time the can was pulled up into the chopper by rope because there was no place to land.

We trekked through the area for several more days, but the only other thing we found was a buried 55-gallon drum filled with rice. We destroyed it in place.

Bravo Company was a professional team, and I believed I had been inducted into their ranks. I was tired but proud.

A new order came encrypted over the radio. Bravo Company would be picked up by choppers, returned to Camp Gorvad to resupply, and then reinserted into a new area. Our timetable was disrupted when a helicopter hunter-killer team spotted and killed one VC. Then a mini-fire base took ten 82mm mortar rounds that inflicted nine U.S. casualties. When we were finally picked up just prior to nightfall, it was too dark for a new combat assault insertion. Consequently the alternative plan was implemented: trucking the company out to patrol checkpoints, and then walking in the dark to security positions. I didn't like the plan, but we were nevertheless in position by midnight.

I was pleased with the results of my first operation with the company. I was firmly established as commander, both with Labrozzi and the troops, and I had confidence in my own experience, training, and intuition. My decisions had been sound, and we had been successful. It was a hell of a start.

July 11, 1970

Darling,

I really don't mind being back in Vietnam but, damn, I didn't think it would be so hard to leave you. Vietnam has changed an awful lot and I expect to see more troop withdrawals soon. It is very frustrating to be here fighting a rear guard for withdrawals.

July 13, 1970

I have been so busy I simply haven't had time to do anything. I hope you will accept this brief letter with understanding and compassion. I am very tired right now, but I feel strong and eager to do a job here. I love you very much, Sandy. I am still waiting to get my first letter.

All my love.

"South Vietnam's war will go on for years. That's the outlook now, as American troops step up withdrawal—and Reds dig in with a new strategy. Fighting has expanded alarmingly in recent weeks and the area of conflict now encompasses half a dozen regions of South Vietnam, Cambodia, and Laos."

—*Atlanta Constitution,* August 3, 1970

27

War Zone D

July 23–August 28, 1970

An earsplitting, blinding torrent of 82mm mortar fire fell on Bravo Company during the black night of July 23. As a result I was already awake when orders arrived from Labrozzi. Early in the morning, Alpha and Bravo companies would reinforce the 2d Battalion of the 7th Cavalry, which was already in combat in War Zone D. The orders presented a logistics problem for me because Bravo Company was still scattered in external security positions outside Camp Gorvad. Overnight, I developed a plan to reassemble them by dawn so we could resupply before we left.

We flew in Chinook helicopters to a French-built airfield on a logging road at Fire Support Base (FSB) Garry Owen, northeast of Camp Gorvad.

There we boarded Hueys to shuttle to a smaller fire base, Patton. Lieutenant Colonel Ed Trobaugh met us there and briefed us before we walked north, our rucksacks sagging with ammunition. Bob Powell's Cold Steel Alpha had been in combat for nine consecutive days. The field strength of Bravo Company was only ninety-one troopers as we began the operation, so I felt short-handed.

We worked in War Zone D, a remote region with practically no civilian population, which afforded free movement for the Viet Cong. This was a free-fire zone: if something moved we shot it before it shot us. Soon after we left Patton, we entered a complex of twenty bunkers but fortunately encountered no resistance. I observed the men exercising strict noise and light discipline without any encouragement from me. Bravo Company troopers set up automatic ambushes on trails approaching our positions every time we stopped. They read the signs as well as I did and prepared for the worst. Bob Powell's company found 400 new AK-47 assault rifles, still in their original wrappings, on a Viet Cong supply route.

War Zone D was covered by tall hardwood trees in triple-canopy jungle. True jungle was not ideal for helicopter operations, so I didn't expect to be resupplied often. The 2d Battalion was already overtaxed logistically, and two additional companies to support further constrained available helicopter support.

* * *

I adapted to the routine of field operations. When mail finally arrived for me, I stored letters from home in my helmet liner to keep them dry. If there was time I read them several times before burning them. I kept letters as long as I could, usually until the next mail delivery came to replace worn-out paper with fresh news from home. It was impossible to keep letters longer than a week in the humidity, anyway. I kept those I had written tucked into my helmet liner until I could send them out with the resupply helicopters. When activity quieted down for the night, I pulled a poncho over my head and, with my flashlight held under my chin, composed letters to Sandy and then made notations in my military journal. These were not the best conditions for writing, but I did my best.

July 13, 1970

Dearest Sandy,

I think the greatest feeling in the world, other than a wonderful family, must be command of a rifle company. The men in the company are the greatest people I have ever met. I never have a dull moment and seldom have a moment to sit down and collect my thoughts. I got up at 0630 hours this morning and it is now 2315. I think this is the first time I've sat down all day. I've done everything from pat men on the back, chew them out, convince them they can operate at night—just like Charlie, break my back to get them anything, almost cry when they do the same for me, search them for pot. In short, I do more in a day here than I did in a month at Fort Benning, and have more of a sense of accomplishment.

* * *

Early next morning I received a report from Labrozzi that Bravo Company's area at Camp Gorvad had been hit again, harder this time, with a combination of 120mm and 82mm mortar rounds. The attack appeared to target my headquarters. Fortunately, most of us were in the jungle and escaped the onslaught. Unfortunately Bravo Company suffered one killed and one seriously wounded; several more casualties occurred in battalion Headquarters Company. Specialist Jimmy M. Mercer was killed in action. He had earned a reputation as the best point man in the company. I didn't know Jimmy well because I had been in the company such a short time, but others did. He had made it through some of the worst fighting in Cambodia, and he was in the rear to prepare for R&R and to celebrate his birthday. The irony is that had he been with us on point, he would have been fine.

Mercer was a good man, as was the headquarters medical platoon leader, Lieutenant Noble, and the circumstances surrounding their deaths visibly bothered the men. Later, we learned the attack was a reprisal for our killing the high-ranking VC in our ambush. Spies inside Camp Gorvad had stepped off the distance to our huts so that the attack could be aimed precisely on Bravo Company. Apparently all the spies inside Camp Gorvad had not been rounded up yet.

* * *

Both companies of the 1st Battalion were extracted from the operation, returned to FSB Garry Owen, loaded on Chinooks, and hauled back to Camp Gorvad. Once there I barely had time to shower, shave, change clothes, and quench my thirst before we launched yet another combat assault. Three Viet Cong had been spotted near Camp Gorvad, suspected by the camp intelligence officer as forward observers for the VC mortar crews that had shelled the camp recently. Bravo's mission was to saddle up with tracker-dog and mine-detection-dog teams and search for the 120mm mortars that had pounded us. Unfortunately we came up empty.

While the patrols were out and I waited for their reports, I reread old letters. Sandy had asked me to include days of the week on my letters, but I couldn't ever remember what day it was. The only significant day was Monday, the day the medics passed out big orange malaria pills: Mondays were unmistakably marked by stomach cramps. I already had difficulty remembering life in the United States. It was hard to reconnect with the situations Sandy faced alone in Columbus. As time marched by, the distance between us became greater.

Sandy,

This is going to be a long, long year, but as long as I am physically miserable and tired, I don't hurt for you quite so badly. I love you very much. Keep writing and please try to understand when I can't possibly write every day. Take care of yourself and thank you for just being you.

"In the wake of the bitter domestic dissent sparked by the Cambodian invasion, the Nixon Administration seemed intent on assuring the nation it was making a sincere effort to negotiate its way out of Indochina."

—*Newsweek,* August 3, 1970

28

Green

August 1970

Fire Base Green was to become our center of operations in War Zone D. The fire base was named for Pfc James A. Green from Boynton, Okalahoma, a rifleman in Charlie Company, 1st Battalion, 7th Cavalry, killed in Cambodia on June 18, 1970, his first day in combat. Efforts over five days to recover his body were unsuccessful, and he was declared missing in action.

Every time I saw a new fire base I was grateful I wasn't building it as headquarters company commandant. I was quite happy in the jungle with an air cavalry company. I was quite content to sit on my helmet under my low-slung poncho "hooch" in a driving rain, feet wet, drinking warm beer and smoking cheap cigars. Life was good—for a soldier.

When palace guard duty ended our battalion was unleashed in the jungle. For one week out of four Bravo Company pulled security duty on fire bases, but in the other weeks we patrolled the surrounding jungle in search of the Viet Cong.

In one area large apes in the trees spooked us. Warriors gazed up in wonder at them, recalling snipers in trees in Cambodia, expecting the monkeys to morph into VC. It was indeed spooky.

Our turn to occupy the fire base rolled around again, and Labrozzi publicly praised Bravo Company. I already knew we were good but I wasn't quite sure what he was praising us for. Nevertheless I was happy to be on Labrozzi's good side. We sweated with fire base construction and improvements, but I found time to take platoons to the perimeter to test-fire weapons. They needed marksmanship training, but I also wanted them to expend their old ammunition and replace it with new. Ammunition of all types became wet and damaged as it was carried in the jungle. I preferred to have ammunition misfire on a training range rather than in combat. In firing the full spectrum of our ammunition in training, we not only honed our weapons skills but also refreshed our mental acuity about the real purpose of soldiering.

One platoon was dispatched on an air cavalry operation in support of the air scouts. In such a minicav operation the platoon flew in helicopters on patrol. If something suspicious was spotted from the air, the rifle platoon landed to check it out. Normally the reconnaissance platoon performed this mission, so we were honored to get the nod. These were real hunter-killer operations, and the troopers loved them—at least they felt like genuine cavalry for a time instead of footslogging Infantry.

> To the LZ we are going, Sergeant Flynn.
> In the breeze the guidon is blowing, Sergeant Flynn.
> High and low, birds of thunder,
> We will drive the bad guys under.
> Drive your bayonet to the hilt for
> Dear old Garry Owen.

* * *

We trudged through the jungle north of Phuoc Vinh for three weeks: steep terrain, crosscut with hills and valleys, complicated navigation and movement. We stayed wet constantly from rain or sweat or both. I pushed the men to their limits in the rough terrain. They were too tired to fight, and their weapons were wet and rusty. It was not unusual for the most experienced of navigators to became disoriented in the rough terrain and have near-miss firefights with another platoon. It was time to reassess these missions.

Bravo Company, like every other unit in Vietnam, was always short on experienced leaders. I wrote home that two platoon leaders were second lieutenants, one a staff sergeant, another a buck sergeant. Lieutenant Kevin Myles was the most experienced of my officers in the field; he reminded me of Lieutenant Considine, a veteran of Cambodia, who was already the company XO when I arrived. Both were quiet, competent officers, who would knock down walls to get the company what it needed, or what we wanted, whether we needed it or not. I protested when Labrozzi announced that Myles would become XO, replacing Considine, whose tour was up, but deep down I knew Bravo needed a good man backing us up. Lieutenant Pete Dencker, a West Pointer, replaced Myles in the 1st Platoon.

Another area where we were understaffed, but well supported, was in artillery support. The artillery forward observer was Pfc Wayne Czajka, who did everything I asked of him. I believed an officer would carry more weight with the artillery battalion, but no one could carry more weight with Bravo. Wayne was backed up up by Spec. 4 Joe Sauble as his radio operator. When Wayne was later wounded, Joe stepped in to adjust fire missions while simultaneously carrying his own radio. I couldn't have asked for better people, but officers should have filled all those positions except radio operator. I was pleased with all of them, but I wondered about priorities when we couldn't staff the leadership in our combat forces. Ironically, the noncommissioned officers and enlisted men who rose to fill those positions did so because of their proven courage and competence under fire. They were great Americans, every one of them!

When we needed supplies, I faced choices of either clearing an LZ or having supplies kicked out from a hovering chopper. I preferred the kick-outs because they were simpler and more secure. Unfortunately, we couldn't send out mail or exchange our funky jungle fatigues for clean ones on kick-outs. When someone was due for R&R, he could not get away during a kick-out. While I preferred this kind of resupply for operational security reasons, I tried to never have two kick-outs in succession. Morale competed with security, and they were interwoven to a large degree.

I didn't like lingering in an open LZ waiting for a chopper to arrive. Consequently I usually pushed the company a considerable distance quickly, just before we were due to receive a sit-down resupply. When we reached the clearing I'd selected, several of us invariably had heat cramps and we were all exhausted. Logistics was a serious constraint in combating guerillas.

After one particular resupply we were air-lifted out of a waist-deep swamp for a combat assault. If the swamp wasn't bad enough by itself, Mother Nature doused us with a driving rain so that we were literally soaked from head to foot. Intelligence reported a hundred VC in the vicinity, and we detected well-used trails running in every direction as soon as we landed. I increased our security posture by prohibiting hoooches, chopping, cooking, or digging that night. We just kept a low profile in the unfamiliar territory.

I had loved the company through the worst conditions, but even surrounded by brave men loneliness of command takes a toll. I wrote Sandy about my feelings:

> Making difficult decisions is challenging. Sometimes, a commander must weigh the merits of safety against the cost of comfort. Being a company commander in the field is a lonely job. You have no peers to talk to, you must make decisions on your own, with little or no advice, and you can show no favoritism. Who says this is the greatest job in the Army?

* * *

After endless days of trekking through the jungle I was ordered to find a new pickup zone. Bravo Company was lifted from another swamp and flown to Camp Gorvad by Hueys, then transferred to Chinooks for a flight to division headquarters in Bien Hoa. I went directly from the swamp to the division headquarters VIP center. That afternoon, battalion officers sat in a roundtable discussion about tactics and operations with Major General Putnam, who had replaced the deceased General Casey.

Next morning, our brigade commander, Col. "Barbed Wire" Bob Kingston, briefed battalion officers. The 1st Battalion, 7th Cavalry, was to transfer from the 2d Brigade to the 1st, move into northern War Zone D, and build a new fire base. I didn't really care much which brigade we were assigned to. Brigade was too far above us to have a measurable impact on our daily life.

That afternoon, I accompanied First Sergeant Royas to the 24th Evacuation Hospital for something I did care about—visiting troopers wounded in the mortar attack. I was buoyed by their high spirits but disheartened by the effects of the war on our country's youth. On the way back to camp, Royas swung by the Long Binh PX to soak up air-conditioning and enjoy an ice cream cone. I had forgotten such pleasures existed. I went along only because the first sergeant insisted, but I was happy when we left. Luxury made me uncomfortable—a moment's pleasure, a diversion from harsh reality, but ultimately a certain return to truth.

* * *

At high noon the next day Bravo Company assembled into a parade-ground formation. Major General Putnam was on hand to present awards to some of our Cambodia veterans. I was proud of them and actually in awe of their courage. At the same time, the company received a Valorous Unit Citation for a battle in Tay Ninh Province in November 1969. General Putnam said, "The 1st of the 7th has a long tradition of this sort of thing. I don't think there's another unit that can wear three Presidential Unit Citations, three Vietnamese Gallantry Crosses with Palms, unit citations of the King of Greece, and a unit citation of the Republic of the Philippines." The Valorous Unit Citation equated to an individual's Silver Star.

Sometimes it takes a while for heroism to be recognized, but it was a long war after all. Soldiers should know what they do will someday be recognized as valuable. We felt connected to men who preceded us in battle under the Garry Owen banner. We only hoped our nation would be grateful to us when the war was over.

When the festivities were finished I wrote a letter to Sandy.

Dearest Sandy,

I'm as happy as a pig in shit to be back in the jungle. The Big PX, traffic, dust, hustle and bustle of Bien Hoa, and the generals make the jungle a better place to live. The VC lives in the jungle because they had first choice. I do miss the showers, clean clothes, and cold beer, but there were other frustrations, too. I tried to call home on MARS every night, but never got through. I really wish I could talk to you now.

* * *

We departed Bien Hoa by Chinook en route to LZ Garry Owen, then made a combat assault into our new area of operations in War Zone D. The LZ was a VC cornfield sculptured from heavy jungle. No farmer this far from a city would need so much corn unless he was feeding an army. We spotted a caretaker as we touched down, but he departed in haste. We found small-animal traps, bunkers, small stores of ammunition, a large rice barn, corn, bananas, squash, and well-used trails leading in several directions. Eventually a sniper engaged us in a feeble attempt to resist. Then it was quiet again.

*   *   *

Our resupply on August 13 was completely screwed up; nothing went right. Immediately after the fiasco we made contact with a VC squad that was trailing us: we killed one soldier and captured a 9mm submachine gun. Bravo Company was the first to pay off in the new zone. Labrozzi was ecstatic, and I loved it. Nevertheless all pleasures were short-lived.

My jungle rot was a fact of life; everyone had it, even in the dry season, because we were wet from sweat when not wet from rain. Mine had mostly cleared up while we had stayed dry at Bien Hoa, but it sprouted again on my right arm and left leg. Festering sores and oozing pus just don't heal well or go away in damp jungles. In addition to jungle rot I was nauseated, sweaty, and suffering from stomach cramps. Many others had the same afflictions, but most bore them with gritty determination.

It rained constantly, and the area was infested with leeches, which dropped off the trees in the rain to fall down inside your shirt, sticking to your arms and wriggling into your boots and pants from the ground. The persistent little pests swarmed to us. Weather, geography, and poor health made short work of my cheerfulness.

We wandered into a Viet Cong camp, which had pigs running around outside and clean uniforms inside a shack. A searcher discovered a letter dated August 10 that said two NVA companies were to arrive on August 14 or 15 to be resupplied. From all appearances, they had arrived early—or we had arrived late.

Darling Sandy,

I'm running completely out of light and I feel I'm racing against time to get this letter written. I don't know why I'm writing so frantically because I'll probably carry it around in the liner of my helmet for a week before I can mail it. Anyway, I feel a little closer to you when I am writing you. I love you so much that I think about you every spare moment.

*   *   *

Bravo Company was picked up again in a driving storm and dumped in a bamboo field. Daisy cutters, 500-pound bombs rigged to go off at ground level, had cleared a landing zone. The ground was so soft the bombs had blown large holes in it, which prevented the choppers from landing. They hovered on the side of the hill while we jumped out with rucksacks, rifles, and helmets jerking and bumping every which way.

Our new brigade commander, Col. Robert Stevenson, landed in his smaller chopper, his pilot managing to find a level clump of ground to perch on. He informed me that we were searching for a Viet Cong hospital. My main concerns were a bad cold, jungle rot, and swarms of damn leeches, all making my life miserable (I wondered if the Viet Cong hospital staff could treat my jungle rot). I finally surrendered to one of the company's medics, who gave me a shot of penicillin. My condition improved immediately. Why had I held out so long?

The sun burst through like rays of hope. We had found no signs of a hospital in the valley, so I moved the company to higher ground to dry out for a while. Patrols were sent out, and I monitored the battalion radio frequency to update the situation. It was then that I heard that Charlie Company had suffered a tragic accident when a trooper tripped his own automatic ambush. Labrozzi was angry, but there was little anyone could do about the awful accidents that occur while fighting a war. Our normal instruments of war were simply designed to be lethal to human beings, and that meant anyone who got in their way.

Bad news came in waves. Delta Company suffered four men killed and two others wounded in a VC ambush. I remembered Bob Powell's admonishment and renewed my dedication to keep Bravo Company's hundred men alive. Somehow the hills, the leaches, the mosquitoes and the bamboo vipers seemed less relevant under the weight of that challenge.

In the hilly terrain we crossed a large stream with fast-running, very cold water. We waded across slowly to provide each man time to drop trousers and wash his funky butt and crotch in the clean, cold water. That helped.

* * *

When we walked out of the jungle onto Fire Base Green, Bravo entered clean-shaven, which impressed Labrozzi again. I wasn't out to impress him—I didn't require the men to shave in the field, but I did require them to shave prior to arriving at the fire base. I wasn't stupid. When Labrozzi was happy, we were all happy!

We all worked to improve bunkers, lay barbed wire and communications lines, organize the battalion ammunition dump, and square away our own basic loads. We dug holes to bury fougasse between the concentric strands of barbed wire that encircled the perimeter. This volatile mixture of gas and oil was buried in 55-gallon drums, to be ignited if VC sappers cut through the wire to infiltrate the base.

I was apprehensive about our marksmanship in the field. We needed additional training, so I oversaw construction of a twenty-five-meter zero range at the edge of the berm. Then I supervised the building of a walking range through the jungle, complete with pop-up targets along the route. As a soldier walked along a trail, someone walking behind him pulled a wire, which raised targets nailed to hinged ammo boxes. Every soldier zeroed his rifle again, and then walked through the range to sharpen basic fighting skills.

At night, I ordered machine guns test-fired with 200 rounds of continuous firing without interruptions. Labrozzi directed the security officer to walk the perimeter every seventy-five minutes. Since it took thirty minutes to walk it, I didn't get much sleep at night, and it was too hot to sleep during the day. I was soon anxious to return to the peace and quiet of the jungle. At least our time on the fire base was productive in sharpening our marksmanship, if nothing else.

Sandy,

Please don't be discouraged at the slow mail. You know I love you; it hurts when you sound so depressed. I count the days until I'll have you in my arms again, Darling. Please take care and remember me in your prayers.

— Richard

29

High-Angle Hell

September 1970

Bravo Company rejoiced to leave the fire base tar baby and be thrown into the jungle briar patch. Sun, heat, fire base discipline, and general hustle and bustle would be exchanged for shade, silence, and independence in triple-canopy jungle.

Bravo would make a direct exchange with Delta, replacing it in the field as it replaced us on the fire base. Delta Company had been following a well-used trail in the jungle, finding little to report except the trail itself. Only VC would use a major trail such as this, slicing through remote regions. Delta had not yet discovered its purpose and preferred to stay until it had, but it had been out for over a month and was due to rotate back to the fire base.

The exchange was especially complicated. Two trees had been cut with C4, creating a single-ship LZ. One load of Bravo's troopers was inserted and one of Delta's taken out, over and over again. The single chopper hovered at the top of the jungle canopy, 100 feet above the ground, settled straight down for 50 feet, turned 90 degrees, and settled another 50 feet before landing. Eight Bravo troopers exited and eight Delta troopers got on each time. Going back up was the reverse of the delicate process. The method was dangerous, and it required three hours to complete the exchange.

Captain Lee Hyslop and I talked for fifteen minutes.

"We followed the trail for three days," Lee said, pointing towards the ridgeline.

"Find anything?" I asked.

"Nothing to report, but you'll see. This trail is heavily used, and there aren't any civilians out here, so it has to be an infiltration route."

"No sightings?" I asked.

"Not yet, but they're close. I didn't want to do the exchange today because we're already here. I don't know if they knew we were here. We moved fast, but I worry about an ambush."

"If they didn't know you were here before, they know it now." I shook my head. Three hours of helicopters going in and out would wake the dead. "I'm surprised they haven't tried to shoot down a chopper. If one crashed here, we'd be stuck with our companies split and no landing zone."

Lee said, "You have more than half your guys in. I'll go out on the next one. Make sure the rest of mine get out, will you? If anything happens, anybody still here will stay under your command."

"Thanks for the brief, Lee. Good luck at the fire base, and kiss the Mad Italian on the cheek for me." I slapped my butt with my free hand.

Lee smiled, gathered up his radio operators for the next extraction, and left me with my thoughts. I decided to look at the trail and took a couple of nearby riflemen and my radio operators, Jim Johnson and Don Verruchi (both were always attached to me by the radios they carried) to examine it. Sure enough, the footpath was worn down to the dark earth and was sufficiently wide for a person to easily pass without touching jungle brush on either side. It reminded me of the Appalachian Trail in the eastern United States, but it wasn't nearly as inviting.

* * *

By the time the exchange was completed darkness and a driving rain had settled over us. I moved the company a short distance from the LZ to set up defenses for the night. It was our first night back in the jungle; everyone was alert. Even the newest trooper recognized the nature of the situation created by the commotion made in exchanging companies that advertised our presence. That, combined with the indications of presence on the trail, aroused a feeling that we were being watched. We knew the 33d Regiment frequented the area. I concentrated on Lee's fear of walking into an ambush and determined not to.

We started out early next morning, anxious to get some distance from the spot where we had entered the jungle. Following a breakfast of dehydrated rations, I directed two platoons and the command group to follow the trail, with one patrol sweeping each side of it. The terrain was quite hilly. Movement off the trail by the security platoons was not difficult, because the ground under the mahogany jungle was open. Tall hardwoods formed a dense canopy that kept the sun off the ground, making it dark and shady underneath, with little ground vegetation. Open space allowed vision for thirty meters most of the time. Visibility worked both ways. Trail watchers would find it easy to follow our movement while remaining out of sight. At times I felt eyes watching me—and I didn't like the feeling. The hair on the back of my neck would stand up when triggered by especially strong suspicions.

While I was pleased to be away from the fire base, I was uneasy about our situation. Delta Company really should have been left on the trail. The noisy exchange allowed anyone to know exactly where we were and to calculate our strength based on the number of helicopters going in and out. The math was simple, the consequences were dire.

Bravo Company moved several kilometers along the trail in a driving rain. We entered a semiopen area unlike the high canopy of the mahogany jungle, a clearing overgrown with low trees with trunks of two to three inches in diameter. This would have served as a better LZ for our exchange. We stopped to set up a patrol base, while platoons scouted in several directions.

One platoon worked each side of the trail, another formed a perimeter around the command group, and the 4th Platoon swept a 100-meter-diameter circle around us.

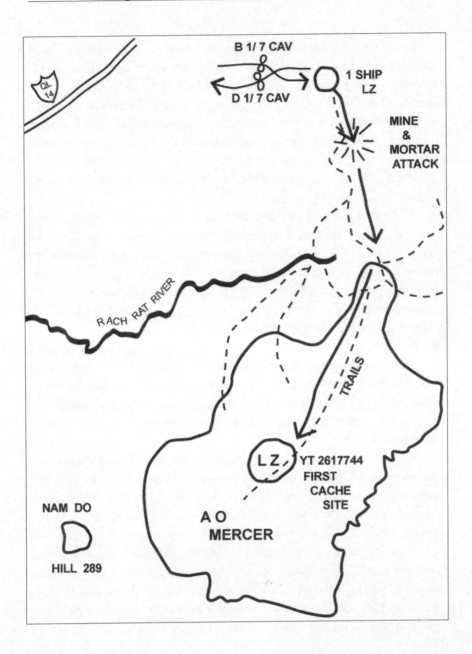

The urgency of diarrhea compelled me to take a walk alone in the jungle, so I grabbed an entrenching tool and my .45-caliber pistol. I looked around before digging a slit trench to complete my business. My stomach was a raging inferno but, despite the cramps, I had a worse feeling on the back of my neck. I positively *knew* someone was watching me—and it was not Bravo Company's security. Nerve endings bristled as I walked slowly back to the perimeter, trying to listen as I trod the soft jungle floor. I stopped once to look back, so strong was the sensation that I was being followed. When I arrived at the radios, I made communication checks with battalion headquarters and the platoons. I called to Pfc Wayne Czajka, the acting artillery forward observer, to ensure that he had radio contact as well.

Before Wayne could make the call, an ear-splitting blast erupted ten meters from where I had been in the jungle. As soon as I fell to the ground, another blast from the same place blew steel pellets through low trees around us, peeling bark and leaves away. Two large round Chinese antipersonnel mines had been command-activated at our perimeter. VC had crawled to place them while I had been there a few minutes before. Perhaps my presence had caused them to aim the first mine poorly, because it was low. Bad aim on the first blast gave us time to fall to the ground before the killer mine was activated. Had we been standing when the second mine erupted toward our position, we would have been mowed down with the small trees around us.

All our radios crackled. Jim Johnson, on the battalion radio net, tried to report our situation and call for helicopter support, while Don Verruchi kept the company net active as the platoons tried to ascertain the situation. Wayne attempted to call an artillery fire mission. I observed him behind a tree trunk two inches in diameter. The tree looked as if it had been attacked with a chain saw. His long antenna was shot off. I told him to replace it. My heart pounded and I felt light-headed as I struggled to maintain a calm exterior to reassure others. Only ten seconds had elapsed since I'd first asked Wayne to make a radio check.

Don had communications with the platoons, but the battalion net Jim Johnson handled had also lost its long whip antenna when steel pellets blasted it away. I told Jim to exchange his broken antenna for the short whip. Precious time was being lost. Rifles around the perimeter fired protective fires into the jungle to discourage a ground attack. I didn't see any enemy targets but I was reassured by the sound of firing.

Operators frantically removed broken antennas and were replacing them with short ones when the hollow plunking sounds of 60mm mortars came like a second wave. Based on the tempo, I estimated that two mortars were firing. We could hear them being fired, yet we had to wait for the rounds to make their high trajectory before they struck. The rounds would hit in only a few seconds. There was nothing we could do but wait to see if we would die. The wait was "high-angle hell," not unlike the pause between a tornado siren and the storm.

We stayed flat on the ground in case enemy riflemen were hidden in the jungle around us. With only twenty-four men in the platoon and five in the command group, I directed the other three platoons to carefully close on our position. Wayne was still unable to contact artillery, but Jim finally reached battalion to report our trouble. Labrozzi would get his chopper airborne as soon as possible, but meanwhile we had no fire support on station and nothing on order.

The initial crash of a 60mm mortar round erupted in the air over our heads. The round had hit a tree limb and burst in the air, sending fragments through our ranks. I had momentarily forgotten about in-bound mortar rounds in my haste to establish radio contact, but I was certainly aware of it now. Noise on the radio was drowned out by the next round, which struck a few feet away. Sounds of men shouting that they had been hit, or calling for a medic, overshadowed everything else.

I estimated twenty mortar rounds had been arced in our direction. The sounds of mortars firing stopped as the first round hit. I knew eighteen more rounds were coming in, and all we and could do was wait out high-angle hell. The mortars pounded us then stopped, but the shouting continued. Our medics heroically rushed about, administering life-saving first aid and assessing the situation. It seemed that everyone was calling "Medic!" at once.

My immediate concern was security. We were too few in the bull's eye. I ordered platoons to approach as quickly as possible. I informed the trigger-happy troops on the perimeter that help was coming in—no more friendly fires. Shouts for "medic" blended with cries of pain. My stomach turned at the sound of my men in agony. I was sickened, and angry as hell that there was little we could do to take the initiative.

When the explosions ceased, the commotion of men making adjustments replaced the momentary silence. Radio operators worked frantically to report, wounded men cried out, troopers shifted to fill gaps, and medics worked rapidly in triage. I wanted to see to the wounded men, but my overriding concern was still security. A ground attack was not likely, but I needed to consolidate the company safely.

Silence extending from the jungle floor into the air was not welcome, either. When a unit is in contact with the enemy, helicopters are on the scene quickly to establish communications and help control fire support. This time there was nothing. The absence of help was due mainly to the second antipersonnel mine knocking out our communications with battalion and direct-support artillery. In addition, the command-and-control chopper was out of the area for refueling. A medevac helicopter was the first on the scene, thank God.

The dust-off helicopter checked in: "Gator Six, this is Dust Off Four-seven-seven. Over."

"Four-seven-seven, this is Gator Six, good to have you on station. Over."

"Gator, is the area clear?"

"We've had no contact for five minutes. Two platoons are still closing on our position, but it seems to be over. We have a clearing to touch down one bird. We'll pop smoke when you're ready."

"What you got there, Gator?"

"About sixteen wounded, but no KIAs. All the wounds are from mortars, no gunshots. Four are serious head wounds. I figure you'll have to make two trips. We'll put the most serious on the first run, over."

"Roger, Gator. Pop smoke now."

* * *

As soon as the first evacuation was out I investigated the area of the attack. A quick check revealed that green wires that had been connected to the mines, having been set up during heavy rain. When I went out of the perimeter to relieve my cramps, the VC who set them were probably crawling back to connect the wires to the generator.

Next I called for a report on casualties and ammunition status. Ammunition was okay; we had not fired that much, but I was wondering whether we had the *right* ammunition. The casualty report revealed the entire command group had been wounded, except for the artillery forward observer, Czajka, and me. I asked Wayne to carry his own radio for Joe

Sauble because I didn't want to pull another rifleman off the line. I carried the company radio myself to control the platoons, for the same reason. I recruited another rifleman to carry the battalion radio set.

I believed we had been scouted during the company exchange the day before. They had followed us, waiting for an opportunity to strike. With the mortars it was easy. Adding antipersonnel mines had been brilliant and courageous on their part. If the first one had been aimed properly, we would have been decimated instead of badly hurt.

I was worried. I called a meeting of platoon leaders to discuss our options. First I asked for ideas, but no one offered any. I waited, but no one wanted to talk, as if they were all in shock. I had to shake them out of that quickly.

So I began: "I'm worried about the intensity of this attack and lack of support. I expect more. We need a plan of our own. We don't have mortars for counterfire, and artillery is too damn slow. We can't keep gunships on station all the time. We can't reach to the 60mm mortars with what we have, and they know it. We had commo problems due to the loss of radios in the first blast. Here are my ideas; I want your comments."

I tried to read their thoughts, but saw only vacant stares.

After a moment, I continued: "I think we should designate a "killer team" in each platoon. The killer team is two riflemen and two M79 gunners. The mortars are fired from about four hundred meters away. The range of the M79 is only two hundred meters." I took an M79 grenade launcher and held it while I talked.

"At the first sound of mortars, the killer team charges straight toward the mortars for two hundred meters, then fires M-79 rounds in that direction. Radio operators will get on the air at the first sound to call for gunships and pre-planned artillery. This is risky, but we need to be aggressive and react quickly next time, or they'll make hamburger of us. What do you think?"

I could read their faces. They didn't love my idea, but no one had a better one, either. I handed the M79 to Sergeant Rogers and said, "At least the killer team will be outside the impact zone of the mortars."

That seemed to dispel concern for the reaction teams and their resistance. Sergeant Rogers, the platoon leader who had conducted the successful ambush, replied, "I'll personally lead my killer team. We need more ammunition," he said tapping the grenade launcher. "And we'll recon-by-fire with M79s as we move."

With Rogers's words of support the others agreed to the plan. It seemed to take the edge off our sense of helplessness.

"Take a few minutes to brief your men and get organized. I'll request additional grenades for our M79s tomorrow. I'll talk to Battalion about getting air or artillery here faster. We'll move in ten minutes and go until it gets dark. We'll stay together tonight. Spread the perimeter out so we aren't bunched up. Let's go."

We stayed on the trail. I figured the mortar crew was long gone, but I suspected they might have been trying to entice us to chase them. Wayne gave advance notice that I wanted artillery spotted around us overnight, and harassing-and-interdicting fires throughout the night. I worked with him on coordinates after we stopped. We planned targets on key terrain features as we moved, to keep the guns pointed in the right direction. I told him to fire white-phosphorus marking rounds ahead or behind us, at least once each hour, to maintain registration points for the big guns.

*   *   *

This was the lowest point of my command. Sixteen men had been wounded in one attack, and the prospects of continued attacks were strong. Slow and inadequate support was an ill omen. I didn't have much confidence in the effectiveness of our killer teams, but I didn't have a better idea and we needed something positive to hold on to. I certainly did not want anyone else to sense my doubts and fears.

Dearest Darling Wife,

I'm terribly sorry about not being able to write for so long. Believe me, it hasn't been because I haven't wanted to. The events of the past two weeks have been almost overwhelming.

"Corruption, short rations, political infighting—they're all part of the price Hanoi's leaders are making the people pay for endless war. Still, aggression is being pushed, with no indications of a letup."

— *U.S. News and World Report*, November 30, 1970

30

Operation Mercer

September 1970

Bravo Company scouted the trail for four more days, receiving rations and ammunition kicked out of helicopters. I preferred helicopters several days apart, believing their presence marked our position for the enemy. But Labrozzi was testing a new concept of daily resupply intended to allow us to move quickly and unencumbered by heavy loads of rations and ammunition. He was concerned about the weight we carried in the jungle, but my greatest concern was security and surprise.

Mortars struck us again after four days' respite. The command group and one platoon were in a patrol base, while three platoons searched the surrounding area. We were thankful that no antipersonnel mines were included in this attack; increased security prevented them from getting so close again. Nevertheless, the enemy was able to pinpoint our position well enough to lob ten 60mm mortar rounds onto the command group and one platoon gathered in a small perimeter. The attack lasted two minutes. I presumed the VC had set up the mortar, fired the mission, disassembled the tubes, and scattered by the time the first rounds struck. When our artillery came to bear, they were already in underground bunkers.

This time, the platoon securing the command post activated the killer team as soon as we heard the mortars plunking. If the Viet Cong forward observer was in position to observe their reaction, the fire mission was likely cut short—exactly what I hoped for. Unfortunately we took four more casualties anyway, including Wayne Czajka. Now I doubled as the artillery forward observer while controlling maneuver platoons. I was glad I had artillery experience in the Delta to draw on, but I simply couldn't do everything. Lieutenant Colonel Carl Vuono, our direct-support artillery commander, stated his intent to send a lieutenant to replace Wayne. Wayne was good, and I didn't want to lose him, but I knew he was due to leave the field soon.

The day after the mortar attack, dreaded news crackled over the battalion net: the battalion commander, plus two others, would join us in the field. He had been doing that with other companies, but I wasn't happy about it. I was already short-handed in the command group, and now I would have three additional people to worry about. Worse yet, I believed my competence was being challenged in the wake of the mortar casualties.

* * *

We followed the trail, worrying about security. Labrozzi was inbound and we needed a landing zone. I told him we didn't have one, hoping he would give up and go away, but I knew that would never happen. Labrozzi never gave up.

He had spotted a bomb crater in a field of bamboo and intended to rappel in. I took a platoon and backtracked to the bomb crater just as the helicopter arrived. Troopers circled the spot, curious to watch the sideshow. The chopper hovered at fifty feet while three passengers dropped their rucksacks to the ground fastened to the end of 100-foot ropes. Since the ropes were twice the distance to the ground, the rucksacks smashed their contents upon impact.

Labrozzi did fine on rappel. He kept his balance, with head higher than his feet all the way to the ground. The command sergeant major and the radio operator were less graceful; they flailed their way down, landing flat on their backs in the bamboo. I bit my lip to keep from laughing aloud as they recovered their belongings. Everything inside their rucksacks had burst, water mixed with the C-rations, and dripped from the corners. Unfortunately their radio and spare battery were also smashed. I confiscated a radio from one of my platoons, enabling the battalion commander to maintain contact while he stayed with us. I collected rations and water to replace those losses as well. Needless to say, they ate ham and lima beans for the rest of their stay; those were the C-ration meals no one else wanted. I was gratified when no complaints were heard from our uninvited guests. I wondered whether Labrozzi actually liked the ham and limas.

During their insertion, a platoon called to report that their point man had spotted a hole that appeared to be a latrine. He was suspicious and had poked around with a long stick. The latrine actually concealed a false floor. Removing the wooden floor, the platoon discovered an ammunition dump of 120mm mortars, B-40 antitank rockets, and unused picks and shovels. They secured the site pending our arrival.

We didn't make it to the cache site until after dark. While my troopers quietly established security for the night, our rear-echelon guests shined flashlights, talked loudly, and banged around noisily. I informed them, including Labrozzi, that they would have to abide by our rules as long as they stayed. My warning helped some, but I could tell my men were made as uncomfortable as I was by our visitors.

The next morning, I designated the cache site as our new patrol base and the platoons fanned out to search the ridge line. The discovery gave us a better concept of what we were looking for and why the enemy was trying to keep us away. Over the next several days, we uncovered several storage bunkers similar to the first and eight more that had been prepared but were still empty.

Mad Anthony was ecstatic. I could hardly restrain him as he rushed alone through the jungle to explore each site. On the positive side good things started happening. Explosives and chainsaws arrived to open a one-ship LZ. Labrozzi wanted to name the landing zone and asked me what we should call it. I quickly looked to others for suggestions before offering one. I told him "Mercer," after Jimmy Mercer, the Bravo pointman killed on his birthday. The name stuck, and eventually became the name of the entire operation.

With a landing zone available, we could easily resupply and shuttle people in and out, including the battalion command group. Unfortunately others found us as well. This was the most productive operation in the division area, so we had more visitors, including Major General Putnam, the division commander, and Major General Wagstaff, chief of staff of II Field Force, in addition to the brigade commander and various other staff officers.

Labrozzi was present when the generals arrived. He pulled me aside. "Do you want to make any instant awards or promotions while we have the opportunity?" he inquired.

"Sure. Let me think about it a minute."

"How about a Bronze Star for the pointman that found the first site?" he asked.

"Yeah." I agreed quickly. I knew I would not have much time, but I followed with an additional request. "I also want to promote one of my platoon leaders. He's a sergeant and has been great. A real leader on this operation, and he was the platoon leader who ran that ambush near Camp Gorvad."

"I'll talk to the general," promised Labrozzi.

In a few minutes, we arranged a quick formation in the jungle clearing and Major General Putnam hung a Bronze Star medal on the chest of the pointman. Then he removed the staff sergeant stripes from his orderly's shirt, and pinned them on Sergeant Rogers's shirt. I was impressed by how easily that was done and appreciated Labrozzi for making it happen. The general's orderly, doubling as photographer but now sans his stripes, took some pictures. At Labrozzi's urging, I led the column of generals on a tour of jungle trails to observe the loot. They were interested in medical supplies, especially Chinese penicillin.

* * *

When the heavies finally departed, Labrozzi sat on a fallen tree trunk and asked me to join him.

"I want to build up to task force level. You'll command it, but I want to talk about what we need to bring in here. I want you to intensify the search to find more cache sites and extend the patrols further out, if necessary. What are your most pressing needs?"

"Well, for starters, I'm short on infantry. Casualties from mortar attacks left us under strength. Digging up and moving explosives, rigging for demolition, and other jobs leave us shorter than ever."

"I'll attach the recon platoon to Bravo immediately. That'll give you more eyes and firepower. I'll round up laborers from the fire base to help dig and haul." Labrozzi quickly met all my first demands. He had impressed me all day, and I realized his visit had been a blessing instead of a curse after all.

I continued, "My next concern is those damn mortars. We can't get artillery fast enough to be effective, and our grenade launchers don't have the range. If we're here awhile, we could use 81mm mortars from the fire base. They could outrange the 60s."

That conversation briefly transformed a small one-ship LZ in War Zone D into the busiest place in Vietnam—LZ Mercer. Task Force Bravo, 1st Battalion, 7th Cavalry, took shape. Over the next few days we grew to include: Bravo Company HQ, with my wounded radio operators returning to man the radios; our regular four rifle platoons from Bravo Company; battalion reconnaissance platoon; three dog teams for explosives detection; two tracker dog teams to track any movement on the trails; an engineer squad to handle the cutting of trees; an explosive-ordnance disposal team to handle demolition of captured explosives; a labor squad from Alpha Company to help with manual chores; a mortar section of two 81mm mortars; and a pathfinder team to handle air traffic.

* * *

I was pleased with the organization and the new sense of responsiveness to our requirements. We received a hot meal every second day and mail every day. Things were working so well that I took a chance. The next day, General Putnam was flying overhead when he called me on my radio net. "Gator Six, this is First Team Six. Over."

"First Team Six, this is Gator Six. Are you coming to our location? Over."

"Just passing overhead, but I wondered if you needed anything down there. Over."

Pushing my luck, I replied, "We're doing well, but we sure could use some ice cream."

"You'll get it. Out."

On the next day a log bird landed with ice cream packed with dry ice in styrene boxes that normally held blood bags. We lapped it up! More important, we got ice cream every other day after that. Someone coined a new motto: "Bravo Kills for Ice Cream."

* * *

Labrozzi continued to visit us daily. One day we sat on a fallen tree to talk. "What do you need?" he asked.

"Well . . . I think we have everything. Ice cream is the icing on the cake."

"No, I mean what do *you* need? Personally."

I was flabbergasted, but I couldn't stop myself from blurting it out. I had received everything I had asked for over the past several weeks. "A shot of bourbon and a good cigar would be fine after a hard day's work," I said jokingly. Labrozzi, who was a nondrinker, didn't comment. I didn't think he appreciated my sentiments.

Next day, a messenger approached me with a C-ration box. He said, "The battalion commander sends this with his compliments."

I couldn't imagine why he'd sent C-rations until I opened the box. Inside were a bottle of Jim Beam and a box of Tampa Nuggets. I couldn't believe my eyes. "I really love that guy!"

Fame is fleeting, however. Following a visit by more generals and the division staff, we seemed to have exhausted the cache sites. Delta Company got into a fire fight nearby and attention shifted there. I expected a new mission soon, and our task force lost some of its attached teams as well as its interest in tramping around the same jungle day after day. Just as I was getting comfortable, we got a wake-up call.

* * *

One platoon patrolling several kilometers away from LZ Mercer was singled out for another mortar attack. Sergeant First Class Furr, who had come to Bravo from recruiting duties at home, commanded the platoon. I didn't believe his past duties had prepared him well physically for the challenges of a platoon command, but he was the senior field NCO in the company. When he arrived, I kept him near the command group for several weeks to become acclimated enough to stand the heat and humidity while absorbing some "field sense." I remembered how Bobby Hurst had kept me under his wing for a few days on my first tour of duty.

My judgment in placing him in leadership so soon was misplaced. He was out of position during the mortar attack and didn't launch the killer team. However, many things happen in the fog of war to cause things to go awry. Fortunately Private First Class Martinez manned the radio and reported the situation to me.

I stayed in touch with Martinez and instructed him what to do as he described the situation to me over the air. I coordinated fire support from the company CP. Martinez barely spoke English, but I credited him with keeping the situation under control during a very stressful time and enabling me to get gunships in support. The mortar attack was brief, but the platoon suffered eight more casualties, taking their total strength down to eight effective troopers. I had to attach them as a squad to another platoon until they were staffed again.

After the attack, I questioned members of the platoon to find out what had happened. As a result, I awarded Martinez a Silver Star and requested that Labrozzi find another position for Sergeant Furr since his platoon was dissolved anyway. After a period, Sergeant Furr joined another company and proved his courage under fire, giving his life leading his men. Sergeant William Furr was decorated posthumously and Fire Base Furr was named in his honor. He was a heroic American, as were those he led.

Additional companies were brought in, and an operations order was delivered to me. The operation was named Operation Mercer.

As Bravo Company mobilized, we lost our section of 81mm mortars. Mortar attacks continued and we were hit three more times. Our best responses were still the killer teams, but now we got artillery faster because there were active battalion-level operations in the area. Helicopter gunships were on station more often, too. The combination of responses reduced the mortar attacks to only three to five rounds each.

Near the junction of a small stream and trail, we found seventeen bicycles near a camp of thatched huts. The bikes were stripped of seats and pedals and rigged for pushing heavy loads. This was a last segment of the supply chain from the Ho Chi Minh Trail into War Zone D.

* * *

I believed the VC sometimes camped on the trail at night; we had found remains of cooking fires on the trails. As I briefed a patrol preparing to search the trail after dark, I leaned my hand against a tree and was bitten by a spider on my palm. The sting hurt like hell, but the shot the medic gave me put me into dreamland. I instructed another officer to take charge until I came out of the stupor and not to do anything I ordered until morning. By the next day the drug had worn off, but my swollen hand throbbed for several days. I walked around holding it over my head to relieve the pain and swelling.

A platoon found another cache with five new AK-47 rifles, twenty magazines, three older SKS rifles, one new B-40 rocket launcher, nineteen B-40 rounds, nineteen rounds for a 75mm recoilless rifle, eighty antitank rifle grenades, and 5,000 rounds of AK-47 ammunition. The new discovery restored excitement at higher headquarters, and we were back on cache-searching duty. Bravo was ready for something new.

While searching we needed a kick-out resupply of rations. We were in tall trees, and a helicopter hovered above the triple canopy of hardwood to kick the C-ration boxes through the trees. A box of C-rations falling from that altitude can kill. I made everyone wear helmets and stand close to a tree trunk. Prop blast from the helicopter hovering overhead blew twigs and leaves through the air. I was sitting on the ground, leaning against a tree, studying a map in my lap. In the swirling wind something landed on my map case. I thought it was a branch, but as I reached to move it a snake looked back at me. I don't know which of us was more startled, but I flung snake, map, and myself apart in one move. I recovered my map—and my composure—before we moved out.

A hot meal was delivered in another interesting kick-out. I wasn't sure how they could kick out a hot meal, but it worked quite well. Hot food was literally poured into long rubber tubes affectionately called "elephant rubbers." The filled rubbers were stuffed into 105mm shipping canisters. On the ground, we cut the ends of the rubbers and poured chili macaroni and green beans onto paper plates. The meals were still hot and tasty and reminded us of real mess hall chow.

Operation Mercer slowly wound down. We returned to Fire Base Green for a couple of days to wait for four B-52s to bomb the area around Mercer. We were to go back after the strike to conduct a bomb-damage assessment.

* * *

Mad Anthony rolled out the red carpet for Bravo Company at Fire Base Green. He met me at the tactical operations center, an underground bunker, and presented me a foot-long cigar. I don't know where he got it, but it was a nice gesture—until I lit it. It was terrible! I liked Tony Labrozzi more every day. Of course it helped to be on his good side, but he was a true warrior, and they were hard to find any more. He brought a flying PX to Green so the troops could buy nice-to-have things like film, candy, and magazines. I bought a pipe. Established as a cigar smoker, I threw a curve ball and changed my image.

Labrozzi suggested I go to Bien Hoa for the day, which sounded good to me. I knew that the first sergeant and XO had the rear in good hands, but I needed a change in scenery. I enjoyed a meal in a real mess hall, barbecued spare ribs, potatoes, and fresh bread. I spent the afternoon talking to the first sergeant, supply sergeant, and company clerk. The first sergeant gave me his room to spend the night. I asked him where he would sleep and he said, "Don't worry about it." I enjoyed his cot with a mattress, clean sheets, an electric light bulb, rotating fan, and radio. I was in heaven!

In the morning, I went to the 11th Aviation Group to complete an application for flight school. Before leaving Green, I had discussed flying with Maj. Wayne Knudson, our S-3 and a superb aviator. Sounding a warning note, he advised me my chances were only fifty-fifty at best, because I had too much time in service.

I completed the application and took a flight physical, which revealed significant problems with my hearing. Two years of being shelled and shot at had taken a toll. The results were so bad that the flight surgeon scheduled me to go to Long Binh for evaluation of my fitness to stay in the army.

I managed to return to Green just before dark. My eyes were dilated from the flight physical, and my vision was just coming back. We took incoming 82mm mortar rounds and sporadic rifle fire that night, but there were no serious attacks. Nevertheless, as commander of base security, I was unhappy with the bunker line. Bravo Company had let its guard down from too much red-carpet treatment and the commander's absence for two days.

Most of the problems were concentrated in two platoons, where I found guards asleep, troopers sleeping without mosquito nets, and beer cans in bunkers. Staff Sergeant Rogers's platoon was perfect. I placed myself on schedule to walk the perimeter every two hours and ordered my lieutenants to walk with me. They weren't happy about it, but the next day the company was back to normal.

* * *

The B-52 strike was planned for September 30, 1970. Before our return to LZ Mercer I took the company, one platoon at a time, to the range to test fire weapons. A grenadier fired a grenade into a tree at the minimum distance to arm the grenade. Fragments flew back to where we were standing: one fragment buried itself into my right thigh near the bone and another sliced my nose. I went to the aid station for treatment, but there was nothing they could do but dab iodine on the wounds. I was lucky the fragment that touched my nose had missed my eye. My lucky day, I guess.

I was leaving the aid station when a helicopter lifting off from the landing pad at Green lost power and fell into the trees. The rotors were ripped apart as they hit them, and the chopper settled almost to the ground. We rushed to help the pilots out. No one was hurt. Their lucky day, too!

* * *

We air-assaulted into the bombed Mercer area immediately after the B-52 strike. Devastation to trees and land was complete. LZ Mercer was so disrupted that we never got oriented again. The big brass expected us to find dead VC or more cache sites exposed by the bombs, but we found nothing except fallen trees and holes in the ground. Tall, majestic mahoganies were scattered like Lincoln Logs. The good news was that if there were supplies hidden there, the VC wouldn't be able to find them, either.

After several days of stumbling about in the damage, Bravo was lifted back to Green and then flown to the 1st Cavalry main headquarters in Bien Hoa for "company refresher training" at the First Team Academy. Thus ended Operation Mercer.

Dearest Sandy,

I'm almost sorry to say—the war is over—over here. The rules and regulations now make it almost unbelievable. It isn't fun any more. I probably should have stayed here on my last tour until I had enough of it. Now, I can only wait anxiously until I return to you. I can see it will be very difficult being a soldier without a war.

"One of our problems is that we didn't have the wholehearted support of the American people. We were doing our job...but the enemy thought he was winning politically and psychologically in the United States."

— General William Westmoreland

31

Reorienting

Early October 1970

While the company settled in for refresher training, I went with the other company officers to 1st Brigade headquarters for the evening briefing, followed by dinner and cocktails with the brigade commander and his staff. The briefing itself was boring and the gathering at the officers' club was rather stilted for field soldiers. I felt somewhat like Alice in Wonderland, pretending to be at a tea party instead of in a war zone. Perhaps I had been too involved in the struggle in the jungle to appreciate the fine points of society. Colonel Stevenson, our brigade commander, was a fine officer and an absolute gentleman, whom I admired very much, and I appreciated his full support in the field, especially ice cream for the frontline troops.

I suspected this occasion was more directed toward bolstering the morale of his staff in their work than with impressing us. On the other hand, it may have been intended to remind all of us that we would have to return to another world someday; this was a glimpse of it. Nevertheless, the event reinforced my comprehension that the war was nearly over and those of us in the jungle were only acting out a part on a crude stage until the final curtain closed.

I was already uneasy about the prospects of peacetime rules, regulations, and staff formalities inherent in an army in search of a purpose. I loved my army and knew I could adapt to those, when it became necessary. But soldiering in a war zone, on the front line of the conflict, was a bittersweet profession, best experienced by feeling, smelling, touching, and tasting, to truly understand it. Our soldiers had shared in the discomforts, pleasures, fears, pains, and exhilarations of a band of brothers. We had only one another—our lives depended on what the person next to us did. Young men from New York, California, Mississippi, and Minnesota were literally thrown together into a crucible to make the best of it, and we did. Whatever we did together could not be shared with the uninitiated.

There was another positive side to the rear area, though as addictive as a drug. Despite grumbling about rear-echelon soldiers, a warm shower, shave, haircut, clean clothes, and cold beer touched someone I once knew, a different person with a civilized mind hidden deep inside. Maybe someday I would find that stranger again, but for now that had to wait.

Company training was well received by the men. For three days Bravo lived in squad-sized huts, devoured hot chow, and practiced basic marksmanship, tactics, and techniques. At night the men drank beer and enjoyed relief from security duties, so they drank even more. Philippine and Vietnamese bands played very bad music very loudly until 11:00 P.M., when beer sales ended. By then, most men had one or more spares stashed in ice chests in the huts. The pleasant routine continued for three days, and Bravo thoroughly enjoyed the change of pace.

> President Nixon proposed a standstill cease-fire in Vietnam, Cambodia, and Laos, immediate release of all prisoners and a broadened peace conference to reach a settlement of conflict throughout Indochina.[2]

* * *

On October 9 Chinooks shuttled us back to Fire Base Green. We were there only an hour, long enough to reorganize for a combat assault into War

Zone D. By October 10 the company was back in its natural element, the jungle. The three pleasurable days had vaporized like a dream.

Quickly a platoon reported a small factory in a clandestine cluster of huts. The place was actually more a repair site than a factory, equipped with a wood lathe, two fans, an electric generator, paint, and two vises. Fields planted with ripening crops, gardening tools, and food preserved for later consumption surrounded the agricultural-industrial complex.

While we were searching the factory, twelve Montagnards from a tribe that usually inhabited the mountainous regions farther north turned themselves in. They included one man, four women, and seven small children who had been in forced labor for the Viet Cong. They were badly undernourished. One little girl reminded me of Edna's little orphan, Kim, who had visited our camp in My Tho three years earlier. When I picked the child up, I was surprised at how at light she was, clinging to my neck as I walked about. I remembered breaking the news to a trooper the week before that he was a father of a little girl, and I hoped he would be a good one. I wondered how it felt to be a father, and if I were up to that responsibility.

*   *   *

Bravo was ordered to a pickup zone for extraction and movement to another area, the company being split between two sites for the extraction. I sat with two platoons in a large open area on one side of a ridge line. The pickup zone was an open field in a valley surrounded by three tall hills. The morning was beautiful with the sun slowly burning off the morning haze. The sun warmed us as it broke over the hilltops.

We had already waited two hours for the helicopters when I received a radio message that the wait was extended another hour. That news chilled me in the warming sun; we had been exposed too long already. My vision strayed to the open hills around us and I sensed the piercing eyes of an unwanted observer. I couldn't tell where he was, but I knew he was out there and I speculated about his location. I requested artillery on the tallest hill across the misty valley, just as a precaution. It was denied because a Mohawk, an army intelligence aircraft, was taking photos. Fate is sometimes tricky that way.

I pulled a novel out of my rucksack and resumed reading. I realized I was acting fatalistic. Whatever will be, will be. I should have roused the company and concealed it in the jungle. I should have learned by then to act on my instincts.

My initial concerns settled into complacency, but when a 75mm recoilless rifle cracked and its round banged into the hillside, we were yanked instantly alert. Fortunately the shot was short of its target, but it had come from the same suspicious hilltop I had earlier identified. We were within range, but the gunner was a poor marksman. Artillery bursting on the hill would have deterred the gunner from risking a shot, and we would have never known he was there—except, I did know. Bravo Company instantly returned fire with grenade launchers, light anti-tank assault weapons (LAW), and a 90mm recoilless rifle, but we were out of range of most of our organic weapons, and they were ineffective. I finally got artillery cranked up, but too late. A futile firepower display signified that a hunch is more than just a guess.

After that incident, we were quickly extracted and landed in a new area. We moved for the short period of remaining light, enduring a drenching monsoon rain in the process. By the time we were oriented in the new area, there was nothing left to do except wait out the wet night. I awoke from a very wet evening stiff, sore, and cold. A strong hunch gripped me again, and I ordered everyone to perform weapons maintenance, including ammunition, and delayed our departure for an hour to complete it.

Within a half-hour of moving, Lieutenant Judge reported that his platoon was in contact with the enemy. Judge led by example, and this time was no exception. He quickly reported two VC killed, a rifle captured, and personal equipment captured as well. He then said that he was going forward to check out the enemy. He quickly reported they had captured a wounded Viet Cong, who was only a boy, about sixteen years old, and the medic was trying to save his life. Unfortunately the wounds were too severe, and the young man died before the helicopter arrived.

Judge had been well forward, and I hoped the close call would make him more cautious. All my platoon leaders were aggressive, and I didn't want to lose one. Judge's actions in contact reminded me of my own, and had he been hit I would have felt somehow responsible. Nevertheless, aggressiveness was needed in our officers or we should concede the battlefield and go home.

Bravo encountered fresh trails running in different directions, unlike the long single trail we had followed into Operation Mercer. I believed the trail into Mercer was a communications route leading to the cache area, whereas these seemed to connect different points—a base of some kind. The feeling that we were close to something or someone was very strong, and I felt watched again. I didn't like the feeling of paranoia, but I was beginning to appreciate these warning of things to come.

Bravo was in among this complex of trails running in all directions, and I wanted to know what they were. I believed I was most aware of our situation and confident of my jungle and marksmanship skills, so I took the point position for a while to try to read the signs better. I left the radios farther back, and had, instead, a skilled rifleman directly behind me. On point, I could read the indicators sufficiently to tell we were within an hour or two of enemy soldiers.

I actually enjoyed the exhilaration of being first man on the trail, expecting to come face to face with an enemy soldier, relying on my skills to detect ambushes or booby traps. I also realized that I enjoyed it too much. If there was trouble there, I would be unable to control the company response; so I relinquished my position of honor, but only after I had a better feel of the area we were in.

Lieutenant Judge and platoon made contact again quickly and pursued. The trail they were on was three feet wide and laced with tire-sandal tracks. Battalion inserted a tracker dog team to lead, and it ran forward with the dog in front. Trackers were extremely aggressive and impervious to the danger ahead, running behind the dog along the trail and relying on the instincts of the dog. However, we didn't catch the fleeing enemy. We seemed to vacillate between successful peaks and empty valleys in our quest to find the illusive enemy.

We had begun the month retraining and reorienting. It was a welcome respite from the rigors of jungle and fire base activity. Retraining was needed because refresher training is always needed in basic skills, but also to help mold a company that, like every other company in Vietnam, was constantly changing with replacements, new areas of operations, and different enemy dispositions. However, it was difficult to orient on a war that was being waged in different directions in Washington, Saigon, and Paris.

> The U.S. pullout from South Vietnam is raising concern among many Americans whether Saigon really can carry on alone against the Communists. The enemy shows no intentions of laying down arms. In South Vietnam, they continue to fight, while waiting for more U.S. troops to leave.[3]

"There are no more inspections on Saturday mornings to delay enjoyment of a weekend pass. No one stands in line for anything for more than 15 minutes. Above all, each man is a soldier because he *wants* to be. That vision of the future Army was soberly presented by the Pentagon as a goal to be achieved within three years in a drive to build an all-volunteer military."

—*Time,* October 26, 1970

32

Bruised Heart

Late October 1970

As a result of withdrawals, soldiers began getting two-week "drops" from their scheduled dates to return home. Those receiving drops were excited to be leaving, but it made us all feel the war was essentially over. We were happy for the lucky ones, but it left us with a feeling of abandonment. Curtailments distracted us from the job at hand—finding and fighting the enemy. One Bravo Company trooper who received such a drop was stranded in dense jungle for two days beyond his adjusted departure date until Battalion sent in a helicopter with a McGuire rig, nothing more than a long rope, to lift him beneath a helicopter so he could go home. I didn't like sending him out that way, but no one relished the idea of having a trooper injured in the jungle when he should be at home with loved ones.

In addition to individual curtailments selected units were leaving Vietnam, not as complete units but as their colors were retired. Soldiers in those units who still had sufficient time remaining on their tours of duty were reassigned to other units as replacements. The result was absolute turmoil in personnel. Bravo received many of these reassigned soldiers. The faces in Bravo were changing weekly, and I dreaded resupply days because I saw so many new faces before me each week.

They were all great U.S. soldiers, just like our troopers, but their turbulent situation was unfortunate. Acculturation of transferees is always difficult: their army family has been broken up, and they have to be accepted by strangers; tactics and techniques invariably differ from unit to unit. Their morale is naturally low, but the biggest operational problem is lack of training in a new unit's standard operating procedures because they always bring different habits and techniques with them from other operational areas.

* * *

Bravo was still operating in the complex of trails when it was due for another resupply. We had people coming in and going out. I was notified that heavy commitments for Hueys made it necessary for a Chinook to deliver our supplies. We didn't have an LZ large enough to land a Chinook, so we would accept an airdrop of rations and ammunition. However, a large number of soldiers were scheduled for R&R and two-week curtailments, complicating my plans. They would have to climb a rope ladder into the Chinook while it hovered above the trees. The climb was dangerous for a man with a rifle and rucksack because it was easy for a heavy rucksack to pull a trooper's head lower than his feet, inverting him in the air. Rifles were easily snagged on the ropes, and troopers were exposed to snipers from a considerable distance while they were in the air. I wouldn't like the operation in peaceful conditions, but my alarms rang loudly with the enemy so close.

If a Chinook was shot down while conducting a resupply or extraction over the company, it would kill most us underneath. Therefore I spread security out as far as practical, both to keep VC snipers as far away as possible and to keep troopers from beneath the large Chinook. I was satisfied that security was as far out as I could reasonably push it and still have a defensible perimeter, but it was still inadequate. My sense of imminent danger rose steadily while we waited, and the longer we waited, the longer the enemy had to act. There had simply been too many incidents like this one to ignore the threat. Something was wrong, and I needed to change the dynamics.

My first concern was in being observed, so I ordered a platoon to send a squad to look for signs that we were being followed or watched. We had been in the area too long already; we were not in a posture to react, and neither was battalion. Communications were stretched, and no air cover was available.

The patrol returned after about an hour and reported that it had found nothing. I was disappointed by the report, but mostly I was skeptical because I had seen so many signs of recent activity all around us. I suspected the squad had cut short the patrol, hunkered down, and returned with a false report. I had heard rumors before. The platoon was now infused with many new people from other units, and they may have operated with a lower standard than I demanded. I had already seen other indications of falling discipline with the transfusion of replacements. Our situation was too serious this time; I would not accept a superficial scouting report.

I ordered 2d Platoon to prepare another patrol immediately, one that I would lead myself because the security of the entire company depended on reliable information.

I led six volunteers outside the perimeter; among them were Steve Martinez, Cleatus Burgess, and Jimmy Denholm, experienced people I completely trusted. We had followed the one-foot-wide trail for about 500 meters when my senses grew stronger that the enemy was nearby. I signaled the others to move off the trail to the right and slightly uphill. We had moved twenty meters farther when the pointman, Cleatus Burgess, froze. About ten meters ahead of him, the brush moved when a dark figure ducked behind a tree.

I yelled, "Fire!" and raised my M16 toward the tree.

At the same time, we were blinded by a bright-red blast that turned the dark jungle into a sunburst. I was thrown to the ground on my back. The explosion deafened us. I yelled, "Fire!" again, but this time I couldn't hear myself. Brush in front of the tree had disappeared; leaves and branches that covered it were stripped away.

We engaged the fleeting figures crashing through brush, going downhill toward the streambed. When I thought they were gone, I spotted another circular Chinese antipersonnel mine resting on its spindly legs on the opposite side of the tree trunk. I yelled, "Mine!" just as the second blast erupted.

An uneven crackle of M16s and AK-47s broke out from both sides. I estimated that our seven were opposed by an equal number of them. Unfortunately, they had achieved the element of surprise and were in concealed positions. They broke away quickly, but the damage had already been done.

I tried to stand to lead a pursuit of the escaping VC but it was impossible and impractical. Burgess and Martinez were sprawled on the ground, and something was wrong with my ankle. Jimmy Denholm checked on them, leaving two men to observe the jungle while I talked on the radio.

I couldn't reach Battalion on the patrol radio, so I contacted the company instead: "Gator Six Alpha, this is Six," I called. Judge was already trying to contact me at the moment of the first blast, but I had been too busy to answer. After the blast my ears were ringing so hard I couldn't hear very well.

"Gator Six, this is Gator One. What's your situation? Over." It was Judge; he sounded like he was in barrel.

"We were ambushed near the LZ. We have casualties. Report to Battalion, call for a medevac, get gunships up to cover, and postpone the resupply," I instructed, realizing that I was shouting into the handset.

"I made an initial report already and I'll take care of the other now. I'm prepared to send out a platoon," said Judge.

"Go ahead and send them out. We'll watch for them. Stay there in control until I get back. I'll tell you more in a few minutes. Out." While Judge made his requests to Battalion, I went to see about our casualties.

They were both in bad shape, but I thought Martinez would be all right if we got him out quickly. Several pellets from the mine had hit him but none seemed life threatening.

Burgess, however, was in much worse shape. Many pellets had struck him at close range in the face, chest, neck, arms, and legs. As pointman, he'd been closest to the first blast; his body had shielded others from the full effects. When the second mine exploded, we were already flat on the ground.

As I moved about to complete my checks, I realized I was dragging the toe of my left foot. I checked it and found a hole in the canvas of my left jungle boot, just behind my ankle. My left boot was squishy inside and some blood oozed from a slit in the side. I noticed cuts on my hips and legs, but I assumed that nothing was broken since I was walking. I ignored them. We had more serious problems.

But our troubles mounted. Confusion at the patrol base and LZ was amplified with the company commander isolated on patrol. The picture of our situation at the battalion operations center was muddier still. While Judge relayed the information I passed, he couldn't answer questions while I was busy and unresponsive. My chief concern was getting my guys out of the jungle to medical care.

Trees were too large and close together for us to clear a landing zone, and we had no C4 to blow them down. The medevac pilot responded quickly, suggesting a jungle penetrator with a basket. He hovered overhead and lowered a cable with an attached basket to winch up the wounded men. But heavy downdraft from the hovering helicopter created severe turbulence, making it difficult to even stand under the ship. We all stood close by under a dead tree that offered the only opening through the dense canopy. The strong air stream from the chopper broke off the dead tree trunk, toppling it on to Jimmy Denholm, who was acting as ground guide. We rushed to the tree trunk to move it, but Denholm had an injured back and now also needed to be evacuated. The patrol was down to four men, three plus me. We no longer had the luxury of attending to security. I had to accept the risk of our vulnerability to get the injured out.

The final four stood below and watched as Burgess ascended into the medevac. As he rose I could feel my strength draining. Life was leaving his limp body as he went heavenward. It was an especially difficult moment for me; grief, guilt, and anger competed for control. I had led the men into the ambush, although I knew the patrol was necessary for the security of the company. I was furious that the first patrol had not done its job better, convinced it had done an inadequate reconnaissance. This should not have happened at all. I was concerned about my own injury, too; the wound itself didn't seem very serious, but walking was difficult, and I couldn't command in the jungle on crutches.

The evacuation was finally completed. I was afraid Burgess had died while suspended in air, but I was confident Martinez and Denholm would recover. We four, lonelier than ever, were left to straggle back to the company. One of the remaining men had a broken finger from the falling tree, and I was using my rifle as a crutch. Thankfully, we were met on the trail by the platoon Judge sent out to meet us.

*   *   *

I wanted to stay with the company, but the walk proved it would be impossible to continue on the trails, much less carry a rucksack. Someone took the radio off my back as I hobbled along. As we entered the perimeter, Judge told me Labrozzi was sending a helicopter with a McGuire rig to ferry the trooper with the broken finger and me to Fire Base Green.

The helicopter arrived and hovered overhead. Two long ropes fell to the ground, one from each side of the bird. The ropes were looped on the ends. We pulled the loops over our heads and under our armpits. When the chopper lifted up, we were lifted with it. We swung to and fro in the wind and we were slammed against the sides of trees, but not injured. We finally crested the treetops and were carried in a forward flight, slow at first but then gaining in air speed. We held our arms out to stabilize ourselves and prevent spinning. The flight to Fire Base Connell was only five miles. I had never been there and it looked unfamiliar as we landed. The chopper let us down gently and then landed beside us so we could climb inside for the continuation to Green.

At Green we went to the aid station to be patched up. While the doctor splinted the broken finger I briefed Labrozzi on everything that happened. I was still talking when the doctor approached us. I had already removed my boot and then dropped my trousers for him to paint the cuts on my legs and buttocks with mercurochrome. I stood with my pants around my ankles when General Burton entered the aid station. Someone called attention and he pinned a Purple Heart on my shirt while the doctor spread purple paint over my buttocks. I made a joke about "the purple butt award" and we shared a laugh, my first in a while and my last for a long time.

When the doc directed me to 15th Medical Battalion in Bien Hoa I was in no position to argue. I informed Labrozzi that Lieutenant Judge was in command of Bravo Company and emphasized that I wanted him to keep it until I returned. I had instructed Judge to investigate the first patrol and intended to see justice served by the Judge.

October 21, 1970

Dearest Sandy,

Right now I have a terrible headache and my eyes hurt. But don't worry, because there is nothing wrong with me that about two weeks time won't cure. I love you and think of you all the time. So please take care of yourself, and don't worry. It all goes to make a year.

All my love,

P.S. Happy Birthday, Darling.

"Selective Service spokesmen acknowledged that a just-issued regulation may permit "dozens, even hundreds," of men to avoid the draft by parlaying administrative delays until they turn 26. The Draft director said men desperate enough to pay the price of such tactics would be more trouble than they were worth."

—*Atlanta Constitution,* October 2, 1970

33

Recovery

October 20–November 8, 1970

I stayed only one night at the 15th Medical Battalion to have the wound in my foot cleaned, but much longer was needed to heal my bruised heart. Later I was moved to the 24th Evacuation Hospital at Long Binh. First Sergeant Royas visited and brought 1st Cavalry Division stationery, a new pipe, and tobacco. The writing paper reconnected me with Sandy; the pipe reconnected me with myself. I needed both because I was feeling very disconnected. He also brought bad news. Lieutenant Judge had been wounded a day after me. He was shot in the thigh with a VC AK-47 round. A clever VC who allowed them all to get into the kill zone before opening fire also hit Tony Daisy and Al Ervasti.

The first sergeant told me that the company had found a grenade factory near where I was ambushed and where the others had been wounded. The VC had fiercely defended their depot. Someone tossed a grenade into the bunker and set off a large secondary explosion, which blew the top off. Steve Martinez, wounded by the Chinese mine that had killed Burgess was also in the same ward next to Judge. After being patched up and stabilized both would be evacuated to Japan. I needed to see them before they left.

My concern for all the troopers weighed heavily on me. Beyond that I realized that the investigation of the patrol incident was now stymied. No one else would investigate it, and time would purge it. I was disappointed because I wanted to know the truth about what had happened—it might have been explainable, but I'd probably never know.

I felt guilty about Judge's wound as well as my own. I believed that when he was wounded he was following my example of assertive, perhaps over aggressive, leadership and took risks that might have been avoided. I kept those thoughts to myself but noted them in my journal. I visited Judge and Martinez for a while and limped back to my bed with my heart as well as my foot, aching.

That night, relentless monsoon rains pounded the hospital so hard that rainwater flooded the floor around me. A nurse pushed my bed into the center aisle, out of the expanding puddle. I could see the television set better, but AFN was replaying the World Series, which I'd already read about in *Pacific Stars and Stripes*. There was no escaping my doubts, a wide range of them. I had to face them.

* * *

So there I lay rusting in bed 8, ward 4, 24th Evacuation Hospital. My ankle and Achilles tendon were sore as hell. Very early in the morning, even before coffee, two nurses rolled me into surgery so the doctors could dig into my ankle.

"We'll remove the fragments from your ankle. How do you feel?" asked one of the doctors.

"I'm okay."

"If you aren't in too much pain, we'll give you a local in the foot and do a spinal block of your legs. That way we won't have to put you out with a general anesthesia. You'll recover much faster."

"Fine by me. I don't want to be put out anyway. I was awake when it went in; I'll be awake when it comes out."

"Roll over on your stomach. Let your feet hang over the end of the bed, so we can get to your heel better."

With a little help I rolled over. The cold air on my butt told me it was exposed to the air conditioning in the operating room. A nurse covered me with a thin sheet.

I thought they would never finish probing my ankle. After a while, the doctors stopped talking to each other and one moved around to my head.

"We're having trouble getting the fragment out. It's lodged between your Achilles tendon and anklebone. Getting it out may cause more problems and damage than leaving it in. What do you think about that?"

"Feels like you're sawing my foot off. What happens if you just leave it?"

"Your body will cover it with a protective layer of tissue. It may move around some, but if it causes any problems, it can be removed later."

"Leave it. I'll keep it as a souvenir."

I had been lucky again, and I knew it. The fragment had gone into the fleshy part of my left ankle. Had it struck an inch to either side, I would have had a more serious problem with either a fragment in the anklebone or a severed Achilles tendon. I recalled my good fortune when Lieutenant Than shot me in Cai Lay in 1967. I had been spared by an inch both times.

*　　*　　*

Customer service is of a different variety in a war zone hospital. Nurses do very little for you; they insist that patients do everything possible for themselves. Pain is a good thing. It means you're still alive. Therefore I went to get my own coffee. Where were the Red Cross "doughnut dollies" when you really needed one? Planning ahead, I took one crutch so I would have one hand free to carry the coffee. Unfortunately once I poured the coffee, I couldn't hop on one foot and still keep the coffee in the styrene cup. After scalding my hand a few times with spilled hot coffee, I sat the coffee cup on a table, hopped past it and reached back, advanced the coffee to another table, and then hopped again. When I got to my bed the show was rewarded with applause from others watching from their own beds. Unfortunately the coffee was cold by then, and the cup was half-empty; a trail of dark puddles on the floor showed where I'd been. Nevertheless I was thankful to have half a cup of cold coffee.

I was depressed in the hospital, where I gave up hope for flight training. I was scheduled for another hearing examination and a flight aptitude test while I was there. I was certain the ringing in my ears from the last mine blast would indicate further loss of hearing. I also missed the guys in Bravo Company, and I was especially worried that I might lose command of the company. I had to get back on my feet and return to the unit as soon as possible.

But for now, all I could do was lie there and think. I would be a father soon, and I wondered whether it would be a son or daughter. The situation reminded me of my own father and how I was born while he was in the Navy during World War II. I missed Sandy so much that it hurt, and I hoped she was getting by all alone. I hadn't figured out what being a good husband meant yet, much less a father.

October 21, 1970

Dearest Sandy,

No! I don't want my son to be a Junior! I want him to be his own individual self. I hope to have his respect, but not to monopolize him. I want him to learn to stand on his own feet much younger than I did. Not that I won't give him all the support he needs, but I don't want to over-shadow him. I want him to absorb my good traits and cast off my bad ones and weaknesses. I don't want a junior. I want a new and better person and we will have one.

I feel very closely associated with my father right now. When I was born, he was in the Navy in World War II. I know how he felt now. I can hardly wait to return to Columbus and my little family. I want to show off my kid when I get back.

Be sweet, darling, and write often. I love you more than I can say. Take care of yourself and our baby. I need both of you.

I wrote a second letter of sympathy to another family—our pointman's. It was the hardest letter I had ever written. Losses were tragic and connected to choices I had made. Mercer had died in retaliation for a successful ambush I had ordered, and Burgess on a patrol I had led. Both deaths had a profound impact on me, as they joined the prodigals who still visit me.

Perhaps they never left. I wish I could see them in life again, with families of their own. I missed them then, I miss them still.

> As I sit in bed with a clean sheet, a hot black cup of coffee and a White Owl cigar, I have time for philosophy. I sit here in the comforts of the hospital bed—even smoking in bed, and desperately wanting to go back to my company in the field. I'm lucky to be alive, but that isn't enough. I'm drawn back to the war to get recharged. Death and danger are not enough. Once you learn to live with them, it is difficult to live without them by your side. Why do young men keep going off to war? Why do countries continually send their sons to war, to waste their blood on fields of battle?

* * *

On October 24, the doctor woke me at 6:45 a.m. "Wake up, Captain. I need to look at your ankle," the doctor ordered.

"The days get real long when you wake me up so early," I replied.

"Do you want to leave tomorrow?" He surprised me.

"I want out now!"

"Well, I have to sew up the hole in your foot, but it looks pretty good. Are you ready now?"

"You mean stitches?" I was being challenged. "Damn right," I replied.

"I don't have any anesthetic here. Do you still want to leave today?" He was testing me.

"Why are you talking instead of stitching?"

"Turn over on your stomach and hold on."

I thought about a million cowboy movies and wished I had a shot of whisky and a bullet to bite.

He stitched my ankle on the spot. Then I walked without a crutch, but as the blood rushed down to my foot, the pain rushed up to my head. Every time I stood up, I had to hold onto something until the flow of blood and nerves were stabilized.

* * *

I hobbled to the ear, nose and throat clinic for the new hearing test the doctor had ordered. Tests confirmed a 55 percent hearing loss at 4,000 decibels. I would need waivers for hearing and time in service to qualify for flight training. Only one waiver was permitted, and none was assured: flight training was definitely out. Later Chaplain Ron Rodeck came by for a visit, timely, I suppose. I liked the battalion chaplain, but I really didn't need a sky pilot right then. Maybe I did but I wanted to fly solo for a while, anyway.

I was released from the 24th Evac at 11:00 a.m. By 11:30 a light observation helicopter from Brigade had picked me up. I was at Fire Base Green by 12:30 p.m., in time for lunch. Bravo Company should have been there already, but its extraction was delayed because it had selected an inadequate pickup zone. I was concerned; selecting LZs was a basic function in an air cavalry company.

Tony Labrozzi greeted me warmly, and he agreed I should go back to Bravo Company as soon as the doctor released me. I was encouraged by his support. I hobbled to the aid station for a release from light duty. Instead I received more bad news. The surgeon told me the incision was wide, requiring two more weeks until the stitches came out. I argued I had been in the field with stitches before, but he would have none of that. Actually I knew he was right. This wound was in my foot, which I kept sticking into the jungle mud. The wound would become infected, creating a more serious problem. So I resigned myself to impatiently waiting a while longer; but waiting was slowly killing me.

The duty of fire base security commander fell to me, but I had no company to man the perimeter because Bravo Company was delayed. I rounded up cooks, clerks, and other warm bodies to do the job that night. I was thankful the motley crew was not attacked, even though my luck had been mostly bad.

*   *   *

Despite my hearing loss, orders directed me to Da Nang for the flight aptitude test. I was discouraged about my hearing, but preferred going to Da Nang to sitting around. Labrozzi agreed. So I took a Chinook to Phouc Vinh, a C-123 to Tan San Nhut, and a Lambretta taxi to Saigon, where I registered at an old French hotel called The Arizona, bachelor officer quarters. It was not as luxurious as I remembered the Rex's being two years earlier, but I was broke anyway. I found enough change to buy two beers at the hotel bar, and a Red Cross worker bought me another. The bar was filled with Vietnamese whores, but they left me alone when they saw the size of my bankroll.

The next morning I sat at the 8th Aerial Port from 8:00 a.m. until 8:00 p.m. waiting for a flight to Da Nang. The first flight had been overbooked, and the next two were canceled. A final flight was cancelled at 8:00 p.m. I was stranded for another night in a fleabag hotel and further delayed en route back to the airfield next morning by a two-hour funeral procession. Consequently I missed the first flight again. By then, I was so disgusted that when a flight to Phouc Vinh was announced, I jumped on it instead, giving up hope of flight training. I went back "home." There is just no place like home.

I was anxious to return to the field, but a typhoon blew through southern Vietnam and choppers were grounded. A crazy warrant officer decided to try to fly to Green anyway and invited Bob Kon and me to go along. We flew through heavy rain for an hour and a half between craggy mountains, buffeted by high winds and with visibility obscured by clouds and fog. As we circled aimlessly, I heard a pilot say on the intercom that we were over Cambodia.

Eventually we landed at Song Be for fuel. Afterward, the pilots aimed the helicopter along the highway five feet above the blacktop, guiding on the faint centerline on the road. Any higher and we could not see the road in the heavy fog and rain, any lower and we would need wheels. If there had been a truck on the road, it would have ruined our day, but no one was so foolish as to drive a truck in that weather!

I made it to Green on October 31—Halloween. I swore I would never leave again! Bravo had returned during my absence, but it was already prepared to return to the jungle. I was a caged animal. It was Sandy's birthday, and I missed her more than I could stand. I wanted to go home and I wondered what she was doing. I wondered what she thought I was doing, if she had any concept of what was happening here. I doubted she could fathom it from my sketchy letters. I wished my writing were more lyrical. I knew my letters were boring; I had lost my inspiration for writing while being careful not to reveal too much. The good stuff was between the lines.

On November 1 Bravo Company conducted a combat assault into War Zone D. I was left to sadly watch their departure from the sidelines. My low morale sagged even further: I had ten more days of light duty, and I was weary of shamming. Ten endless days!

* * *

I ventured back to the rear, restless and wanting to stay occupied. I found Capt. Ted Plucinski, the battalion surgeon, at morning sick call and we shared a cold beer while we watched a football game on television. That was the best therapy Ted had to offer until brigade headquarters announced an officers' call for 3:30 p.m. We found the former Alpha Company commander, George Lovelace at the officers' club. George had left Alpha following a successful command tour and was on his way home. We celebrated his good fortune with a drink Pete called "skip and run naked": beer, limejuice, and gin. We talked and joked for a while, ambling after dark to the 11th Aviation Group club to teach the pilots some of the finer arts. At 2:00 a.m. we stumbled arm in arm back to our base for a private nightcap from Ted's personal stock. My ankle no longer hurt when we were finished. I was feeling no pain and I spent the night on a litter at the clinic.

*   *   *

The sun rose early and brighter than usual the next morning. It was followed by the first sergeant who informed me I had been selected to go to division headquarters as "king for a day." Had I not been so hung over, it would have been the funniest thing I had ever heard. The commanding general selected one company commander each week to give his rear-echelon staff the smell from the field. Actually it was a great program, but I believed I was a poor selection, because I was shamming in the rear area, not coming directly from the field. I was simply available.

I was chauffeured in a jeep to division headquarters at 11:00 a.m., and shown to the general's mess. There I met a gaggle of lieutenant colonel staff officers who all appeared harassed, busy, and preoccupied—but determined to make the "king for a day" feel important. After lunch, I followed an agenda that included office calls on staff officers responsible for personnel, intelligence, operations, supply, and civil affairs. Each one wanted me to tell him how to do his job better. They all listened politely when I said they were doing a fine job already. I didn't want to offer any great new ideas that might make me a candidate for the staff.

By the time I finished the day I knew the war effort was really screwed up, otherwise we would not need kings for a day and air-conditioned officers' clubs. My mind had probably been warped, but I still believed if we concentrated more time and effort on winning the war, we could.

At 6:00 p.m., I attended the evening briefing and was seated between Major General Putnam and Brigadier General Burton, both of whom I knew and liked from their visits to the field. The briefing officers wore heavily starched uniforms, and their hair was shaved into white sidewalls. They were stiff, formal, and clearly nervous as they stood at attention. I was relieved for them when it was finally over: I didn't find the spectacle especially entertaining, as some did. The dog-and-pony show reinforced my intention to face Viet Cong mortars, not briefings. Little did I know!

When the show ended I accompanied the generals to the mess for cocktails and dinner. I was seated between General Putnam and the chief of staff, Col. Rex Newman, during dinner. The conversation started by Brig. Gen. "Smokey" Hyman dealt with why troopers carried their weapons on "rock and roll," full automatic, thereby firing all their ammunition at the first indication of trouble. General Hyman put his question to me, "How do your troops carry their weapons, automatic or semiautomatic?" He intended to solicit my help to prove his point, which was lost on me.

I knew I would have to justify my answer, whatever I said. "We carry them on safe, unless on point." That was, of course, a blatant lie, but it was the textbook answer. There was some laughter at the general's expense, and the subject was quickly changed.

After dinner, General Hyman graciously offered me one of his trademark cigars and, of course, I graciously accepted. It was like a peace pipe offered to a cavalry officer by a renegade Indian chief. I was pretty sure Hyman saw himself as the cavalryman. Nevertheless it was an unusually fine cigar, not the Tampa Nugget or White Owl I was accustomed to. The commanding general presented me a Penguin lighter with the 1st Cavalry Division horse blanket on one side and "King for a Day" on the other. I was touched by it, and I still have the lighter even though it leaks. I replaced it with a Zippo, the real Vietnam lighter.

"A lull settled over Indochina battlefields and for the fourth time in six weeks communiqués reported no American combat deaths. But U.S. Air Force B52s continue a blitz of the Ho Chi Minh supply trail in Laos."

—*Atlanta Constitution*, November 12, 1970

34

Artillery Ambush

November 4–11, 1970

Fire Base Green had become so familiar to me that it almost felt like home; but all things must end. We departed and closed the fire base in early November. The battalion moved lock, stock, and barrel to another region of War Zone D, and I was temporarily posted to the battalion tactical operations center to assist with planning and control of combat operations. The underground operations center was hot, dusty, and cramped. But when the day finally arrived to remove the stitches from my ankle, I was happier than I had been in weeks.

Rains ceased and the monsoons appeared to be over. Dry felt good for a change, but it necessitated carrying additional water, increasing loads on the backs of soldiers in the field.

* * *

An eight-man squad from the reconnaissance platoon had hidden near Green when it was closed. The men concealed themselves in the jungle at the edge of the clearing, established good fields of fire over the old fire base, and registered artillery. Viet Cong frequently scavenged deserted bases for anything useful, such as ammunition, rations, wood, or scrap metal. This time enticements were deliberately left in plain view to tempt them. The trap was set. The first day several VC took the bait and came on the base. While they were unprotected in the open, 105mm howitzers from the 1st Battalion, 21st Field Artillery, at Fire Base Durall hit them and killed two. Our reconnaissance element stayed in position in the belief that the others would return to remove the bodies.

* * *

I had been working as assistant S-3 in the operations center with Maj. Wayne Knudson. I was taking a break outside the dusty bunker when a light observation helicopter limped toward the landing pad and slammed down in a swirl of dust. On hitting solid ground Plexiglas in the fuselage crumbled. I rushed to the crippled chopper.

"Hey! What happened?" I yelled.

The crew chief was first out, while the pilots let the engine wind down to avoid a fire. Shakily he said, "We were on a scout mission with a gunship and spotted bunkers. We hovered over the bunkers, and I lobbed a grenade into one. It set off a secondary explosion that almost blew us out of the sky. We were just a few feet above when it exploded."

No one was injured, but the crew was visibly shaken by the self-inflicted surprise. While we laughed about the close call, Command Sergeant Major Florio ran breathlessly from the operations center to report that six VC had returned to Green. Employing more of the preregistered artillery, the reconnaissance troopers had killed two more, but the remaining VC had fled in the direction of recon's hiding position. The recon troopers fired in self-defense, wounding several of the enemy but exposing their own position. The platoon leader, who was with the squad, believed it was unwise to stay another night and requested extraction. Labrozzi overruled him and directed him to stay in place. Our mission was to cover their move to a new hiding position.

The sergeant major, who was running the operation, was rounding up volunteers to go to Green, remove the VC bodies, and cover the recon squad while it relocated. He wanted me to join him because he believed I was crazy. I was, and I did, along with a radio operator and three others. We piled into the helicopter with a tracker-dog team. Major Knudson pointed the helicopter toward Green. This was the cavalry, all right: I felt like Custer riding to the Little Big Horn.

We lay flat on the floor as we approached so that it would appear from the ground that the chopper was arriving empty. Once on the ground, I accompanied the dog team as it trailed the wounded VC. We chased for 200 meters into the jungle before the dog lost the scent. We were not equipped or armed to go very far into the jungle. Also, two weeks of convalescing had not prepared me for the exertion; I found myself sweating and breathing hard.

As our chase team trudged uphill onto the old fire base, the sun sizzled. The dead Viet Cong on Green had already decomposed in the heat, generating a stench. Disgusted by the necessity, I helped the sergeant major stuff them into body bags, gagging on reflex. I feared an arm or leg would pull off as we strained to get them into the bags. I was already dizzy from chasing through the jungle; the ripe bodies pushed me toward nausea.

Major Knudsen circled in the helicopter, returned quickly, and landed nearby. We shoved the body bags into the helicopter and crawled in with them. The recon squad had taken advantage of our diversion to change positions. When we lifted off we sat in the doors in plain view, legs dangling outside, with the wind in our faces. The rush of fresh air cleared my head. We had gone in hidden and wanted it to appear that the stay-behind squad was being removed on the way out, hoping the VC would return to the base one more time.

Twice was stupid, but falling into the same trap three times would have been suicidal. The Viet Cong were smarter than that and did not return to Green again.

*   *   *

Labrozzi was ill tempered for several days, and he passed it along to everyone he came in contact with. I liked Labrozzi, but I liked him best when several miles of jungle separated us. Now that I was trapped on the fire base with him, I was exposed to a heavy dose of his temper. But on a positive note, Dr. Thompson, who had replaced Ted, finally released me to rejoin Bravo Company. I had been away from the company for three weeks, but it seemed like an eternity. I wondered how the men would feel about me after my patrol had been ambushed.

My long absence had created other worries as well. I wondered whether the company members had changed and whether they would respond to my aggressive leadership. I wondered whether they had embraced other bad habits while I was away. With all the replacements, I wondered if this was still the same company at all. I also had questions about whether I could keep up in my poor physical condition. I would find out very soon if I could pass the test.

Darling,

Things are very hectic around the operations center, and it is hard to concentrate. I just wanted you to know I'm fine and gaining weight again. I love you very much and think everyday about you and the baby. Time is indeed getting near. I guess about two more months and we'll be proud parents. Please take care of yourself until then. I love you very much.

Write often, your letters mean everything to me.

November 12, 1970

Dearest Sandy,

One thing I do know. I hate spending Thanksgiving, Christmas, and New Year's out here in War Zone D. If I could only be with my family for that, I would be very happy. I love you very much, Darling, and with only 230 days left, I think of you more every day.

— Richard

35

Back to Bravo

November 1970

As I feared, the company had changed in my absence. Its leaders had changed tactics, and the troopers had developed sloppy habits. It was not the same outfit as before. But this happens to the best of units in a leadership vacuum, especially when people are coming and going every week. I had left unexpectedly three weeks earlier, knowing the infusion of replacements would create lack of unity in the organization. The patrol incident on the day I was wounded had already indicated as much. I could not squelch it then, but I had to deal with it now. I had to reverse a corrosive trend. Lives depended on it.

Facing this new challenge, I was concerned that the company might be suspicious of my leadership following the ambush: either afraid that I had lost my touch or would make an irrational decision. After three weeks' absence I'd become a stranger in my own company. A new commander gets the benefit of the doubt, but I no longer felt this was "my" company, and I had to reclaim the position of leadership to continue as commander. Bravo and I had both changed, so I had to reshape my style and the company to a new mission and a changed situation.

An unexpected test of my resolve came to me in short order. Doubts about the war had seeped into my mindset while I was in the rear. Contemplating my soldiers, war protesters at home, personal loneliness, and continuing unit withdrawals affected my perspective about our continued presence. I had new doubts about the usefulness of tramping through the jungle. I was not afraid of combat, even after the ambush, but I harbored stronger misgivings about the purpose of a war that my country no longer seemed interested in winning. I knew we would adapt to what we were asked to do, but I recognized my personal reservations about putting these soldiers at risk. Was the United States sufficiently committed to justify placing lives in jeopardy? It was not a question of right or wrong, it was a matter of commitment.

I had sensed an attitude that the war was over in the rear. I had not recognized those thoughts while I was there, but they were clear from the perspective of the jungle. We were an army in retreat, verified by units' departing the battlefield. At our level the mission was to find the enemy and kill him, disrupt his operations, and capture and destroy his supplies. At division and higher levels the mission was to delay until a settlement could be worked out in Paris. At home, the country was divided. Pressures to withdraw came from elsewhere, not from the battlefield. We were winning on the battlefield, but losing on Main Street.

November 14, 1970

Dear Sandy,

My spirit really isn't in it like it should be. It seems everywhere you look everything is negative as far as the war goes. We haven't lost the war, but we seem to have lost the cause. Right now, I just feel like I am marking time. I'm just not motivated for this thing anymore. It isn't

that I like the army any less, or my job—it is just that it seems pointless
to stay here any more.

Strategically we were bargaining chips in Paris. In War Zone D, Bravo
Company kept the enemy at bay so others could go home. This was a
retrograde operation. Increased safety procedures, limits on flying time, and
the shrinking pool of replacements confirmed my beliefs about where the
war was headed. In such a situation rumors prevailed. So what were we to
do? I felt we had to continue with aggressive operations, or complacency
would take over. Once a fighting organization becomes complacent it is ripe
for ambush, attack, or accident. The situation we faced was more
psychological than physical: if the war was over in our minds, then we would
certainly be defeated in battle. We continued our mission aggressively, but
cautiously, to avoid endangering lives needlessly.

*   *   *

Driving rains dampened our spirits as well as our clothes. I worried
about cracking branches and crashing trees in monsoon storms. Not even a
hot meal could cheer me up. I was depressed by my conclusions and the
direction we were taking, but I was careful not to let others see it. I wore a
soldier's mask—a war face—to conceal my doubts. When I gave orders for
new patrols, I wondered whether they could see my true feelings in my face
or hear them in my voice. I was determined that no one would.

Late in the year, Wendell S. Merick, a reporter for *U.S. News & World
Report,* visited Green to report on "Sagging Morale in Vietnam: Eyewitness
Report on Drugs, Race Problems and Boredom." The report didn't appear
until late January 1971, but it upset me immeasurably, partly because of the
truths it revealed publicly while I was trying to avoid exposing my own
doubts.

> The most persistent enemy a soldier faces these days is not
> Communists—it's boredom. With the war ebbing slowly away, one
> day merges into the next. GI's resent being exposed to combat in a war
> no American has any intention of winning. Even so, many prefer
> fighting to dull garrison duty, and more than one infantryman would
> trade the "spit and polish" life at a relatively safe headquarters for a
> jungle patrol.[1]

*   *   *

A platoon approached a stream with steep banks on both sides. To cross, Lt. Ed Sweeney sent a squad ahead to secure the far side, exactly as I would have done. As the pointman climbed over the top, a Viet Cong soldier shot him in the stomach. After a brief fire fight, the shooter escaped and we evacuated the wounded man. This was the first casualty we had taken since I returned. I was upset, but Mad Anthony was furious. He was convinced that Sweeney had made a mistake. I defended his decision to Labrozzi because I didn't see any other way to conduct the crossing. Labrozzi couldn't seem to get over it. I wondered whether he was having the same doubts about the high cost in casualties. But I knew we would continue to endure casualties as long as armed men walked the jungle stalking one another.

I quickly lost the ten pounds I had gained, but my ankle bothered me more than I had anticipated. The doctor had been right to restrict me as long as he had. I could feel the fragment working around as I walked about—a constant warning of the danger around us. I sat on my rucksack at every opportunity instead of walking around to talk to my troops. Maybe that was a good thing, considering my true feelings.

After finding a high-speed bicycle trail—four feet wide and covered with bamboo mats, slicing through dense jungle—Bravo was alerted to move back to FSB Durall. I accompanied two platoons there, while the other two went to Fire Support Base Connell. Battalion planned to reopen Green and close Durall. After five days on base security Bravo made a combat assault to follow more trails. We seemed to be on a merry-go-round, going around and around but getting nowhere.

> One of the worst things is when we lose a guy, somebody getting killed. We're a lot closer being in small units, so everybody knows everybody else. And you feel it when somebody gets it.[2]

*   *   *

On Thanksgiving Day we followed a large trail indented with elephant tracks. I wheezed with a chest cold, but we wanted to catch the elephant, so we pushed hard. I didn't want to stop chasing it for our Thanksgiving meal. None of us wanted helicopters to mark our location either. When the log bird arrived I refused the meal. I was afraid a reminder of Thanksgiving Day would create sadness. The arrival of a family holiday in the war zone was unwelcome, from my point of view. The helicopter left with our meal.

Before long, the log bird returned with the battalion S-4 aboard. I really appreciated the S-4, but it was a thankless job, probably right up there with headquarters commander.

"Gator Six, this is Mushroom Four. I'm en route with your Thanksgiving meal and we'll kick it out. Pop smoke. Over."

"Negative," I replied. "We're on a hot trail and we don't want to give away our position. Over."

"Gator Six, I have orders to deliver the meal. The cooks worked hard to make it special. Pop smoke and we'll drop it and be out of here."

"Negative. We're not in position for it today."

"Gator Six, you have to take it! If I go back with it, the Mad Italian will kill me. He sent me personally to deliver it. If you don't take it, I'll drop it in the jungle for the VC, but I'm not taking it back. Over."

I thought while the helicopter circled. I didn't want to make that decision.

"Smoke is out," I relinquished. "My compliments to the chef . . . . Thanks, Four." I wasn't sure if I relented in sympathy for him, in appreciation for the efforts of the cooks, or whether I really wanted us to receive the Thanksgiving meal after all. I certainly didn't want Labrozzi to deliver it himself on the next bird. I wondered whether I had been selfish. Anyway I hoped the men would enjoy it.

The meal was wonderful even though we squeezed it from elephant rubbers. It was complete with printed menus bearing a message from General Abrams. Some of the guys made jokes about catching the elephant to give him the rubbers.

Later I read an article in *Pacific Stars and Stripes* about Sergeant Tee Shaw, who had wanted to rejoin his unit, Bravo Company, 1st of the 7th Cavalry, for Thanksgiving, but couldn't because the company didn't have an LZ. Shaw said, "I just wanted to spend Thanksgiving with my buddies." I was touched when I realized that Shaw was aboard the helicopter helping with the delivery, trying to catch a glimpse of his buddies—his only family-on Thanksgiving Day.

Commander's Thanksgiving Message

This Thanksgiving Day we find ourselves in a foreign land assisting in the defense of the rights of free men. This has placed you a long way from home on a holiday that is historically a family affair. Traditionally, Thanksgiving means attendance at your neighborhood church, a visit with friends and family, watching your favorite college football game and a dinner with turkey and pumpkin pie. The day also stands for much more—a nation founded on the principles of hard-won freedom, a grateful nation with equal opportunities for all. We should never forget that in Vietnam our actions defend free men everywhere. We pray that our efforts will lead to peace in the world and the opportunity to return to our own land and loved ones in the near future.

Creighton W. Abrams
General, United States Army
Commanding

"The communists today rejected a U.S. offer to exchange prisoners of war and said if there were any more American commando raids to rescue captive U.S. pilots, the United States will have to assume full responsibility."

— Marietta Daily Journal, December 3, 1970

36

Backs to the Wall

December 1970

The war zone was quieter than usual after Thanksgiving. A rumor circulated that Labrozzi would leave around Christmas. That raised questions for me, but the one that alarmed me most was whether I would retain command of Bravo Company after Labrozzi left. In fact Bravo Company was my only real reason for being there in the first place. But the war continued despite how we felt about it.

While I was on Green with Bravo, one of Alpha Company's patrols had an accident with a Claymore mine and Pfc. Gary Bivens was severely wounded. Word came in while I was seated between Labrozzi and Merick, the *U.S. News & World Report* reporter at the evening briefing.

The briefing was nearly over when someone handed Labrozzi a note from the operations center. "Good God!" he murmured under his breath. I knew there was trouble.

"Forget about everything else," Colonel Labrozzi ordered. "Just get that kid out of there."

> There, in the middle of War Zone D, medic John D. Swan took charge. It was pitch dark, but Specialist Swan managed to apply tourniquets. Four volunteers stretched out on the ground beside the wounded soldier to give him direct blood transfusions.[2]

Once Private Bivens's evacuation was underway The Mad Italian's concern gave way to anger. He pointed a finger in my direction. "These accidents shouldn't happen. You will hold an inquiry, and from now on, no more 'automatics' until we've had a chance to put these guys through training again. From now on, command-detonated Claymores are the rule until we've put our guys through training again."

Obviously I agreed with him, but I knew Bravo had never had an accident with Claymores. We were fortunate, but we were also careful, and I had emphasized training. In fact we had been on the range firing our ammunition that same day.

* * *

In early December Charlie Company made contact and had a running engagement for several days. I sat in a patrol base while Bravo Company squads scouted for other signs of activity. I listened to Charlie's engagement in case we were called to help. I heard a report that my friend, John Fuller, was shot in both legs. A platoon leader was also hit. The details were confusing, but it sounded similar to the incidents involving Judge and me. AK-47 rounds had broken both John's legs; the platoon leader died of wounds. John went back to the United States for treatment, and he was engaged to be married when he returned.

Bravo was redeployed to Green on December 10, 1970. I was met by more bad news. First Sergeant Royas had received a drop and had already gone home, one of my best lieutenants was reassigned to the 75th Rangers, and the division would begin a redeployment home in March. Worst of all,

Labrozzi informed me I would be the battalion intelligence officer at the end of the month.

I didn't want to stay on the fire base one day longer than necessary. I pleaded with Labrozzi to leave me in Bravo Company; it was no use. But this time he explained his decision, which was rare for him. If I was not in a principal staff position at battalion, I would be reassigned to the brigade staff or sent home early. The only way to stay in the battalion until the end of my tour was to accept the S-2 job. I realized I was not being offered a choice. It was an order with which I had to comply, clinging to the false hope that I would find another way to stay.

My morale sank into my jungle boots. Meanwhile Bravo Company prepared to move out once more. Our mission was to return to LZ Mercer and search for signs that the Viet Cong had returned. Going back to the Mercer area of operations was like going home again.

* * *

At Mercer 4th Platoon was ambushed on the familiar trail network. One trooper was killed and two were wounded, including a new platoon leader. A Vietnamese Kit Carson scout—a former VC who switched sides—guided the platoon and was also wounded. We came up short on the surprise attack, and that bothered the men. We had once been able to shake off setbacks quickly and go about our business, but now the strain was accumulating into a burden. I felt that it was my personal responsibility to keep everyone safe, but I just couldn't do it.

Lieutenant John Lynch of Alpha Company had been leading a platoon behind another Kit Carson scout when one of his men collapsed from heat prostration. I was following the action on the radio because heat was a real problem for all of us. Labrozzi snaped out instructions: "Keep wet towels on that man. Wrap him in wet blankets. Keep his head up."

"It's my fault," Lt. Lynch reported. "I guess I've been moving the man too fast."

"Take it easier," Labrozzi advised. "Don't run the platoon into the ground."

> There have been times in this war when a commander would not have compromised an operation to save a single man. But this was a new phase of the war.[3]

*   *   *

On December 21 we needed a resupply. The pilot called on the final approach, "Gator Six, this is Log Bird Four. I have a load of rations and ammo for you. Pop smoke, please."

"This is Gator Six. Smoke is out. Just push it out right on top of the smoke. Over."

"I see grape smoke."

"Roger. Kick out on the purple smoke." Boxes fell through the air.

"Gator Six, the goodies are unloaded. Merry Christmas, buddy!"

His words were like an electric shock. I had forgotten Christmas was coming—or had pushed it out of my mind. No one had talked about it. The thought smothered me: I felt a year's homesickness drop on me all at once. I wondered what others thought about Christmas. How would I lead these guys through that challenge?

On Christmas Eve, we received a resupply that included another hot meal of turkey and the trimmings. I didn't want to stay in the same place because we had been there too long already, but Labrozzi ordered me to stay at the LZ so that we could take a regular meal, instead of another kick-out. While we were there Labrozzi and Colonel Stevenson visited us. The Catholic chaplain came along to conduct mass. There were not enough chaplains to go around, so each company either had a Catholic or Protestant service. All were invited to the "religion of the day." Otherwise Christmas was completely uneventful. I moved the company into the jungle for shade to wait out the ceasefire. I sat alone and remembered the violations of the one in 1968.

*   *   *

After Pfc Wayne Czajka was wounded, I had trouble keeping an artillery forward observer, despite Colonel Vuono's best efforts. One caught pneumonia on his first night in the field in a driving rain; another one was hit in the knee by an artillery shell fragment while adjusting direct fires on the fire base in his first hour with the company; and I can't even remember what happened to the third one. Finally, Lieutenant Jones arrived; he was a "keeper."

We had trouble with communications after Christmas. Jones bragged that he could climb a tall tree to erect an RC-292 antenna near the top;

however, he set the condition that he would climb the tree only if I would take the antenna down. I knew Jones had been a gymnast at the University of Oklahoma, but that made the challenge even sweeter. Jones made going up the tree appear easy, and the antenna worked beautifully. The next morning I had more difficulty bringing the antenna back down, but tried to make it look as easy as Jones had. My arms and legs trembled, but I covered up with a smile.

December 31, 1970

Dearest Sandy,

I love you very much. I need you more and more every day. I long for the day we'll be together again as one happy family.

Here it is New Year's Eve and I don't have any resolutions. I guess I'll just try to be a better husband—(better than what?)—and, I will be a good father.

* * *

On New Year's Eve a patrol reported a fresh trail, so I moved up front to see for myself. As I caught up with the lead squad, the point man signaled movement ahead. The lead platoon spread out on line, flat on their stomachs. Rifle fire erupted from the jungle. We were twenty meters from approximately twenty VC, and bullets ripped through leaves around us. We stayed flat on the ground returning fire. I was on the front edge and saw a VC in black pajamas. Just as I squeezed off a shot, a flash burst directly in front of my face that blinded me; I couldn't see if I had hit my target and wasn't sure whether I'd been hit. The VC broke away and fled downhill through the jungle, and our firing subsided. I knew I had been hit by something, but was unclear about exactly what had happened. I'd never seen a flash like that one before, and it was very close. The trooper next to me lay on his side, examining the muzzle of his M16 rifle. As my vision slowly returned I looked at his weapon.

A bullet had struck the flash suppressor on the rifle's muzzle; metal splinters from the bullet and rifle had burst over several of us, accounting for the blinding flash. The splinters had sliced my face in several places, as well as my arms and legs. Others, including the trooper whose rifle was hit, were also bleeding. None of our wounds was serious, but looked bad because of all the blood.

A radio operator reacted quickly as I had trained him to do, reporting our situation to battalion. Labrozzi wanted to send a chopper out for me, but I refused to leave. I insisted on having a field medic dress the cuts and stayed until our scheduled extraction on January 3. I knew that if I left again, I would never return to Bravo Company. The medic shot me up with penicillin, and I stayed with the others.

Before we left the field Lt. Ed Sweeney's platoon found an old elephant skeleton, proving we had been right about elephant tracks on Thanksgiving Day. I directed Sweeney to bring the skull back as a trophy for the fire base, but his men couldn't lift it. So they dragged up a ten-pound elephant tooth and some bones as proof. Somebody took a picture of Sweeney, wearing his classic army-issue sunglasses and holding an elephant bone. Funny!

* * *

I met with Labrozzi at Green. I tried to feel him out and confirm my earlier suspicions.

"Thanks for leaving me in the field. I've seen enough aid stations," I said.

"Don't get too used to it. Brigade and Division both wanted you out when you were hit again. There's an unwritten rule: second Purple Heart, you depart."

"Tell them to keep it."

"Doesn't work that way."

"I won't survive in the rear. Will you leave me in Bravo Company?"

"You'll stay as long as I do," he promised. "But you'll come out the day I do, unless you get hit again. If you are, you're out—no questions asked!"

"That's the best I can get?" I left with my head hanging.

I appreciated Labrozzi's support. I really loved the guy. This war would be no fun without him.

* * *

Sandy's pay allotment was still fouled up. On January 5, 1971, I was unsuccessful making a MARS (Military Affiliate Radio System) call to the States and Labrozzi suggested I go to the Saigon USO (United Service

Organization) office in Saigon. Unfortunately a commercial call cost $54. I hated to spend the money, because I knew Sandy was also struggling without enough money. I didn't have any to send her because we were salting as much as possible into savings. I had to book the call, so while I waited a Vietnamese sketch artist drew my picture.

My name was called before the artist had finished, but he completed the sketch while I talked. Since it was a commercial call instead of by short-wave radio, we didn't have to say "over" and "out" as we talked.

The call left both Sandy and me with a strange, vacant feeling. We thought we knew each other through our letters, but on the phone we were strangers. This needed to be addressed by us, but it would have to wait until we were reunited in five months. I didn't like leaving it that way, but it was too much to handle right then. I couldn't deal with my future life while struggling to handle my responsibilities there, along with my doubts about the war. Were we really still in love, or were we just accommodating each other during a difficult time? Unasked and unanswered questions, and unrequited doubts, remained to be resolved later, if there was a later. If there was not, it wouldn't matter.

I was haunted by my uncertainties as I walked along Tu Do Street, buying souvenirs of Saigon. I wanted to have a good time in the city but I had forgotten how, or had lost the motivation. I had forgotten how to celebrate, or relax, or just hang out. I was depressed to be leaving my company, which was my closest family. I was uncertain about my future as a staff officer, and more uncertain about my next posting in the army. I was disturbed by the timetable and conditions of the army's redeployment from Vietnam and distressed over protests at home. I was afraid that those of us on the battlefield were being sold out at the Paris peace talks. I missed Sandy so much that my heart ached, but I wasn't sure whether we even knew each other any more. I was confused about how to be a father even though I knew I would be one very soon.

I was just in the damn dumps! So I bought a small battery-powered radio and prepared to live the life of a fire base rat in a culvert. I remembered my pet rat in My Tho, and wondered whether I was any better off now than I had been then, any better off than the rat.

November 30, 1970

Hello Darling,

I was really shocked at the newspaper headlines I received today—"GI's Enter North Vietnam," "Russia-Red China Ties Restored," "Bombing Started Again," and general activity seems to be picking up—at the same time units are going home. I stay puzzled and perplexed most of the time.

Your letters mean so very much to me. There isn't much else to look forward to.

"Stroll around the fire base at night and chat with the guards and the men manning the artillery. There is no consensus about the Army or Vietnam duty. Few want to be in Vietnam. But many—even though they don't want openly to admit it—are proud they served here."

—*U.S. News & World Report,* January 25, 1971

37

Staff Wars

January–February 1971

My purpose for being in Vietnam had vaporized as fast as my command. Now, with a steady dose of news from AFN radio and *Pacific Stars and Stripes* I could see more clearly that we were just hanging around the war zone. I would stay for another five months, but no longer, and no extensions; my enthusiasm had waned.

The military custom for change of command signifies passing authority and responsibility from one commander to another. Bravo Company, jungle fighters, not parade ground patriots, straggled onto a dusty road that sliced through the center of Fire Base Green. The ragged line reminded me of a similar formation six months earlier, when I took command. Remarkably, the troopers settled into fairly straight lines before the mortar platoon's sign: "High Angle Hell."

Labrozzi walked stiffly into the street and said a few unmemorable words, probably the same ones he had said before. I didn't listen or care what he said. His litany sounded as depressed as I felt. The same guidon I had received so unexpectedly from him six months earlier had been rushed in from the rear. The first sergeant handed it to me; I held it until Labrozzi pulled the staff from my grip and passed it to Capt. Dana Gary, a good man.

I wanted to leave then, disappear. I wasn't interested in hearing his remarks, either. Nevertheless, I stayed to congratulate him. I liked Dana; I just didn't want to hand him Bravo Company. It was all over after that. I felt as if I had been stripped of my purpose, been made obsolete.

*   *   *

Now I was officially a forward-area staff rat; more specifically, I was intelligence officer for 1st Battalion, 7th Cavalry Regiment. I was proud of my skill at finding the enemy in the jungle. I credited that to being able to read and interpret signs—and gut instincts when there were no signs. Sometimes I relied only on feelings in the pit of my stomach or a chill on the back of my neck. I presumed that I'd been handed this particular job because of that ability. I was less confident in my capacity to find the enemy from an underground bunker. Finding the enemy and discerning his intentions from radio reports and intelligence summaries were not my idea of how to "close with the enemy." The indicators would still be there but they'd be different. I just had to learn to read them in another way.

I knew Labrozzi was upset at losing his own command, and I appreciated his efforts to retain me in a staff job in the field rather than in a rear area. But I found it difficult to forgive him for taking away my purpose. It amounted to trading a hundred warriors in the jungle for a dirt bunker and map board. Ensconced with Master Sergeant Kress, I swapped the quiet cool of the jungle for a blazing hot sun and the constant commotion on a fire base. Instead of engaging the enemy face to face, I would fight indirectly with a staff notebook, map, and grease pencil.

Kress had arrived at the battalion about the same time that I had, but he had been intelligence NCO the entire time. He knew the area of operations and the enemy very well from reports. I knew them face to face. I didn't know why we needed an intelligence officer with an NCO as competent as Kress; but it didn't matter, I was there.

I moved into my new residence in a sewer—literally half a culvert for sleeping. After a long day in a dirty, underground bunker, I crawled into my sewer pipe to sleep, like the rat I had become. I selected one near the tactical operations center so that I could be found easily in the dark. To customize my hole for human occupancy, I stacked sandbags at one end to slow the constantly flying red dust that blew through the openings; now it just settled on top of everything. Inside the cramped space I assembled my luxuries: air mattress, poncho liner, rucksack, and rifle, a small battery-powered radio, and a dry-cell-generated airfield landing light for reading and writing at night. All the comforts of home!

* * *

An accidental shooting on Labrozzi's last day in command threw him into a rage. I stayed out of the operations center and out of reach throughout the day, moping quietly. Kress could easily handle the job for a day, and I didn't want to be near the Mad Italian in his final hours. I was quite familiar with the demons he wrestled. After the change of commanders I would find out what the new one wanted.

Dearest Sandy,

Yesterday I mailed you a nasty letter that I'm already sorry for. There was no excuse for me responding in such a manner. More than anything, I want our marriage to work, and it will as soon as we have a chance to build on it together. A year apart like this may strengthen character, but it doesn't strengthen the home—especially one as new as ours. I'm sorry for the things I said—truly sorry.

* * *

On my first full day on the job as S-2, I gave separate briefings to Labrozzi before his departure, to Lt. Col. Alfred E. Spry after he assumed command, to the brigade commander, to the assistant division commander, and to the division commander. That was merely my first day on the job, and I didn't think I knew much about it. I assumed the briefings were intended to lock me down and witness that I was actually out of the jungle. I wondered whether the powers-that-be didn't trust Labrozzi, or me, to actually make it happen.

The ceremony was on the large helipad. To my surprise the flags, music, color, and pomp and circumstance were impressive. Loudspeakers broadcast a musical rendition of "Garry Owen." Generals flew in to participate in or witness the parade. The troops were sharp, including Bravo Company, and I found my place in a row of staff officers composed of staff principals. We did it without a rehearsal. As Labrozzi had said several months earlier, "If you've been in the army more than a day, you don't need to practice this stuff!"

Spry and Labrozzi were poles apart; Spry would certainly command differently. The Mad Italian had been a pure and simple field commander, relying primarily on his company commanders for advice and action. Spry relied considerably on the staff, reflecting his own staff background. I'd been fortunate to command under a commander-oriented leader and serve as a staff officer for a staff-oriented boss. Each was effective in his own way.

* * *

Immediately after the ceremony, a platoon engaged fifteen Viet Cong during a patrol. Graciously, the VIPs departed to get out of the way. Two VC were killed, but the others escaped, leaving their rifles behind along with a large Chinese radio with an estimated range of seventy-five miles. The radio belonged to the Viet Cong 81st Rear Service Group, which was responsible for the arms and ammunition caches and factories we were uncovering. I climbed aboard the helicopter with Spry and Capt. Robbie Robinson, the new operations officer, to overfly the scene.

As soon as we arrived at the site we dropped a rope with a grappling hook attached. The three of us attempted to haul up the radio and captured rucksacks attached to the end of the rope. The take was so heavy that it pulled the helicopter down, and had to be separated into two loads. We finally managed to get the 120-pound radio equipment aboard, but we were tired and sweating, with trembling muscles and stiff backs as we hauled the second load up. Spry was familiar with the radio and explained its capabilities to Robbie and me off the cuff. I wondered whether this job might be interesting after all.

Spry relied heavily on intelligence, constantly prodding me for information. He understood the relationship of sound analysis to success from his own experience in the Pentagon and with the 1st Cavalry Division during the Tet offensive. He demanded good assessments and could quickly discern intelligence from bullshit. I often worked past midnight, but I found the new job challenging, stimulating, and interesting. Spry was an uncompromising teacher. His questions were intended to direct my investigation and analysis rather than get a quick and easy answer.

Spry shared his helicopter, too. He permitted me to take it for a visual reconnaissance one day. His only guidance was: "Don't fly low enough to shoot Viet Cong with your .45!" I laughed at his remark, but I privately wondered whether he was sending me a message. Did I have a reputation for recklessness? I considered the question for some time, which was, I believe, exactly what he intended.

*   *   *

A hunter-killer team was composed of a light observation helicopter and a Cobra gunship. The low bird searched low and slow, peeking under jungle canopy and enticing the enemy to fire and thus give away his position. The high bird, a Cobra attack helicopter, circled high above like a hawk and waited for the scout to find something. Then the attack helicopter would strike quickly from above. An infantry squad, either in the air or at the helipad, remained ready to respond.

Master Sergeant Kress and I were responsible for briefing the teams before they went into action. We accompanied one team on a mission to get a better feel for it. Kress flew in the Cobra, and I took the scout, reflecting our personalities. The warrant officer pilots invited us to fly the choppers for a while. We drifted around aimlessly all over the skies, trying to master the art of flying helicopters, which was more difficult than we'd imagined. Perhaps flight training had not been right for me after all; I would keep my feet planted firmly on the ground, where my instincts were more reliable.

When we returned to Fire Base Green, General Burton joined us for lunch. He spoke excitedly about the new triple capability division forming at Fort Hood, Texas: it was being assembled from returning units of the 1st Cavalry Division. He informed us that 3d Brigade would remain in Vietnam with the 1st of the 7th Cavalry, 1st of the 5th, and 1st of the 12th. The three battalions would form Task Force Garry Owen, and Burton would command it. That meant I would stay with the 7th Cavalry. My family and my army remained in conflict; I wanted to go home but I also wanted to stay.

I envisioned the new division and began to feel a growing excitement for a hot, dry prairie in Texas. Finally Sandy and I had a place to visualize in our future—the first step in construction.

* * *

Unit withdrawals accelerated. I felt that the few of us remaining were the only ones blocking a large army in Cambodia and North Vietnam from our escape hatch in Saigon. It was not a comforting thought. I believed that our backs were against the wall and that the Paris peace talks were only buying time because we became increasingly outnumbered and outflanked. I feared we were being duped again as we had been during the Tet cease fire in 1968. To the Communists diplomacy was another means to achieve victory: "talk, talk, fight, fight, talk, talk, fight, fight."

* * *

The reconnaissance platoon was an intelligence unit and therefore fell under my staff control. One day the platoon found 114 Montagnards wandering in no-man's land. The "Yards" were brought to Green for interviews and taken to Song Be for resettlement. At 2:00 a.m. next morning, I was awaked from my rat hole near the operations center when the recon platoon troopers detected movement outside the perimeter. They believed the VC were preparing to attack them, but I was afraid that other Montagnards were moving about in their vicinity. I hated second-guessing people in the field, but I worried about killing civilians. I urged the battalion commander to have the platoon hold fire unless attacked. Tension mounted in the op center and in the voice of recon's radioman.

At 4:30 a.m. events sprang to life.

"Cymbal Two, we are being penetrated," was the initial alert. I heard sounds of firing in the background as the radioman spoke.

"Scout Six Alpha, more details, please," I requested, wondering whether I had been wrong.

"We had movement around our perimeter. A trip flare was set off. We blew a claymore and started firing."

"Are you taking fire now?" I asked.

"I don't think so," he replied. That puzzled me. I knew that if Viet Cong were attacking, they would be firing. I was afraid civilians had wandered into our defense position and been shot.

"The firing stopped. We got something. We need artillery flares to check it out." Tension increased as we held our breath for the next report.

"Roger," I replied. "I'll get the guns cranked up. There should be light over you in a few minutes. Be ready!" I cranked the hand generator on the field phone to wake the artillery fire direction center.

I heard artillery fire one round, then another, then three more spaced a minute apart.

"Cymbal Two, we found one KIA." I was bewildered. One person wouldn't attack alone. I hoped it was not an old man.

"Anything else?" I asked.

"It's a tiger, four feet long, about ninety pounds, I'd guess." Deep breathing. "He smelled our C-rations and decided to sample some." Laughter erupted in the op center. I envisioned a shaved-head briefing officer telling this story at the evening briefing for the brigade staff!

* * *

I was getting a handle on the job after three weeks. From my position, I actually influenced operational plans. I also made improvements to my living conditions by adding a poncho flap over the open end of my culvert to keep out more red dust. I acquired a cot and styrene blood box to ice my beer and Cokes. A large cable spool served as a table under my poncho flap, and an ammunition box worked for a chair. Life on easy street! I found more time for letters and to contemplate the future.

I missed Sandy, and the baby was nearly due. Bravo Company called to ask if I was handing out cigars yet. I had spoken about my family more than I realized. Sandy and I argued in our letters over the baby's name. If it was a boy, I wanted to name him Zachary—Zachary Scott Taylor—but Sandy vetoed Zack. We settled on Scott.

* * *

Our intelligence picture improved as we gathered information on the VC 81st Rear Service Group. Maneuver platoons managed to win most engagements with the enemy, but they were harassed with friendly fire and plagued by noncombat accidents. Occasional trips to the field for firsthand intelligence helped my morale. Spry sensed that I needed to occasionally get a "fix" on the war in order to stay in touch with reality. I still missed Bravo and wished I could return to a cavalry company. But an old proverb says, "Be careful what you wish for, you might get it."

> Defense Secretary Melvin R. Laird left Vietnam on January 11 with a promise that the current withdrawal target—48,000 more men by May 1—will be met or exceeded. To the 322,000 Americans still in the war zone, this word was welcome. For most GI's, leaving Vietnam means an end to dull routine or the daily challenge of staying alive.[2]

"A large and well-protected bunker complex…was recently the scene of one of the most grueling and bitter firefights faced by 1st Battalion, 7th Cavalry Skytroopers since the long, hard days of Cambodia."

— *Pacific Stars and Stripes*, 1971

38

Delta Demons

January 28–February 2, 1971

The Delta Company Demons stumbled into an unexpected encounter with the security company of the VC 81st Rear Service Group. Specialist 4 Steve Zolecki, on point, found a trail that looked as though it could accommodate a deuce-and-a-half truck. Staff Sergeant Jesus Carillo moved up to reinforce as the Demons moved into a complex that had been dubbed "Bunker City" in *Pacific Stars and Stripes*. When Carillo hit a bunker with a fragmentation grenade, enemy fire opened up on all sides, pinning down a squad with .30-caliber machine gun fire. These were NVA troops and they hung on fiercely to the complex.

We listened to the vicious initial contact over the radios in the tactical operations center, searching for ways to help with fire support. In the initial onslaught Delta had five wounded, including the company commander,

Capt. "Skip" Rozelle, who had been doing a fine job with Delta. His elbow was shattered, so he had a one-way ticket to Japan—if we could get him out of the jungle.

Another disturbing report quickly followed: one man was missing, along with his radio. That chilling news swept over everyone tuned in to the battle. We simply did not lose our troopers; they might die in battle, but we just didn't lose them. Leaving Private Green in Cambodia had been too much for any company to have to relive.

On the ground Earl Wilkes, a medic who had been in the bush only four days, moved about caring for the wounded. Meanwhile a medical evacuation helicopter was dispatched to recover Skip and the others, but heavy ground fire wounded one of the crew. The helicopter, full of holes, fled for survival without recovering the wounded. A flight of F-4 Phantoms with iron bombs circled over the area. We hoped the display of U.S. fire power would swing the fight in our favor before another chopper attempted to go back in. Nevertheless, the second medevac bird encountered heavy ground fire, as well, and took a round in the windshield. It also departed hastily without making the pickup. Another bomb run followed. We were testing the waters in a very risky manner. Meanwhile, the troopers on the ground clung to the periphery of Bunker City as relentlessly as the NVA defended it. Delta was decisively engaged.

The situation didn't improve much. The command-and-control (C and C) helicopter circled overhead at about 500 feet with Spry aboard, trying to regain control of the battle. But the NVA fighters were persistent. The C-and-C chopper took three hits and lost hydraulic fluid; it barely made it back to Fire Base Green. It landed so hard that the impact bent the skids outward. Fortunately no one was injured in the crash landing, but the command helicopter could fly no further in its damaged condition. A Chinook lifted it out, but a replacement was not immediately available. Delta's situation appeared to be on the verge of getting out of hand.

From reports and background noise on the radios in the operations center, I could tell that the company was heavily engaged by enemy rifle and machine gun fire. The company was scattered in small groups, unclear about their own situation, much less the enemy's, and unable to effectively use air strikes. Delta continued to bring helicopters into the threatened environment, further endangering itself and the helicopter crews. A ground commander must make sound decisions under fire, but Skip was incapacitated, and Delta was experiencing a shortage of experienced leadership at that level.

A platoon leader was now in charge. He had taken up to his unwelcome role but was in over his head with the responsibilities thrust on him in this crisis. It was not the lieutenant's fault, but everyone involved was at risk. At long last a medevac chopper got in to extract Skip and the other wounded. We were relieved by that turn of events, at least.

Radios in the tactical operations center buzzed constantly with gibberish. One man, a radio, and several weapons were still missing. We received frantic calls for help with more fire power, which was available but ineffectively employed. Nevertheless a Shadow gunship, the modernized version of the old Spooky, was scheduled to stay on station all night to provide close fires and flares around Delta's position. Spooky had saved our ARVN unit several times in my first tour, and I was confident that Shadow could do the job unassisted here. Artillery fires were plotted for defensive purposes and registered in by an airborne forward observer before dark for the acting ground commander.

I huddled in the operations center with the battalion commander, who was grounded after his command helicopter was shot down. We listened to each update from Delta, and were shocked when the lieutenant on the ground released all fire support at midnight. Spry went ballistic. I used the opportunity to give him my assessment that the lieutenant was plainly too inexperienced for the situation. Spry already had a good picture of the tactical situation, but from the viewpoint of the operations center and the C and C helicopter. I tried to paint a clearer picture of the situation on the ground for him based on my personal experience.

"Sir, the company is disorganized," I began. "Platoons are separated, not linked for a solid defense. One man, a radio, and several weapons are still missing. The lieutenant doesn't know how to use fire support, so it may be just as well that he dismissed it. He might bring fires on top of the company. More likely, it'd be too far out to be effective.

"They brought in helicopters without security and endangered the crews. We need to get an experienced leader on the ground, before there's worse trouble."

Spry nodded. "I'll relieve the platoon leader, and Colonel Stevenson is sending someone from Brigade to command the company."

"Don't punish the lieutenant; he's at least trying. I think he's doing the best he can under the circumstances. You need someone to direct actions on the ground. The whole company needs that now—not later."

"Captain Turner will be here in a couple of days, as soon as he can turn over his other responsibilities."

I raised my voice in exasperation. "I'm sorry, but that won't cut it, sir! Those men deserve better. Their lives are at risk. Let me go and help now."

"No. Absolutely not! You'll stay here. I don't want to hear any more about it."

* * *

I felt that I had made my case convincingly, but Spry was adamant. A little after midnight I went to my culvert, cleaned my rifle by my dim airfield light, and packed my rucksack. My old instincts had returned; I could see the future, and it included my joining Delta the next morning. I knew that no matter how much Spry meant what he said, he would eventually relent. There simply were no other viable options. I intended to be prepared when he realized it was the right thing to do. I assumed he would discuss his options with the brigade commander first, but both were good soldiers, and neither would endanger the men in Delta needlessly. There had to be incredible moral pressure to locate the missing man. We just do not lose people, even dead soldiers. That was not negotiable.

* * *

I was in the operations center early next morning catching up on Delta's situation and waiting to hear from Spry. Nothing had changed in the field. Even though the battle had quieted down, the picture on the ground was still an ugly one. Faced with the prospects of having the company resume operations and search for the missing man, radio, and weapons, Spry had indeed considered my logical argument. He knew I was the most experienced company commander in the brigade, and the only qualified person available and ready to go immediately. Another life could be lost while we twiddled our thumbs. He had discussed it with Colonel Stevenson in light of the delay in getting Captain Turner ready to take command. But the short-range solution did not change the long-range plan.

Finally he approached me. "Do you really want to go?"

"Absolutely!" I replied with no hesitation as I stood up.

"When can you be ready?" he asked.

"I'm packed," I replied. "But if I have to rappel, I'll need to prepare my ropes. Ten minutes."

Spry looked startled. I guessed he expected to have a longer discussion, or thought maybe I would change my mind, letting him off the hook. Instead I had anticipated his question, and now he was faced with the decision, which he had expected to have more time to consider.

He quickly regained his composure. "I've discussed this with Colonel Stevenson," he told me, "and Captain Turner will assume command in a few days. So don't get comfortable out there. You'll get the company organized, find the missing man and equipment, and don't take any chances!"

I rose to leave. "I understand. Can I go?"

"Go ahead. Take the log bird. And give me a report as soon as you can."

"Roger that. And thank you, sir."

I headed for the log bird, which was idling on the pad. I had packed sparingly because I didn't expect to stay long, but I was surprised how heavy my equipment had become since I'd last carried it. It doesn't take long to lose jungle footing and strength. Despite the logic of the decision and my desire to go, I doubted I was physically ready. There was no time for lingering doubts, however; I was going, regardless.

*   *   *

Delta still had no landing zone, so the helicopter hovered over a ten-foot-wide clearing between fifty-foot trees. I would use ropes to rappel into the opening in the jungle. I dropped my heavy rucksack on the end of my rappel rope, but I didn't have a firm grip on the heavy bag and it slipped from my gloved hands and crashed to the jungle floor. Images flashed of the command sergeant major making the same entrance to Bravo on Operation Mercer. I knew how it had looked on the ground then, so I was determined avoid embarrassing myself further on rappel. I remembered how Labrozzi remained under control during his descent, with his head above his feet. I kept that image in mind, determined to do it like Labrozzi.

The crew chief tapped my shoulder. "Drop far enough that you don't hit your head on the skids," he advised.

I made it down safely and intact. I felt awkward, and I know it probably amused the people on the ground—or maybe not. The situation on the ground was not very funny.

I found a spot just outside the clearing and sat on my rucksack, which had a broken frame, while the acting commander briefed me on the situation. He really didn't know the situation as well as he should have, but instead of criticizing I got on the radio with each platoon, informed them I was in command, and found out what they could tell me. The company was split up; not only were the platoons separated, but troopers were separated from their rucksacks. One man was still missing, along with a radio, two rifles, and Skip's carbine. I got on the battalion net and informed Spry it would take all day just to clean up the confusion, and we would probably be ready to move the next day.

I spent the rest of the day doing just what I had told Spry I would do. We found the missing trooper, who had been killed, as we suspected, and located all the missing equipment. I managed to get the platoons tied together to form a single perimeter. Everyone got his own equipment back, and we conducted an inventory. We evacuated the dead trooper and all the excess equipment through the clearing in the jungle. Then I had the men clean their weapons in shifts.

Next morning was Tet, 1971. This was a momentous anniversary for me, but I kept those thoughts to myself, as I usually did. The morale of the company seemed to have improved already: military order was restored, and confidence had returned. I felt better and reported to Spry that our situation was stabilized. He told me that Captain Turner would be ready to assume command on February 2.

I led the company into the bunker complex where the battle had occurred to search it. We moved very cautiously because the complex was covered with unexploded cluster bombs from the air strikes. I didn't want casualties from our own munitions. Moving painstakingly into what had been termed in the press as "Bunker City," we found four dead NVA among strewn clothing, six rucksacks, two AK-47s, a B-40 rocket launcher, three B-40 rockets, eight Chinese grenades, a 25-pound Chinese antipersonnel mine, and a U.S. Claymore mine. I was surprised by the find; normally, the enemy took everything with them when they left. Delta Company had really surprised them—as much as it had surprised itself. This had been a desperate and unexpected fight for both sides. The Delta Demons had acquitted themselves well, individual troopers at the point of battle doing exactly what they know how to do, and with little direction.

After the search, the 2d Platoon established an ambush and killed three NVA out of four, capturing two more AK-47s and all four rucksacks. Despite the fiasco of a few days earlier, this was a good company. They had a long tradition of good commanders like Lee Hyslop and Skip Rozelle. The Delta Demons quickly accepted me and I enjoyed being with them. I only wished it could have been longer.

*   *   *

On February 2 Delta was extracted back to Green. In only a few days I had grown quite attached to the company, but Spry had forewarned me. It was very hard to relinquish control again, although I was never officially commander. However, Captain Turner was waiting for us at the fire base when we arrived. He made a crack about my trying to steal his company. He intended it as a joke, but it really pissed me off. I let it drop. I was leaving a company in combat for the third time, and it felt as bad this time as either time before. I was in no mood for jokes.

Meanwhile, battalion had opened a new FSB named Noble, in honor of the medical platoon leader killed at Camp Gorvad in the attack that killed Jimmy Mercer. The XO, Major Langbein, ran operations from Noble and I was responsible for security, operations, and intelligence at Green.

*   *   *

Mail. A notice arrived from the Department of the Army, informing me I would be going to Fort Hood, Texas, in June. Fort Hood was a large corps-level installation, but I knew that somehow I would get to the new 1st Cavalry Division when I arrived. It was being reorganized as a test triple-capability division, combining the air-mobility lessons of Vietnam with armor and mechanized infantry. I was excited.

I could not have known that when I did report to Fort Hood in August 1971, that Colonel Stevenson had already contacted Maj. Gen. James C. Smith, the commanding general of the new 1st Cavalry Division, easing the way for me.

February 3, 1971

Dearest Sandy,

These are just a few lines to let you know I love you more today than yesterday. Every day I miss you more and more. I received a nice three-page letter from you today. I think by now we must surely be parents, but I just haven't gotten word yet.

Love.

"South Vietnamese troops, supported by heavy U.S. airpower and artillery fire, cross into Laos for an extensive assault known as Operation Lam Son 719 on the Ho Chi Minh Trail."

—*The Vietnam War Day by Day*

39

News from Home

February 1971

I waited impatiently for official news to confirm what I already suspected. At 3:30 P.M., Colonel Stevenson arrived at Green with an American Red Cross representative. He gleefully informed me that I was the father of a nine-pound boy named Richard Scott Taylor. "Both Scott and his mother are doing fine." I was relieved to know that much.

Finally the momentous event was verified, but I was still unsure about all the ramifications. I didn't know much about being a quality father, or husband for that matter. I would learn on the run—like I had learned to command an air cavalry company in combat. The fact that I didn't understand everything did nothing to quash my unabashed delight. The first box of cigars was gone instantly as I joyfully handed them out to everyone I knew, whether they smoked or not. I ordered another box for Bravo Company.

I learned later that Sandy's mother had died at almost the same moment Scott was born, a stark reminder that the interval between crib and grave is brief and tenuous. I was very concerned about Sandy's state of mind and how she would cope with her mother's loss while caring for a new baby. I was powerless to do anything, isolated and out of touch as I was. Until then Vietnam had been reality, and home just a dream. Suddenly another world was thrust sharply back into focus, imposing a new reality. Meanwhile I was trapped in a continuous nightmare far from my dream.

*   *   *

I squandered a day at FSB Noble as a diversion from my altered focus. Noble sat atop a small mountain with a panoramic view of higher peaks to the north. However, the terrain consisted of heavy red clay, which turned to thick dust in the dry season until monsoon rains transformed it to sticky red paste. When the clay was wet, our boots adhered to terra firma and walking was difficult. I watched a soldier step off with a bare foot, leaving a boot stuck in the mud.

However, the clay was dry this month, and every thing or person was covered with red dust. It was difficult to discern features of people and equipment from the ground because all were the same red hue.

A mangy, crippled, ignoble old dog was one permanent inhabitant of Noble. The dog lapped up beer and stayed drunk all day because people were continually sharing. The mutt stumbled around looking for his next drink, or slept where he dropped.

Master Sergeant Kress handled intelligence functions at Noble, but when he and Major Langbein left for R&R, I returned as base commander. Approaching Noble by air, I spotted the base from miles away by a tall red dust cloud. Something had to be done about the dust after a helicopter nearly crashed and others refused to land due to safety concerns created by the dust. We spread a cover of oil on the ground to hold the dust down.

General Burton visited Noble with Colonel Stevenson. They graciously invited Spry and me to join them on a trip to Bravo Company, which had discovered a fortified enemy base camp. We were going to investigate. I found the hill forgettable but thoroughly enjoyed my reunion with old comrades in Bravo. I yearned for our lost purpose in Vietnam.

*   *   *

Heart-warming news arrived in the mailbag. A card from Sandy contained a poem about little boys, along with Scott's footprint in ink on a piece of paper. I was surprised and touched. Sandy was having trouble getting her military pay allotment for the two of them to live on. Because of the baby, I was given a high priority for a MARS call. As usual I could not get through via MARS, even with priority, so I made a commercial call instead. Sandy was upset about the pay, and I understood why: she now had serious additional expenses, as well as rent and other needs. I was puzzled how pay could stay snarled for months.

Sandy had also taken a roommate to help with the rent. That annoyed me, especially because I knew I was not adequately caring for my own family. Even though she was fine, except for the money, and Scott was growing. A strange sentiment emanated from her real-world troubles that reached me even in the combat zone; I felt her vulnerability and my powerlessness. I went to Bien Hoa and pleaded with a pay clerk to fix it for me. A copy of our marriage license and Scott's birth certificate, both colored by red clay stains, finally solved the problem.

*   *   *

By the middle of February, the battalion had closed Green and moved to an old fire base known as Aries, originally constructed by 1st of the 12th Cavalry. Changing bases is dangerous because troopers, communications, and firepower are split between two bases. This time we were stretched even thinner because Noble was still functioning. Now we had three bases to protect! One company worked on the new base and another was split between the other two. That left only two companies for patrols, with no emergency reserve.

*   *   *

On a lighter note, a CH-47 converted to a flying store—the flying PX—landed at Noble, and I went on a shopping spree. I bought a photo album to protect the photos Sandy sent. Red dust had covered my pictures, and they became moist in the humidity and stuck together. I was wearing out the pictures, looking at them so often. I loved them and hoped we could make a go of it when I got back to the States. I was uncertain; Sandy and I had been through tough times that year.

Scott had become ill and my mother was helping Sandy with him. My father wrote, "Scott looks like a general, but sounds like a drill sergeant!" I wanted to go home.

February 5, 1971

Darling Sandy,

I knew today was the day as soon as I woke up this morning. My sixth sense seldom fails me and all the other days were just waiting, but today I knew the news was coming.

I love you, Sandy, and thank you for the greatest gift of my whole life.

Always.

Dearest Sandy,

I think of a million things I want to tell you during the day, but when I sit down to write, it all seems to slip away. But I never forget how much I love you and need you.

— Richard

40

All or Nothing

February–March 1971

Life, love, and money can slip through your fingers without leaving any evidence that they'd previously existed.

In late February the 7th Cavalry CP moved to Aries from Green. In its first life, Aries had been made infamous by a CBS television special about pot smoking in Vietnam. Moving command and control is always risky because communications are tenuous at best. But old fire bases are never pleasant to reopen. When a unit leaves all its trash is buried in old bunkers and resurfaces during reconstruction. The only advantage to reopening an old base is that the clearing in the jungle already exists. Flying restrictions, due to a constrained budget to fight the war, limited our supply of building materials. Consequently we used chain saws to cut raw timber from the surrounding jungle to construct overhead protection.

I shared a sleeping bunker with Lt. Tommy Adams, the assistant S-3. He did most of the digging, while I manned the tactical operations center for both of us. One could say rank has its privileges, but Adams preferred to work outside. So did I.

Accidents continued to happen and were of great concern to all commanders: the accidents seemed especially tragic in the waning phase of the conflict. Since automatic ambushes had racked up a poor safety record, Spry instituted a policy that none could be established without first getting his permission. I don't think he intended to deny any, only to issue a safety reminder with each approval.

Daylight faded, bringing darkness earlier in the jungle than on the open fire base. The battalion commander was aboard the C-and C helicopter when it went to Bien Hoa for refueling. Aries was in its normal state of disorganization when the Alpha Company commander radioed, requesting to speak with Spry. As the senior officer on the fire base, I was summoned to the operations center from digging duty.

Alpha Six, this is Two," I answered his call.

"Two, this is Alpha Six. We're on a very hot trail and I want to set up an ambush before dark."

"Alpha Six, you know the policy. Wait till Big Six returns or is back in range of the radio."

"How long will that take?" He was clearly impatient.

"I don't know. They had to refuel at Bien Hoa; maybe another half-hour till they're back in range."

"That's too long. It's nearly dark now. Can't you approve it?"

I sensed his frustration. "Six hasn't delegated that authority."

"Look, this is important. This trail is hot and there aren't any good guys around here. What happens if I just do it?" We had reverted into our peer-to-peer relationship.

"I don't recommend it." I kept the mike open a moment while I thought. "But . . . in this case, Six would probably want me to approve it for him. Go ahead and set it up, but be careful. Our butts are in this together. I'll take responsibility for approval here, but you're still responsible for safety!"

"Roger. I owe you one. Out."

Alpha's string of recent accidents had triggered the new approval policy. I felt justified in approving it, but I was uncomfortable with the company's safety record. Nevertheless I made the decision, true to my man-on-the-ground principle. I logged my approval into the operations journal and worked on another intelligence assessment Spry had requested, leaving the digging to Adams. When Spry returned after dark I briefed him on the special report he had assigned, but I forgot about the ambush.

I was awake early next morning, when Alpha Company reported that the 3d Platoon's ambush had been sprung. A patrol searched the site. I was apprehensive, remembering that I'd logged the incident into the journal but had not briefed Spry. When I told him, he was unconcerned and agreed with my decision. The ends justified the means, and in this case more than usual. Alpha reported killing five NVA and capturing packs and weapons. We quickly dispatched a chopper to recover the booty.

Dearest Dick,

I thought I'd better write while Scottie is sleeping. He awoke last night at 3:30 and threw up all over the place, so he is back on the hypoallergenic milk. It costs twice as much as the other, but if that's what it takes to keep him well, it's worth it.

The phone bill came in today—$68.00—your call was $48.00 plus tax. I didn't think we talked that long. If you should call again we'll have to time it—that is really high, although I loved every minute of it.

Love.

*   *   *

As soon as the chopper arrived at Aries, I directed that everything be brought to the briefing tent; I had a table and chairs set up to search the packs for any useful intelligence. I examined the rifles first, four AK-47s and an M1 carbine, but they were standard with nothing remarkable except damage from the ambush. All the rifles were still loaded, so I cleared them myself, remembering another intelligence officer who had carelessly shot me with a captured AK-47.

I eagerly turned my attention to the packs. They were tan canvas bags and smelled strongly of sweat, dried blood, and fish oil. The packs were the grungiest I had ever seen, and I didn't relish rummaging through them. It was apparent the Alpha troopers had not bothered with them, either.

I methodically emptied the contents, piece by piece, looking for documents. Food and ammunition were on top; dirty, sweaty clothes were next, along with a few letters and documents. I examined each item, spreading the contents on the folding table as I went. Near the bottom of the last pack I found three mysterious bundles. Each was about the size of a brick, two the same size and one slightly smaller than the others. All three were wrapped tightly in brown paper, taped shut, and tied with string. Each bore Vietnamese inscriptions on the corners. I was unable to read them but I knew I was holding something important and I was curious what it was.

My excitement rose as I saved the special packages for last. I studied them carefully, since I didn't want to damage the inscriptions when I opened them. My curiosity peaked as I hesitated, taking a big breath before unlocking the mystery.

I examined the exterior of the packages a final time. I concentrated first on the smaller of the bundles, finding a corner and carefully tearing the end away. My hand trembled, but when I saw inside the tear I sat the package down like a hot potato. I breathed heavily as I stared at a green "50" in disbelief. It was something familiar. I was seeing, but not believing, a U.S. S50 bill. It was a stack of $50 bills as large as a brick, a thousand of them.

Never had I held so much money in my hands. There I was, alone in a tent in a jungle with $50,000 in cash in my hands. No living person knew I had it. The NVA couriers were dead. The company that had recovered the money had failed to search the packs. No one was in the tent nor had there been any curiosity about what was in the packs. With my heart pounding, I tore a corner of one of the larger packages to reveal Vietnamese currency in large denominations, totaling 500,000 paper piasters and one 50-piaster coin in each bundle. It totaled over a million piasters, worth about $40,000, and $50,000 in cash: $90,000. With shaking hands, I stuffed the three bundles back into the pack and out of sight.

I paced in circles around the tent for several minutes, trying to grasp the magnitude of the situation. I jammed my hands in my pockets to keep them from shaking, breathed deeply and wrestled with my conscience over what to do. I wondered whether I could keep the money and somehow get it out of Vietnam. But would I? Could I really do it? It was not mine, but it was no one else's, either! Sandy needed money then—but it still wasn't mine to keep. On the other hand, it was the spoils of war.

I continued to pace, mentally going back and forth. I slowly regained control of my breathing, and my heart rate slowed. I casually walked to the sides of the tent and lowered the flaps, leaving only the door open. I hesitated in the door a moment, and then called for Colonel Spry. Several people ran to investigate, but I waved them away—I wanted to see only the battalion commander.

As Spry approached the tent, he wore an expression that indicated he knew I had found something important. An inquisitive smile tickled his lips when he asked what I had found. I reached into one pack and removed the package of U.S. currency. I showed him the exposed corner. His smile vanished; he turned pale and said only, "Don't let anyone in here!" He rushed to the operations center to call Brigade. I assumed a guard position next to the packs, just inside the door, using a reloaded AK-47 to keep onlookers away. And I did have curious visitors. The smell of money was in the air!

A Huey landed at Aries in under an hour, spilling out the task force commander, the brigade commander, the task force finance officer, and a special security detail. Soon I watched the entourage fly off with "my" money. It was gone. Oh, how I could have used it! Sandy needed it, too. That money would have changed our lives.

Dearest Sandy,

My mom informed me that your mother died in the same hour that Scott was born. I'm so very sorry, Darling, and I really worry about you now. We have to take life and death together, because both are an integral part of each piece of humanity. It is sadly ironic that something as beautiful as birth obligates you to death.

Always.

Dearest Sandy,

"The only thing that keeps my morale high now is that R&R is only thirty-six days away. I miss you terribly, and long to hold you and talk to you for hours and hours."

— Richard

"The problem, of course, is that there is no one TRUTH about the Indochina Wars. Instead, many different truths co-exist and compete. To be sure, there are facts, a myriad of them—the tonnage of bombs dropped by the U.S. during the war, for example. But facts, while useful and necessary, do not lead to understanding . . . past events and actions become part of the historical sense of self and society. . . . The sense of self connected with these wars is still very much a contested issue. . ."

— John Tegtmeier, Vietnam War Internet Project[1]

41

Which Way Home?

March 1971

Fragments of my life were scattered on both sides of the world. Time had come to pull them back together again. Finally our long-awaited reunion was due—past due. After ten long months I would finally be joined with Sandy in Hawaii. I anticipated our reunion with tremendous excitement and some apprehension.

Fears swept over me.

What would I see in her eyes after all this time?

Would we still have something in common, or had either of us changed so much under these circumstances that we could no longer make it work?

Dearest Dick,

I love you.

I am so excited about R&R, that I can hardly contain myself. But what really made my day was the mail.

You make me so happy with your sweet letters and they make me even more anxious to be with you again. I just can't settle down and write the sort of letter I wanted to. Just know how happy I am thinking about being with you so soon.

Always.

* * *

Sandy and I met alone in Hawaii. Scotty was too young to make the trip, and we had important issues between us to deal with. When I arrived in Honolulu my knees were shaking and my heart was in my throat. I was a warrior returning to claim my woman, yet I was as nervous as I had ever been. I half-expected Sandy to still have the look of an expectant mother, but the person I saw standing before me was a beautiful young woman so in control of herself in a Pacific island paradise. Was this the fictional woman I had been writing love letters to and dreaming of? Did I deserve her? I knew I might lose her.

Sandy looked great. I was a mess on the inside, and later would learn that she was, too. Looking at her, I couldn't imagine that she possibly shared my doubts.

It was a stretch for me—from an Asian jungle to the beaches of Maui. We were strangers. (Everyone was a stranger to me.) I nurtured great expectations about "the real world," but I was no longer sure there was such a place. I reassured myself that once the war was behind us and I had settled down with my family, everything would be fine. But would it?

I had glorified Honolulu to Sandy when I was stranded there en route to Vietnam. I dramatized the convertible and the beauty of Oahu. I rented another convertible for our special dinner on our first evening. Rain pelted us as we left the hotel garage for the restaurant to hear Don Ho, but we were oblivious to it, anticipating our special evening. When we stopped at a red light, I noticed the canvas top of the convertible sagging under the weight of collecting rainwater. I reached up to push the water off, as I had done so many times in my poncho shelter in Vietnam. This time a gallon of water poured between the cloth top and the front windshield—directly into our laps. We sputtered and shuddered as cold water drenched us. Alas, we were forced to return to the hotel room to change clothes.

We started out again, in our second-best clothes, in a dour mood. Dressing well was a big deal to Sandy; it was no laughing matter. Our wonderful evening—the launch pad for our future—was under water.

The undertow got worse. We arrived at the restaurant late. The window seat with an ocean view that I had reserved was no longer available; we had to settle for another table behind a post, near the door. Nevertheless we ordered and pretended to be in high spirits. Don Ho asked for people celebrating anniversaries, birthdays, or other important events to identify themselves for recognition with a special song. I clammed up, withdrew into my shell, and sat stoically and silently, wishing I was back in the jungle. Sandy was properly devastated. I was irritated with myself and upset at Sandy for being mad at me. Our evening in paradise had turned into a disaster.

Unfortunately this was typical of our entire week in Hawaii. The time we had anticipated so breathlessly became worse than no time at all. How could everything so important to both of us go so wrong at the very moment we needed something to go right? I had believed Vietnam was a living hell, but I was wrong. Hawaii was hell: Vietnam was only purgatory.

Sandy and I spent our time together in Hawaii on different wavelengths. We spoke strange languages; we were from different planets. I realized for the first time that I had changed in ways I didn't realize or understand. I'd expected the world and everything in it to change with me, but it had not.

Her hopes and dreams for our reunion were shattered. She had struggled alone in her private world and had prepared herself to play all her chips to win this one roll of the dice. She suffered nightmares about her mother's untimely death and sometimes became violently ill. Money had been a problem for her and Scott, yet she made it all work because she had no choice. But I remained aloof, as if she wasn't the most important part of my life.

She was hurt, and her doubts about our ability or willingness to save our future were reaffirmed. I was unable to address her needs and unable to understand my own insecurity with a loving relationship. I was lost in the wilderness without a compass.

She, too, had blunted her senses to summon strength for all the things she thought she had to do. Our week of R&R ended with neither Sandy nor I able to comfort one another or confront the real issues. We were discomfited by our reunion, assaulted by doubt, living casualties of war.

> The spring season for rallies and demonstrations broke out in mid-April with the war in Vietnam as an old target and pollution of the earth as a new one.[2]

* * *

At the airport, I saw Sandy standing in a sundress on the observation deck after I boarded the plane. I took a window seat, and could see her just standing there. I couldn't take my eyes off her. She was so beautiful, slender, and tanned, while I was so disturbed, churning. I was uncertain what was going through her mind, and I could not make a connection with the scattered fragments of my own life.

March 30, 1971

Darling Sandra,

> I'm somewhere over the Pacific between Guam and the Philippines. I've finished reading my book and the diversion helped displace my anxiety of leaving you in Hawaii. I saw you standing on the observation deck after I boarded and I couldn't take my eyes off you. I couldn't see your face but I'm sure you weren't crying—you have been such a brave and wonderful wife for such a soldier as me. I wonder what a fool I am that I haven't seen my precious son and I've found only one fleeting week with my wife—only three weeks together and about forty separated. I too, like you, was afraid I had forgotten you after all that time, but the one small moment of time we shared in Hawaii sent the realization crashing down on me that I love you more than anything on this earth. I have never in my life felt so totally committed to anything as I do to our family. I know you have the same desire for these things that I have and this whole year you have born the entire burden, all alone. It is more than any one should have to stand in a lifetime. . . .

Republic of Vietnam

"To see you standing there, alone, waiting for your husband to rush off to his phony little war, with questions in my own mind: Is it all for myself? The Army? Or the United States? And will it do anyone any good?

To see you standing there, alone, just as you've been alone for nine months already, and bearing your burden so resolutely, I begin to wonder which of us is the real soldier. I have never in my life, or could I ever again, feel for anyone what I feel for you. . . .

I'm afraid to take out the photographs and look at them because my loneliness is bad enough already."

— Richard

42

Fragments

March–May, 1971

I was disoriented when I returned to Vietnam, pretending like everyone who returned from R & R that the break had been wonderful. In reality, I was stunned by a realization that the war had taken its toll on lives in ways other than death and destruction.

Tony Labrozzi, who shared my warrior spirit, appeared out of nowhere to rescue me from my morose mood again. I never knew what prompted his visit that day—he and Spry were barely on speaking terms—but it was as if

Gabriel had sent him to firm up my crumbling foundation. Mad Anthony arrived in a helicopter and suggested we take it for a reconnaissance flight. We relived former times even though few words passed between us. We reenacted a reality that he and I had shared before; the pilots and door gunners were only supporting cast in this scene.

Labrozzi instructed the crew to take the chopper high for a better view of the horizon. Once we were up he spotted garden plots carved out of the jungle. He spoke into the intercom to the pilots: "Make a low pass over those gardens for a closer look."

We made a low and slow approach, buzzing the ground as if daring someone to take a shot. I wished, as I am sure he did, that someone would test us—but no one dared. Here we clearly saw crops waiting to be harvested to feed a Viet Cong army. After the third low-level pass without a shot, we regained altitude. Tony reached under his seat and pulled out a box of white-phosphorous grenades.

White phosphorous explodes and burns for a long time in a white-hot fire. It burns green crops, and if even a sliver touches human skin it must be cut out or it will literally burn for hours. A white-phosphorous grenade exploding inside a helicopter would ignite fuel to create an inferno and turn the helicopter into ash before it hit the ground.

Tony calmly pulled the pins out of five grenades, one at a time, and handed each one to me. I pressed each grenade against my chest to keep the handles attached. Once the pin is pulled and the handle flies off, the grenade is activated to explode in five seconds. After handing me five, he removed the pins of six for himself. My adrenaline pumped while I wondered whether he had a death wish. I thought the two of us might be better off as ashes in Vietnam than as misfit soldiers in a tame world.

"Okay, go back to altitude," Tony instructed the pilot. "When I give you the word, dive over the center of the garden, with guns blazing to cover us. We'll drop the Whiskey Papas."

We had done this before: this was how he cultivated his persona of Mad Anthony. I respected who he was, and he thrived on it—he could not live without action and danger.

We dropped quickly and began a high-speed pass over the gardens with doors wide open. While the door gunners fired their machine guns from each side, Tony and I hung out the doors and released the grenades one at a time. The chopper gained altitude so we could watch the emerald-green field turn to a white sea of smoke. All my cares were washed away.

Seeing Labrozzi again and taking that high-speed, high-risk mission of zero consequence just for the hell of it was exactly what I needed to clear my mind. Thank you, Gabriel, for sending the Mad Italian!

* * *

Army First Lt. William L. Calley, Jr. was sentenced to life imprisonment for premeditated murder of at least 22 South Vietnamese men, women and children at My Lai three years ago.[1]

* * *

Drudgery quickly replaced the excitement of seeing Tony Labrozzi again. Dirt, heat, and a hole in the ground were a long way from Hawaii. Enemy sappers had been testing base defenses around Vietnam, breaching perimeter wire and attacking from inside. The brigade commander personally checked defenses. I had staff responsibility for security, and had noticed inconsistencies between company procedures at different times. My analysis of the variations led me to some conclusions: nighttime inspections revealed that alertness was highest on the first night that troopers were on the base. On subsequent nights, they gradually relaxed until they sensed how insecure they were. After that security improved until the final night before returning to the jungle. But the last night on the fire base turned into a party night, and then security was worst of all.

The normal cycles of insecurity were exacerbated by the cycles of darkness. The moon provided the only light on the fire base at night. As light increased, security increased, and as light decreased, security dropped—just the opposite of how we wanted it. I reluctantly briefed Spry on my findings, and we changed our security planning. I think that was when Spry decided that I really had the potential to be an adequate intelligence officer, even by his high standards.

* * *

One night, at the evening briefing, Spry expressed annoyance that our contacts with the enemy were too infrequent.

"Staff, we have three companies in the field, with four platoons each. If we exclude one platoon as reaction force . . . that leaves three platoons per company. Each has four squads. That adds up to thirty-six possible ambushes each night. Is that correct?"

"Yes sir," replied the S-3. "They set up ambushes every night, but with poor results."

"I don't think we're putting them in the right places," replied Spry.

Robbie explained, "We assign the company an area and they select the best locations based on what they find on the ground."

Spry turned to me. "What do you think, S-2?"

"I agree with Robbie, sir. I believe the man on the ground can best make those decisions." I reinforced my "man-on-the-ground" principle.

"Bullshit!" he retorted. "You sell yourself short. You have better information than they do. They've done their own thing for weeks with poor results. We won't do that anymore! S-2, you personally select the fifty most likely ambush sites by tomorrow morning. S-3, you select thirty-six of those fifty, and assign them to the companies. By tomorrow night I want those ambush sites manned."

"Sir, I don't think that's the best way. May I suggest another way?" I beseeched.

"No! I gave an order, and that's it. If you can't find the ambush sites, S-2, see me and I'll help you." The meeting ended abruptly.

It was an all-nighter. Sergeant Kress and I poured over records of every enemy contact in the area of operations from the journals of the 12th Cavalry and our own for two years. We plotted every contact or sighting on a map using acetate overlays and grease pencils. When the sun broke in the morning, we had established fifty hot spots from historical evidence. I gave the list to the S-3. Robbie divided it into sections and assigned them to the companies.

Following a day of protests and grumbling, by dark thirty-six of the ambush sites were manned. By next morning seventeen ambushes had been activated. Everyone was amazed, especially me. Spry was smug. His smile proclaimed that he was the master and we were apprentices. He had made me do my own thinking, and I was amazed by the results. Spry graciously gave me credit—another prime lesson in leadership.

* * *

Fire Base Charles was a new base, designed in a new way. U.S. fire bases were usually round; French firebases had been triangular. Spry asked me why the difference. I had absolutely no idea and couldn't have cared less. He asked for my reasoned response in a couple of days.

I gave the geometry quiz some thought and concluded that the French made their bases triangular because they were designed with security in mind. The points of the triangle were strongpoints that provided grazing fire along the sides without being exposed. Each point of the triangle provided security for the other two points. On the other hand, U.S. bases were built to optimize logistics: they accommodated military supplies, weapons, people, and equipment, plus helicopters flying in and out. The round shape gave the most area inside the base, but offered the least security. Security was enhanced by additional artillery and air support. I was satisfied with my answer.

Surprisingly Spry accepted my conclusions immediately. Then he asked, "What's the ideal shape?" After two more days of pondering and drawing, I decided a pentagon offered increased security with its five points, and sufficient area for our logistics. Surprising me again, Spry accepted my proposal and directed Charles to be built in a pentagonal shape. Good idea? I didn't know. But I was puzzled that my analyses were accepted without question. Maybe I was getting too good at this job—or worse, maybe I was not so good, but he thought I was!

Just as pentagonal Charles neared completion, orders were changed to occupy Mace instead. Mace was a former brigade headquarters near Xuan Loc. All the work at Charles was for nothing, except as an experiment in fire-base architecture. Fortunately Mace was fully developed, having been a former brigade headquarters.

*　*　*

As of April 29 the 1st Cavalry Division was no longer officially in Vietnam. The 3d Brigade (Separate) stayed to control the remaining forces, all of them. The pace was invigorating, and the tempo of operations significantly increased. Yet I believed the Viet Cong were filling the vacuum left by departing Americans.

On April 14, the battalion had had a pitched battle with North Vietnamese forces near Xuan Loc for over three hours. The commander of Charlie Company was wounded, and I made my best case to replace him, but I was again denied. Instead, I was called to the morgue at the 15th Medical Battalion to identify a Bravo Company trooper killed in another action. I had seen death and I thought this would just be another unpleasant episode. It was worse.

I was unprepared for what I found. I was accustomed to soldiers dying on the field of battle. Bloody uniforms, strewn weapons, shot-up equipment, and loose boots with feet still inside were part of the landscape. Battle was an honorable death for a warrior—a crusader lying on his shield. That was what I expected to find, but it was not what I encountered.

First I was escorted into a walk-in refrigerator. Then, instead of a warrior in battle dress, I found a young American boy, completely naked, mouth and eyes open, lying awkwardly on a freezer floor. I had believed I was callused about death, but I felt the ground move under my feet. Where in hell was I? This was no place I had been before. I could not accept it my mind would not fathom it.

I averted my eyes toward the doctor.

"I don't know this boy," I muttered.

"Are you sure?" he pressed. "Think back. He would have been in uniform and looked different," the doctor implored, trying to complete his paperwork.

"I'm sorry, I just don't know him. I don't know anybody. I don't know myself anymore." I left.

* * *

Another battalion had had a significant engagement with an NVA intelligence unit and captured a large number of documents. Every day, Spry requested the brigade intelligence summary for information gleaned from the documents. Nothing appeared. The next time the assistant brigade commander was at Mace for a briefing, Spry asked him about the assessment of the documents.

"We heard about the documents captured a couple of weeks ago. What did you learn from them?"

"Our analysts went over them and can't make any sense of them," he replied.

"I can't believe that!" Spry shot back. "Those are obviously important papers. If you can't interpret them, Taylor and I will do your job for you."

The colonel jumped to his feet. "If you're so damn smart, I'll send them out here. If you can't figure them out, you owe me a bottle of Jack."

"Quit drinking. You'll never get it from us."

I had never heard an exchange between colonels like that before. Furthermore, I was not sure I appreciated being included in the challenge. I had had no intelligence training except under Spry.

Nevertheless, a large pouch marked "Top Secret" arrived from brigade, and I had to sign for it. I wasn't very happy about signing my name to the control sheet. Spry said sarcastically, "Don't worry about it. The enemy already knows what's in it. Our people don't have a clue. That isn't intelligence—it's stupidity!"

Master Sergeant Kress and I spent a couple of days studying the translated documents. We made little headway, and I wondered how much a bottle of Jack Daniels cost. Spry pestered me for progress reports until I informed him it was an interesting system of checkpoints but that we were unable to break the code and connect them to map coordinates.

The next morning Spry came to me. "Take my helicopter and go to Long Binh. Do two things and don't come back till you accomplish them. First, go to the main exchange and get a set of india ink pens so that I can color maps. Second, go to the U.S. Army–Vietnam map depot and requisition a complete set of 1940-through-1950 French maps of our entire area of operations."

I thought Spry was crazier than Mad Anthony, but I spent the entire day at Long Binh doing exactly as he asked. When I returned that evening, Sergeant Kress and I spent another night assembling the brown French maps. All the next day and well into the evening, Spry helped us plot checkpoints on the French maps. Surprisingly everything fell into place. Kress and I spent another day creating a grid system to transfer the checkpoints from the French maps to the U.S. maps.

Now our companies could find the checkpoints on the ground. At each one we discovered that the checkpoints on the 1950 French maps were villages, cemeteries, or other structures that no longer existed and did not appear on our newer maps.

Spry was ecstatic. As we connected the dots, Spry shouted, "You've unlocked the entire communications-liaison routes from the Cambodian border into the heart of Vietnam." And he was right about every thing except one: he had visualized it. I was only an instrument in his great discovery.

The next time the assistant brigade commander came to Mace, Spry directed me to brief him on our findings. At the conclusion Spry turned to him and said, "We handed you the entire enemy communications-liaison routes from the Ho Chi Minh Trail through War Zone D. You should have handed it to us. If you'll send your intelligence analysts out here, we'll train them to do their jobs. Send the Jack Daniels to Taylor."

I never got it.

Needless to say, there was bad blood between Spry and the burly full colonel. Later he returned for another briefing. I was well into my presentation when the sounds of the colonel snoring had everyone looking in his direction. I stopped talking, unsure what to do next. Spry stood up quietly, took my long wooden pointer from me and stood in front of the full colonel. He waited a moment, with the pointer raised over his head. Then he suddenly slammed it on the wooden desk directly in front of the sleeping officer. The bird colonel almost flew the coop; he jumped straight up into the air. The two stormed out the door yelling at each other, and I thought there would be blows between them. A few minutes later Spry walked back into the briefing room, smiling from ear to ear.

"I'll bet that son-of-a-bitch never sleeps in here again."

*   *   *

I was just telling Lt. Adams that I went to Hawaii and fell in love with my wife all over again. I feel like a high school kid. I haven't stopped thinking about you for one minute since I've been back. I am twice as impatient to have this tour over now as ever before. Please think of me and write every day, as time will pass just a little faster. I must close now. Even though there isn't anything really to do, the longer I write the lonelier I become. I love you.

*   *   *

April 10, 1971

Another day without mail and frankly I'm beginning to worry. Today, most of our mail came, which had been delayed because of this operation, and everyone seemed to get a stack of letters except me. I'm worried about something being wrong because I haven't gone even two days without hearing from you for months, and now I've only received one letter since R&R.

If you are angry for something, please don't be. I love you more than anything in the world. I'm going to stay up again tonight and attempt to make a MARS call. With today ending I have only 80 more days left and that is another 10-day milestone.

I'm so sleepy I can hardly keep my eyes open. I'll close for now and hope to hear from you by tomorrow.

"The *New York Times* begins the three-day publication of leaked portions of the 47-volume Pentagon analysis of how the U.S. commitment in Indochina grew over a period of three decades. The Pentagon Papers disclose closely guarded communiqués, recommendations and decisions on the U.S. military role in Vietnam during the Kennedy and Johnson Administrations, along with the diplomatic phase in the Eisenhower years."

—*The Vietnam War Day by Day*

43

Saint Christopher

Late June 1971

The war was over, for me at least, and in any other measurable and meaningful way it was finished.

June 26, 1971, was my last day at Mace. In a few hours, I would depart for Bien Hoa to catch a freedom bird to the real world, if it really existed. I could hardly wait to go, and my thoughts were concentrated on a life with my new family. Sandy was always in my thoughts now. I began to measure myself by the yardstick of my future as a husband and father. I remembered how disappointing our R&R in Hawaii had been, and I was afraid that I would make the same mistakes again. I hoped not.

My experiences in Vietnam had marked me in ways that could never be changed. I carried with me experiences that shaped my behavior and my view of the world. I had met people whom I admired considerably. I had seen Americans and South Vietnamese die for causes that neither country was fully committed to. I had experienced courage, fear, pain, hunger, hate, and love. I would always have those by my side, along with fellow prodigals who shared them.

Abruptly, I found myself standing in the mess hall with Lieutenant Colonel Spry beside me. I heard him speaking, but I really wasn't listening; my thoughts were elsewhere. Then it hit me that I was actually leaving, and I found that my eyes were misty. I was, surprisingly, pulled between my strong desire to go home and a reluctance to leave the family I had bonded with in the cavalry. Spry placed a prized cavalry bugle in my hands, I muttered a few forgettable words, and I was on my way to Bien Hoa before I absorbed what had happened.

Dearest Sandy,

My fondest dream is to have you meet me at the airport in Columbus so we can begin exactly where we left off one year ago. A lot of things have changed and we have missed a lot during this year. However, I think when we meet at the airport this time we'll be a lot closer to each other than at the same spot a year ago. You know our marriage has had every opportunity to fail, but because we both wanted it, we held it together. I love you and I'll see you soon.

* * *

The corrugated tin roof radiated heat downward like a convection oven into the passenger terminal at Ben Hoa Air Base. Heat transformed oppressive humidity into steam off my khaki uniform shirt. It smelled musty from storage in a damp metal container for twelve months, waiting for its owner to recover it—if he left Vietnam alive. How many times had survival assistance officers shipped the uniform and other possessions to the next of kin? In my case, I wore my uniform. Amazed to actually be alive at my own departure, I was happy to have made it this far.

A line of uniformed young men, lost in their own feelings and thoughts, meandered ahead of me. I believed that, like me, they contemplated their futures. For some that meant leaving the army and finding a civilian job, for others it meant being reunited with a girlfriend or wife, and for some it foretold only uncertainty or unhappiness. As for the future, none—not a single one—would return to the same world had left only a year before.

Our world had changed during that year. It changed in the hometown drugstore; it changed in the houses where we grew up. Ball fields, streets, and pool halls had all changed, as had the people who frequented them. Our friends and neighbors were changed: those fine people would never see us in the same way again. But the most profound changes were in ourselves. We were afflicted by our experiences, some more, some less, some just differently; some would recover and adjust completely, others would not. Hardly any of us knew he was different, but would soon encounter the inevitable truth.

For me the minutes clung like the sweaty shirt to my back. Time would allow me to cross the tarmac and climb the long ladder of the Flying Tiger 727. Once on board the freedom express, nothing in the world would stop me from leaving an insane place and winging to a better one. The only thing between freedom and me now was a dwindling line of soldiers—and a lone military policeman.

I finally reached the head of the line. There I stood, a captain, veteran of two years in combat in the only war we had. A warrior, resplendent in a uniform distinguished by two and a half rows of ribbons, stood where a youth once stood.

The MP stopped me. "Sir, I'll need to see your orders, ticket, and identification."

"Here you go, Sergeant." I offered the documents to him. I had observed those ahead of me in line and was prepared in advance.

"Thank you, sir. I need to inspect your carry-on bag."

I sat the bag on the metal table and unzipped it for the customs inspection. I knew I had no drugs or war trophies, so it was no big deal.

I was startled by his next words. "You can't take this with you, sir," the MP said, pointing to the green ledger in my bag.

I stared incredulously at the book. Routinely, for the past year—in rain, heat, and darkness—I had hidden under my hot poncho, smelling my own unwashed armpits, using a flashlight to write letters home, and then entered our military activities and my personal thoughts into my journal. The letters were mailed every week, but my journal stayed with me, wrapped in a plastic bag and carried around Vietnam on my back. The journal had aided in tracking our daily activities, planning future operations, and recording experiences and lessons learned. I poured thoughts into my journal that I could never send home. Deep feelings, which were mine and mine alone, resided there. My journal was the bridge between the past incredible year and the future. Without my journal the past would be lost in shifting sands of time and a fading memory.

I panicked. I could not part with my own history. I would rather give up a limb than my journal. The journal represented an irreplaceable part of me. I could substitute a leg or an arm with a prosthetic, but I could never replace my own history.

I protested. "Sergeant, this is a personal diary which has no military value. I won't leave it. I'm taking it with me for my personal records."

The MP represented a serious obstacle to freedom. "I don't care what it is, sir. It's written on a government ledger. You can't take government property. Drop it into the 'no-questions-asked box,' or I'll detain you for an investigation. You can't leave until it's completed. The choice is yours, but decide now, because the airplane is loading!"

Why hadn't I just mailed it home? Why hadn't I written on notebook paper? Why had my government, for which I had willingly placed my life on the line, decided I was a criminal for stealing blank paper worth $2 in the supply store? Didn't he know I had turned in $90,000 I could have kept? Why couldn't I just go to San Francisco to be spit on by hippies? Why was my beloved army persecuting me? Why all of it? Why now?

I felt sick at my stomach. My knees were weak and my hand trembled. An entire year flashed before my eyes. Not only the last year, recorded in a green ledger, my personal history was at stake. What was a future without a past?

The son I had never seen waited to get his life under way with a real dad. My wife held her breath for my return. My parents prayed for my safety every day. And new challenges waited for me at Fort Hood. Why this dilemma? Why now?

At the moment of decision I caved in. I surrendered to the arbitrary forces of bureaucracy. Dropping my precious journal into the box, I recovered my orders, tickets, and identification card, glared at the robot military policeman, and trudged across the hot tarmac to my freedom flight. I wanted desperately to turn around, attack the MP, and recover my notes.

I remember little of the flight home—but I'll never forget the fury I felt at myself for capitulating. I had never surrendered to any challenge in two years in Vietnam, yet I felt my final act there had been ignoble. I had witnessed incredible sacrifices by good people, and I had given up their stories without a fight. I had let them and myself down. We were cheated—the final insult of an ungrateful nation.

*   *   *

In San Francisco I eventually encountered hippies who spat on my uniform. Far worse were the looks from white men in business suits: their scorn for a returning warrior.

*   *   *

We flew through heavy fog to the airport in Columbus, Georgia, forcing the pilot to make two passes. On the second approach, he powered through the fog and the ground appeared just before the landing gear touched the wet runway. I had not known what time I would arrive in Columbus until I made the connection in Atlanta: I called Sandy from the Atlanta airport and rushed to my flight. The flight to Columbus was only forty-five minutes, so she was not there when I arrived. As I waited in front of the terminal I reached inside my shirt and found my dog tags—and the tangled Saint Christopher medal—realizing the blessing of Saint Christopher had brought me back safely. I thanked God and peered into the street until I saw an old Chevy approaching. Greeting me was my beautiful wife in a sundress that clung in the heat, and in her arms was the son I had never seen. It was my future—a sight I will never forget.

My life was changed forever by Vietnam, and my only hope was that my family would become my anchor in the storms tormenting me. Sandy would have to forgive my many faults. The army had been a wonderful life, and I intended to blend a military career with my family's life for the next quarter-century. I didn't know whether that was possible, but it was my hope.

*   *   *

I forgot the journal for a long time, blocking it out of my mind along with everything else that had accompanied those years. Once, though, I was cleaning out a footlocker in a crowded basement, preparing for yet another move, and found a shoebox. I expected to find canceled checks when I opened the box, but instead, discovered a stack of letters. My first thought was that my wife had a lover and that she was saving his letters. I was right. My hands trembled as I examined the envelope containing one letter. It slowly registered that this was a letter in my own hand, written to Sandy from Vietnam. All of them were in the box. I didn't know she had saved them. Ghosts from the past assembled around me.

As I read my own words from long ago, I remembered the journal. Then I cried for a long time. I live with the pain, and I will never give it up. Pains, like scars, are our history.

So this is where it ends. This is the last real chapter, but it is also the beginning of the real story. To reassemble it all I worked backward through the letters, recapturing my journal through the words written home each night in the rain. Then I used the pictures from my first year, annotated and saved for me by my parents. Armed with those little jewels I was able to resurrect the first year.

Once the journals were composed, they were tucked away to gather dust. Attempts to type and edit them were too personal and painful. Each effort ended in failure; I invariably stopped typing with one page written and a bottle of Scotch emptied. The story finally unfolded, like dark figures emerging from a dense fog, hardly visible, yet fully recognizable, images in letters and pictures, names on the Vietnam Memorial Wall—bastard stepchildren who appeared unwanted and unloved before now greeted me like prodigal sons.

Here patriots live, who for their country's good,
In fighting fields were prodigal of blood.

—Virgil

44

Postmortem

Two sons were given their inheritance; one stayed home and invested wisely, the other went away and wasted what he was given in foreign lands. But upon returning to his father's home he was welcomed back, forgiven all transgressions, and appointed to a place of glory. What if the father had not welcomed his son's return? Such are the prodigal sons of Vietnam, who as patriots, wasted their blood and returned home. I welcome those who return in my dreams. I wish our nation had done so well.

I attended my first Vietnam Veterans of America meeting more than thirty years after getting off the airplane in Columbus. When an overweight and aging vet with a ponytail shook my hand and said, "Welcome home, brother," I knew for the first time I was really, finally, home.

I have tried to write this story before, each time quitting after the first few pages. When I started this time, I discovered the most important element was not the chronology I had documented so well, but the feelings and thoughts that rested under the surface. When those feelings were exposed, the memories of a time some would say "are best forgotten" spread before me in a mosaic.

I set about reconstructing the journals, using the letters and pictures as crutches. Once the journals were rewritten, they were stowed away—too tender to touch.

When I went to Vietnam the first time, I was eager to test my manhood. I genuinely wanted to experience the feelings and emotions encountered in war, and I wanted the opportunity to test my mettle against the highest challenge man or nature presented. By my second tour, I was anxious to prove myself as a professional soldier because that was the path I had chosen.

This is a story of a journey through life, a war story, but it is also a love story. It involves thoughts and emotions of a simple soldier and those close to him. The minute experiences and personal struggles are contrasted against world events.

My purpose in writing this was as an exploration of thoughts, feelings, and actions of a young man traveling in unknown territory, chronicling actions and emotions. It is a story of a divided life, half professional and half personal. And it exposes lives divided by the war—just as the nation was divided.

So many are due credit for the contents of this book that it is difficult to know where to begin, and it is impossible to mention all. Nevertheless, some of the indispensable ones who made this book possible are mentioned below.

This is first a war story. The participants in this story include Vietnam veterans—those who survived the experience, those who died in it, suffered through it, shared in it, and were changed by it.

I'm especially thankful to the men of Advisory Team 75 in the Mekong Delta, notably Bobby Hurst and Master Sergeant Mendenhall, who taught me to walk and talk as a soldier, and survive. And I'm just as thankful to the troopers of the 7th Cavalry, the Garry Owens of 1970 and 1971. Every last one of them struggled with the same hopes, fears, disappointments, and dreams that I did, but we never left a trooper behind. Even Private First Class Green is with us in our hearts and minds. Bravo Company has formed its own LZ on the World Wide Web with a battle cry: "As long as it takes!"

All Vietnam veterans were affected by the war in some way, but the combatants who laid it on the line were a breed apart. Prodigals who wasted their cherished blood, time, lives, hopes, and dreams, and then returned home unrecognized, are the heroes here.

But it is also a love story, certainly a story of love for comrades in arms, but also love for families, friends, waiting spouses, and the children whose lives were affected by the war and the way it changed their fathers and mothers. They join the long line of walking wounded.

The Vietnamese, both southerners and northerners, were torn by battles raging on their farms and in their neighborhoods. Too often they saw their children die before their eyes. They had suffered through hundreds of years of struggles and oppression. Their numbers include warriors on both sides and civilians.

This book would have neither a beginning nor an ending without my wife Sandy, always waiting for me. She appeared in the middle of my Vietnam experience and gave me reason to pull through it, inspired me to be better because of it. I was one of those lucky enough to have someone to stick it out with me despite my shortcomings. By saving my letters she returned the bits and pieces, enabling me to reconstruct my second journal and providing the inspiration to create the first. The letters brought me in touch with painful feeling, fears, and hopes from a time buried deep inside and long forgotten. As we studied the draft together, her insights helped me get those parts right, but also brought closure to old wounds. To Sandy I owe the most.

And there were others who helped me through the trials of Vietnam and writing about it. Peggy, Bonnie, Bobby Hurst, Tony Labrozzi, and Earl Spry each came along when I needed someone to guide me through trying times. They touched me in ways that kept me focused on survival and yet remain a member of the human race.

Cindy Bowlin, a woman born of the Vietnam War era, questioned me about the war. Her genuine interest in my answers finally started my reexamination of the story to its completion. She read my handwritten journals, encouraged me to write the book, and helped with it. Without her encouragement, I would have avoided some of the most important aspects of the story. I approached those parts reluctantly and unwillingly, but her objective questions and encouragement kept me going when I would have quit.

And my editor, Nancy Koesy Parker, not only edited my manuscript but also helped me remember how to write. Without her help, my notes would have languished as a manuscript instead of taking life. She gave me the courage I needed to submit it.

Eric Hammel at Presidio Press recognized it as worthy, pushed it along, and encouraged me to make it better. I hope I have. And to Jamie Lozano, a special soldier, thank you for your help with the maps.

Unfortunately I must acknowledge the policymakers who gave our country this bungled disaster. Unseen except in news clips, they created the environment we lived in; hiding in carpeted offices, they sent us away and turned their backs when we returned. They made us the bastard prodigals. America's children, the young and idealistic, will always fight our country's wars, but when they return as grizzled veterans, they should be received—if not as heroes—then at least as returning sons and daughters. "Welcome home, brother!"

My memory alone would not have permitted me to complete this book without the vital props of my letters and pictures. However, as I relived the experiences on paper, I was surprised by the clarity with which they returned. Any errors of perception, clouded by many years, are mine and mine alone. The views in this story are mine, and reflect the way I recorded them then and as I recall them still.

A few names were protected to avoid hurting people, but most names remain unchanged. Those were decisions I made and take responsibility for.

"Garry Owen" verses are from song sheets I saved from my days in the cavalry. I understand that a great American of the 7th Cavalry in the Ia Drang Valley and, later, the World Trade Center, Rick Rescorla, wrote and sang most of them. Letters are excerpts from originals, and any poor poetry is by the author from the period. Please excuse its quality.

Autopsies of the war reveal many mistakes, accidents, and misconduct—and heroism. After so much time has passed fixing blame and responsibility is an intellectual exercise, while what is needed is an exorcism of our spirits. Most of us, but not all, prevailed despite their experiences. The United States survived despite Vietnam, not because of it. Conflict tore the fabric of democracy, as it tore the lives of those touched by the war. I hope our nation is stronger because of it.

As for me, I've done well. Vietnam stamped me with indelible ink that never washes away. I was driven by the war into the life of a professional soldier. I loved soldiering, and I loved soldiers. It came naturally to me—for reasons I never questioned. I wanted to be among the elite and I was, as a cavalryman, a ranger, and a paratrooper. At Fort Benning I trained young men in the fundamentals of fighting and survival, and instilled discipline and a desire to win in battle—and succeed in life. At Fort Leavenworth I taught career officers the principles of joint and combined operations and lessons from the world of insurgency and counterterrorism. In Brussels and Vienna I soldiered for peace in Europe, seeking disarmament in the Cold War through the negotiations for reductions of forces.

The Soviet Union was disassembled, the Berlin Wall fell, and Eastern Europe opened its fortified gates. For my final duty, I returned to the Philippines to chase the ghosts of Nick Rowe and Peggy, and to taste the sweet, warm rains of Asia once more. I saw the U.S. flag fly for the last time over Subic Bay and a Clark Field covered in ash from Mount Pinatubo. Finally I placed my helmet on the closet shelf to stay, and hung my uniform below. I can look back with pride and with no regrets for my service as a soldier. I would eagerly serve my country again, anywhere, anytime.

*   *   *

A Tale of an Army Tent

An army tent is a perfect place
To think about your wife.
If you've never tried that, my friend,
You're wasting away your life.

The warmth of the pot-bellied stove
Is like her warm arms around me.
The cold, hard cot is my bed
When she is gone.

The sound of the lantern burning
Is water she left to boil.
The ringing of the field telephone
Is my child crying.

The cold wind blowing in the door
Is my love when she is angry,
And the rustling it makes
Causes my canvas house to shake.

> The warm coffee on my lips
> Are her lips, and the touch makes me warm inside.
> You know, my friend, an army tent
> Is nothing at all like home.

—Richard H. Taylor, 1971

* * *

A final postscript occurred after this manuscript was boxed for delivery to the publisher. A letter arrived from our daughter, a medic in the 3d Armored Cavalry. She was on her way to the battle zone of Iraqi Freedom.

Dear Mom and Dad,

I made it on the plane and am surprised how great the flight was. One of the flight attendants was a nurse in Vietnam. . . . The support is what makes this worth it. It's been great to just hear a 'Thank You!'

Love

Amy

Someone wrote the following on Amy's envelope: "We were deeply honored to have served your very brave soldier today! Thank you.

— United Crew/Flight 9956.

History does repeat itself.

End Notes

Chapter 1: History Repeats Itself

1. Mike Feinsilber, "Paratroopers, Gun Ships Trap Red Regiment," *The Atlanta Constitution*, August 17, 1967, p. 2.

Chapter 2: The Long Journey

1. Edwin Q. White, "Stratoforts Bomb Big Buildup Base," *The Atlanta Constitution*, August 19, 1967, p. 1.

Chapter 3: Good Morning, Vietnam

1. Editor, "Showdown in U.S. Over Vietnam War," *U.S. News & World Report*, Volume LXIII-No.9, August 28, Washington, D.C. 1967, p. 21.

Chapter 4: Sliders

1. Peter Baestrup, "Thieu Joins Tour With His Rivals" and "Viet Cong Mortar Attack Kills 50 Civilians in Delta," *The New York Times*, August 27, 1967 pp. 1:7, 2:3.

Chapter 5: Assignment: Mekong Delta

1. Editor, "End of Vietnam War in Sight?" An interview with the Army's Chief of Staff, General Harold K. Johnson. *U.S. News & World Report*, Volume LXIII No. 11, September 11, 1968, pp. 44-45.

Chapter 6: Rude Awakening

1. Editor, "U.S. Forces Under Fire; Lands on Shore of River," *The New York Times*, September 16, 1967, p. 5:2.

Chapter 7: Storm Clouds over the Double Y

1. Editor, "Inside the Vietcong," *Time*, August 25, 1967, p. 21.
2. Ibid., p. 20.

Chapter 8: Trouble at the Double Y

1. Editor, "March on the Pentagon," *Newsweek*, October 30, 1967, p. 20.

Chapter 9: Friendly Fire

1. John W. Finney, "McCormack Scores Foes of War Policy," *The New York Times*, October 12, 1967, pp. 1:1, 5:2.

Chapter 10: River Assault

1. Editor, "Hanging on With Giap," *Newsweek*, October 23, 1967, p. 36.

Chapter 11: Into Snoopy's Nose

1. John W. Finney, "Pilots Loss Linked to Bombing Curbs," *The New York Times*, October 24, 1967, p. 1:2.

Chapter 12: Changes

1. Lloyd Norman and Edward Kosner, "Why Is McNamara Leaving?" *Newsweek*, December 11, 1967, p. 3.

2. Ibid., p. 25-26.

Chapter 13: Sudden Death

1. Max Frankel, "President Visits Base in Vietnam After Thai Stop," *The New York Times*, December 23, 1967, p. 1:8.

2. Editor, "McNamara: Under the Gun?" *Newsweek*, October 30, 1967, p. 16.

3. R.W. Apple, Jr., "Pacification Moves Slowly in Mekong Delta Region," *The New York Times*, December 23, 1967, pp. 1:5-6, 8:3.

Chapter 14: East of the Sun

1. Editor, "Drive to Send Gifts to Troops Gets Big Response," *The New York Times*, December 23, 1967, p. 8:4.

2. Editor, *The Atlanta Constitution*, "Atlanta GI Gets Asylum," March 6, 1968, p. 6:1.

Chapter 15: Unfriendly Fire

1. Editor, *The Atlanta Constitution*, "Jets Hammer North in Effort to Cut Flow of Supplies South," December 7, 1967, p. 1:8.

2. Editor, "Three Holiday Truces Set by Viet Cong," *The New York Times*, November 18, 1967, p. 18:1.

Chapter 16: Big Storm

1. John S. Bowman, ed., *The Vietnam War Day by Day* (London: Bison Books, 1989) p. 119.

Chapter 17: Gates of Hell

1. Military Assistance Command – Vietnam, "Instructions to United States troops in Vietnam," *The MACV Observer*, January 31, 1968.

Chapter 18: Storm Unremitting

1. Oberdorfer, Don, *Tet*, Avon Books, New York, 1971, p. 169.
2. Bowman, p. 120.

Chapter 19: Mopping Up

1. Joseph Kraft, "More Troops Not the Central Issue," *The Atlanta Constitution*, March 5, 1968, p. 4:7.
2. Bowman, p. 121.

Chapter 20: Rats of a Different Sort

1. Bowman, pp. 121-122.
2. Editor, "U.S. Creates Command Along DMZ," *The Atlanta Constitution*, March 8, 1968, p. 1:3.

Chapter 21: Blessed Respite

1. Art Pine, "Widen Strategy, Russell Urges," *The Atlanta Constitution*, March 13, 1968 p. 3:1.
2. Milton Benjamin, "He Would 'End the War' if Elected, Nixon Pledges," *The Atlanta Constitution*, March 6, 1968, p. 2.

Chapter 22: Clock Winding Down

1. Bowman, p. 124.
2. Editor, "Seven Days in April," *Newsweek*, April 15, 1968, p. 26.
3. Editor, "Postponing the Blow," *Newsweek*, July 15, 1968, p. 44.

Chapter 23: Revival

1. Hedrick Smith & Neil Sheehan, "Westmoreland Requests 206,000 More Men, Stirring Debate in Administration," *The New York Times*, March 10, 1968, p. 1:8.
2. Bowman, p. 132.
3. Lewis Gulich, "Johnson is Cautious on Peace Expectations," *The Atlanta Constitution*, May 4, 1968, p. 1.

4. Bowman, p. 163.

Chapter 24: Returning

1. Editor, "The War in Indochina," *Newsweek*, July 6, 1970, p. 51.

Chapter 25: Garry Owen

1. Editor, "Garry Owen tradition," *Pacific Stars and Stripes*, 1968.

Chapter 27: War Zone D

1. Editor, "Fighting to Continue," *The Atlanta Constitution*, August 1, 1970, p. 8.

Chapter 28: Green

1. Editor, "The War in Indochina," *Newsweek*, August 3, 1970, p. 34.

Chapter 30: Operation Mercer

1. Editor, "Inside North Vietnam: A Tidal Wave of Troubles" *U.S. News and World Report*, Nov 30, 1970, p. 21.

Chapter 31: Reorienting

1. Editors, "Vietnam 'Failures'—A Military View" *U.S. News and World Report*, Nov 23, 1970, p. 51.

2. Editor, "Complete Pullout Planned," *The Atlanta Constitution*, October 7, 1970, p. 1.

3. Sol W. Sanders, "Can South Vietnam Survive After the GI's Leave?" *U.S. News & World Report*, September 28, 1970, p. 72.

Chapter 32: Bruised Heart

1. Editor, "Toward an Ideal Army," *Time*, October 26, 1970, p. 26.

Chapter 33: Recovery

1. Editor, "New Regulation May Permit Hundreds to Avoid Draft," *The Atlanta Constitution*, October 2, 1970, p. 2.

Chapter 34: Artillery Ambush

2. Alan Dawson, "No GIs Reported Killed," *The Atlanta Constitution*, November 12, 1970, p. 6.

Chapter 35: Back to Bravo

1. Wendell S. Merick, "Sagging Morale in Vietnam—Eyewitness Report on Drugs, Race Problems, and Boredom" *U.S. News & World Report*: (January 25, 1971) p. 30.
2. Ibid., p. 32.

Chapter 36: Backs to the Wall

1. Editors, "Reds Turn Noses Up on POW Exchange Offer," *Marietta Daily Journal*, Dec 3, 1970, p. 88.
2. Merick, pp. 31-32.
3. Ibid., p. 32.

Chapter 37: Staff Wars

1. Merick, p. 33.
2. Ibid., p. 30.

Chapter 38: Delta Demons

1. Alan Brown, "Stiff resistance at 'Bunker City'" *Pacific Stars and Stripes*, 1971.

Chapter 39: News from Home

1. Bowman, p. 176.

Chapter 41: Which Way Home?

1. John Tegtmeier, The Vietnam War Internet Project, May 25, 2003, www.vwip.org/vwiphome.html/.

2. Editors, "Rallies—And Riots—For Peace," *U.S. News & World Report*, April 27, 1971, p. 78.

Chapter 42: Fragments

1. Phil Gailey, "Calley Draws Life, Appeal Under Way," *The Atlanta Constitution*, April 1, 1971, p. 1.

Chapter 43: Saint Christopher

2. Bowman, p. 181.

INDEX

Abrams, Gen. Craighton W., 257-258

Adams, Lt. Tommy, 288-289, 304

Advisory Team 75, 24, 26

Armed Forces Network, 112, 240

Agency for International Development, 46

Ap Bac 1, 50

Ap Bac 2, 50

Ap Bac, 84, 90, 128

Army of the Republic of Vietnam (ARVN), 14, 18, 35-36, 39, 46, 101-106, 112-113, 118, 121, 126, 132, 150

Army of the Republic of Vietnam, Military Units: 2nd Infantry Battalion, 135; 3rd Infantry Battalion, 135; 7th Infantry Battalion, 24, 26, 28, 50, 58, 87, 118, 145, 147, 150, 166; 10th Infantry Regiment, 58; 11th Infantry Regiment, 34, 42, 85, 125; 32nd Ranger Battalion, 28, 135; 42nd Ranger Battalion, 129, 131

Atlanta Constitution, August 17, 1967, 1; August 19, 1967, 5; August 3, 1970, 193; December 7, 1967, 93; March 13, 1968, 139; March 5, 1968, 125; November 12, 1970, 249; October 2, 1970, 239

Ben Hoa Air Base, 308

Ben Luc Bridge, 153

Ben Luc, 152

Ben Tranh, 128

Ben Tre, 58, 60, 118

Benewah, USS, 152

Bien Hoa, 170-171, 176, 200-202, 223-224, 236, 285, 288, 307-308

Binh Duc Training Center, 28, 31, 38-39, 43, 46-47, 55, 65, 77-78, 87, 96, 101, 113, 122, 134-135, 150, 157

Binh Phu, 35

Bivens, PFC Gary, 259-260

Bonnie, 141-144

bonus marchers, 49

Bouie, Maj. —, 32-36, 60, 64, 72, 77

Bowlin, Cindy, 315

Brady, Col. Morris J., 188, 190

Braniff Airways Military Airlift Command, 6

Brickhouse, Lt. —, 96, 100

Bunker City, 276, 280

Burgess, Cleatus, 233-235, 240, 242

Burton, Gen. —, 236, 247, 271, 284

Cai Be, 67-68, 71, 78, 102

Cai Lay, 35, 81, 93-95, 133

Calley, Lt. William L., 299

Cambodia, 28, 85, 162-163, 167, 170, 173, 195, 201, 245, 276

Camp Alpha, 14, 139, 152

Camp Gorvad, 174, 178, 182, 190-191, 193, 195-196, 200, 218, 281

Camp Zama, 148

Can Tho, 25-26, 69, 152

Carillo, SSGT Jesus, 275

Casey, Gen., 167, 200

Civilian Irregular Defense Group, 90

Clark Air Force Base, 9, 14, 19, 165

Coker, Maj. —, 148
Columbus, GA, 311
Combat Infantry Badge, 36
Consedine, Lt. Tom, 177, 199
Corps, IV, 24
Custer, Gen. George A., 169
Cuu Long, 62
Czajka, PFC Wayne, 199, 209, 211, 213, 216, 262

Da Nang, 244-245
Daisy, Tony, 239
Demilitarized Zone, 100
Dencker, Lt. Pete, 199
Denholm, Jimmy, 233-235
Dinh Toung Province, 26
Dinh Toung, 46, 58
Dodson, John, 166
Don Ho, 294-295
Dong Tam, Mobile Riverine Force base, 39
Dong Tam, 46, 100-101, 108
Double Y, 43, 47, 49-50, 57, 84, 88-90, 130, 134, 147
Dragon's Mouth, 62
Drake, Peggy, 6-7, 9, 11, 14, 19, 37, 39, 60, 123, 141, 152-153, 165, 315

Ervasti, Al, 239

Fayetteville, NC, 157
Fire Base Aries, 285, 287, 288-289, 291
Fire Base Charles, 301
Fire Base Connell, 236
Fire Base Durall, 250, 256
Fire Base Green, 197, 204, 222-223, 226, 236, 244-245, 249-251, 256, 259-260, 264, 267, 271-272, 276, 281, 283, 285, 287
Fire Base Mace, 301-302, 304, 307
Fire Support Base Connell, 256
Fire Support Base Garry Owen, 193, 196

Fire Support Base Nobel, 281, 284
Florio, CSM —, 250
Fort Benning, GA, 39-40, 42, 157, 161-162, 166-167
Fort Bragg, NC, 3, 24, 91, 150-156
Fort Hood, TX, 271, 281
French Quarter, Saigon, 20
Fuller, Capt. John, 166, 260
Furr, SFC William, 220-221

Gary, Capt. Dana, 268
Giap, Gen., 61
Go Cong Province, 26, 62, 148, 166
Gorvad, Lt. Col. Peter, 174
Grant, Johnny, 88
Green Berets, 90-91
Green, PFC James A. 197, 314

Ho Chi Minh Trail, 85, 93, 134, 221, 283, 304
Hong Kong, 139-143
Hue, 117
Hurst, Capt. Bobby, 28-29, 31-34, 36-37, 39, 46-47, 51-53, 55, 57-58, 63, 70-72, 74, 95-97, 101, 106, 129-131, 139, 147, 221, 314-315
Hyman, Gen. —, 247
Hyslop, Capt. Lee, 206, 281

Ia Drang Valley, 316
Infantry Officers Advanced Course, 44

Jefferson, Lt. Mike, 18
John F. Kennedy Special Warfare Center, 24
Johnson, Spec. Jim, 206, 209
Johnson, President Lyndon, 83, 123, 148, 158
Johnson, Sherry, 88
Jones, Lt. —, 262-263
Judge, Lt., 228-229, 234-236, 239-240, 260

Keopler Compound, 14-15, 23
Kiem, Lt. —, 40, 44, 52, 54-55, 57, 60, 95, 137
Kien Hoa Province, 26, 58, 83, 118
Kien Hoa, 60-61, 88
Kien Toung Province, 26
King, Martin Luther, 148
Kingston, Col. Bob, 200
Knudson, Maj. Wayne, 223, 250-251
Kress, SGT. —, 268-269, 271, 284, 300, 303
Ky, Gen. Nguyen Cao, 17, 147

Labrozzi, Col. Anthony, 170, 174-178, 187-191, 193, 195, 198-199, 202-204, 215-220, 223, 236, 244, 250-251, 256-257, 259, 261-262, 264, 268-270, 279, 297-299, 315
Laird, Melvin R., 274
Langbein, Maj. —, 281, 284
Laos, 28
Landing Zone Garry Owen, 202
Landing Zone Green, 224
Landing Zone Mercer, 219-220, 224, 261
Landing Zone Springfield, 42, 50, 84, 90
Long An Province, 128
Long Binh, 166, 201, 223, 239, 303
Long Dinh Bridge, 50
Long Dinh, 34, 42
Lovelace, Capt. George, 246
Lundberg, Louis B., 181
Lynch, Lt. John, 261

Marietta Daily Journal, December 3, 1970, 259
Martinez, PFC Steve, 221, 233-235, 240
McBain, Diane, 88
McCormack, John, 57
McNamara, Robert S., 77, 82
Mekong Delta, 24, 100, 153, 171, 186, 314
Mekong River, 28, 43, 62, 67, 108
Mendenhall, SFC —, 29, 33, 53, 74, 96,

101-105, 108-109, 111, 113-114, 147, 314
Mercer, Spec. Jimmy M., 195, 217, 242, 281
Merick, Wendell S., 255, 259
Military Affiliate Radio System, 264
Military Airlift Command, 9
Military Assistance Command Vietnam Observer, January 31, 1968, 111
Military Assistance Command Vietnam, 3, 14-15
Mobile Army Surgical Hospital, 95, 101
Military Units: 1st Cavalry Division, 157, 166, 224, 271, 281, 301; 1st Battalion, 5th Cavalry, 271; 1st Battalion, 7th Cavalry, 167, 197, 200, 219, 257, 268, 271, 275, 287, 314; 1st Battalion, 12th Cavalry, 166, 271, 285; 1st Battalion, 21st Field Artillery, 250; 2nd Battalion, 7th Cavalry, 167, 193; 9th Infantry Division, 58, 60, 87, 95, 118, 120, 125, 146, 152; 9th Infantry Division Mobine Riverine Force, 24, 73, 121; 11th Aviation Group, 223, 246; 15th Medical Battalion, 236, 239, 302; 24th Evacuation Hospital, 201, 239-241, 244; 32nd Ranger Battalion, 83; 75th Ranger Battalion, 260; 82nd Airborne Division, 91, 128, 150, 156-157, 167; 101st Airborne Division, 3, 18; 187th Regimental Combat Team, 175
Mobile Riverine Force base at Dong Tam, 39, 58;
My Lai, 299
My Phouc Tay, 90-91
My Tho, 25-26, 46, 58, 62, 65, 88-89, 101-103, 112, 118-120, 122, 125, 128, 130, 135, 148, 227, 265
Myles, Lt. Kevin, 199

National Highway 4, 28, 34-35, 38, 50, 62, 68, 89, 128
National Liberation Front, 58, 118

National Road, 50, 221
Neely, Maj. Cecil N., 34, 37, 51, 68-69
New York Times, August 27, 1967, 17;
    September 16, 1967, 31; October 12,
    1967, 57; October 24, 1967, 67;
    December 23, 1967, 83; December 23,
    1967, 89; March 10, 1968, 155
Newman, Col. Rex, 247
Newsweek, October 23, 1967, 61;
    October 30, 1967, 49; December 11,
    1967, 77; July 6, 1968, 163; August 3,
    1970, 197
Nguyen Van Thieu, 119
Nixon, President Richard M., 144, 162,
    226
North Georgia College, 3
North Vietnamese Army, 39, 51, 53, 55

O'Malley, Capt. —, 90-92, 137, 157
Oakland Army Depot, 4-5, 164
Operation Lam Son 719, 283
Operation Mercer, 221-222, 224, 228,
    279

Pacific Architects and Engineers, 46
Pacific Stars and Stripes, 275
Peace Corps, 46
Phoenix program, 146
Phouc Vinh, 171-174, 198, 244-245
Plain of Reeds, 24, 43, 53, 55, 64, 85,
    89-90, 134
Plucinski, Capt. Ted, 246
Powell, Capt. Robert, 167, 176, 194, 203
Putnam, Gen. —, 200-201, 218-219, 247

Quan Loi, 170-172, 178

Rach Bao Dinh River, 26, 118
Ranger training, 150, 156-157
Reitz, Maj. Bob, 166
Rescorla, Rick, 316

Rex Hotel, 19-20
Rich, SSgt —, 29, 43, 50-53, 59, 85, 96,
    147
River Assault Group, 58
Robinson, Capt. Robbie, 270
Rodeck, Chaplain Ron, 244
Rogers, Sgt. Dwayne, 184, 186, 188-189,
    212-213, 218, 223
Royas, SFC Francisco, 177, 182, 185,
    189, 201, 239, 260
Rozelle, Capt. "Skip," 276-277, 280-281
Rung Sat Special Zone, 62
Russell, Senator Richard B., 139

Saigon, 14-15, 25, 100, 112, 117, 152-
    153, 244, 265
Sauble, Spec. Joe, 199, 212
Scharf, Sabrina, 88
Shaw, Sgt. Tee, 257
Smith, Gen. James C., 281
"Snoopy's Nose," 67-70, 74, 78
Song Be River, 178
Song Be, 245, 272
Song My Tho, 43
"Spooky," C-47 Cargo plane, 20, 53,
    129-131, 277
Spry, Lt. Col. Alfred E., 269-271, 274,
    276-281, 284, 288-289, 291, 297, 299-
    304, 308, 315
Stevenson, Col. Robert, 203, 225, 262,
    277-279, 281, 283-284
Student Mobilization Committee of End
    the War in Vietnam, 145
"Swamp Fox," 86-87, 119
Swan, John D., 260
Sweeney, Lt. Ed, 256, 264

Tan San Nhut, 14, 25, 244
Tao, Capt., 84, 106, 147
Tay Ninh Province, 201
Taylor, Richard Scott, 283, 285-286, 291,
    294
Taylor, Sandy, 159-167, 176, 191, 194-

196, 200-203, 205, 224, 237, 239, 242, 245, 252-254, 263-265, 269, 272-273, 282, 284-287, 289-291, 293-297, 308, 311-312, 315
Tet holiday, 93, 96-97, 89, 119
Tet Offense, 100-107, 111-115, 117-120, 123, 134, 271
Tet Truce, 100
Thanh, Lt. —, 40, 44, 46, 60, 83-84, 94, 97, 241
Thieu, General, 17, 77
Time, August 25, 1967, 41; October 26, 1970, 231
Tokyo, 148
Tong Doc Loc, 43
Trobaugh, Lt. Col. Ed, 167, 194
Turner, Capt. —, 278-281

U.S. News & World Report, 255, 259, August 28, 1967, 13; September 11, 1968, 23; November 30, 1970, 215; January 25, 1971, 267
United Service Organization, 264

Van Tao, Capt. Nguyen, 33, 40, 50, 58-59, 77
Vann, Lt. Col. John Paul, 26, 50, 128
Viet Cong, 54, 58, 62, 93, 106-107, 126, 134, 228
Viet Cong Military Units: 1st Infantry Regiment, 128; 1st Main Force Regiment, 67; 9th Infantry Division, 118-119; 33rd Infantry Regiment, 207; 81st Rear Service Group, 270, 273, 275; 261st Battalion, 67, 94, 118, 128-129; 263rd Battalion, 67, 69-72, 74, 83, 118, 128-129; 514th Local Force Battalion, 84-85;
Verruchi, SPEC Don, 206, 209
Vietnam Memorial Wall, 312
Vietnam Veterans of America, 313
Vietnamese Air Force, 42-43
Vietnamese Popular Forces (PF), 34

Vietnamese Provincial Reconnaissance Unit, 146
Vietnamese Regional Forces (RF), 34
Vung Tao, 96
Vuono, Lt. Col. Carl, 216, 262

Wagstaff, Gen. —, 218
War Zone D, 193-194, 197, 200, 202, 219, 221, 227, 249, 253, 255, 260, 304
Westmoreland, Gen. William C., 123, 132, 155, 225
Wheeler, Gen. —, 132
Whitley, John, 166
Wilkes, Earl, 276
Wilkinson, Maj. —, 28

Xuan Loc, 301
Xuan, Capt., 39-40, 44, 60, 63, 67, 70-74, 78, 85, 102-109, 112, 114-115, 118, 131-132, 147, 301

Zolecki, SP4 Steve, 275